MICHAEL INGRAM

The Voyage of
ODIN'S
RAVEN

Clearwater

I·O·M

Published by
Clearwater Publishing Limited,
'Thie-ny-Chibbyr', Surby, Port Erin,
Isle of Man, British Isles.

© Michael Ingram 1982
Designed by Peter Hearsey

British Library Cataloguing in Publication Data
Ingram, Michael.
  The Voyage of Odin's Raven.
  1. Odin's Raven (Ship)   2. Voyages and travels
  – 1951 –   3. North Atlantic Ocean
    ISBN 0-946363-00-5

Typeset in 12 pt Photon Plantin by
Keyspools (IOM) Ltd.,
Second Avenue, Onchan, Isle of Man

Printed in Great Britain by
Redwood Burn Limited,
Trowbridge

To my wife, Wendy

'This is *thy life*: Indulge its natural flow, and carve these forms. They yet may find a place on shelves for them Reserved. In any case, I bid thee carve them, knowing what *I know.*'

Old Manx Poem
1887 Braddan

ODIN'S RAVEN

Robin Bigland (Chieftain)

Richard Tomlinson

Eddie Kaighin (Skipper)

Nigel Wood

Colin Bowen

Richard Young

Brian Cousins

Odd Børstad

David Eames

Knut Hoff

Michael Ingram

Rolf Hansen

George Kneale

Knut Skøgoy

Shane Lucas

Arne Wisth

Alan Binns (Trondheim to Lerwick).

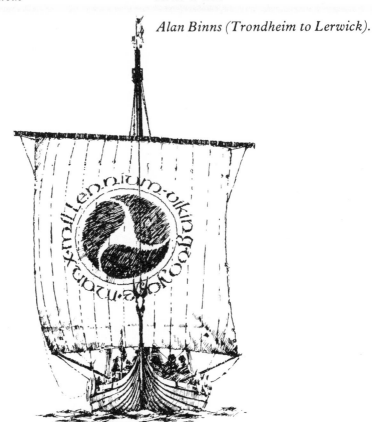

Contents

Introduction by Magnus Magnusson   11

Preface   14

CHAPTER ONE   Prelude   15

CHAPTER TWO   Oslofjord   24

CHAPTER THREE   Oslo Interlude   39

CHAPTER FOUR   Departure   45

CHAPTER FIVE   The Storm   59

CHAPTER SIX   The North Sea   72

CHAPTER SEVEN   Landfall   101

CHAPTER EIGHT   The Minch   110

CHAPTER NINE   Capsize   126

CHAPTER TEN   Corryvreckan Whirlpool   142

CHAPTER ELEVEN   In the wake of Godred Crovan   160

Appendix – Odin's Raven   180

Bibliography   190

Acknowledgements   191

The Kingdom of Man and the Isles

All districts conquered by the Norse were claimed by the King of Norway as being under his control, but in practice powerful Viking Chieftains fought each other for Supremacy. Thus at one time Man might be ruled by a king who lived in Dublin, at another time by a king who lived on the Island itself. There were other occasions when the Earls of Orkney claimed to rule the Island, especially during the eleventh century.

As time passed Man came to be linked particularly with the other Norse islands of the Hebrides along the west coast of Scotland, and the whole domain was called the Kingdom of Man and the Isles. There are in fact several hundred islands in the area if each islet is counted separately, but officially they were together reckoned as thirty-two in the days of the kingdom, Man being the most important of all.

For the purposes of administration the Hebrides were divided into four groups, based on the main islands of Lewis, Skye, Mull and Islay. These were further sub-divided into two groups, a northern and southern, by the promontory of Ardnamurchan Point, the North Isles, namely Lewis and Skye, being regarded as the Out Isles, from the Manx point of view.

With the ascension of Godred Crovan, 'King Orry', to the Manx throne in 1079, the history of the island assumes a more continuous pattern, instead of being the mere collection of unrelated scraps that it had previously been. But while Godred is the first king about whom anything very definite is known it must be admitted that much concerning him is very obscure. His nickname Crovan is supposed to be due to the fact that he always wore white gauntlets when he went to war. Godred's home was possibly Islay, though he's said to have spent part of his youth in Man. He fought with the Norwegians under Harold, King of Norway, against Harold of England at Stamford Bridge in 1066, and fled to Man following the English victory. Nothing is heard of him for some years, but he then appears on the scene as the leader of three expeditions against Man, having somehow gathered together an army and a fleet. His first two attacks were unsuccessful, but in 1079 he made an attack which gave him possession of the Island.

Godred was the ruler who was responsible for the union of Man and the Isles into one Kingdom, and to administer this great maritime unit he devised the political system known to this day as the House of Keys, the thirty-two members of which reflected the number of Isles in the original kingdom.

(*from* 'The Isle of Man' by R. H. Kinvig.)

INTRODUCTION

by Magnus Magnusson

In the summer of 1978 there was much talk in the Isle of Man about holding a Millennium. The year 1979 seemed as good as any. An opportunity to celebrate a thousand years or so of Viking inheritance and tradition associated with the Manx Tynwald. At dinner one evening, a young Manx insurance company director and entrepreneur, Robin Bigland, who has reason to believe that his family originally came 'west-over-sea' with the Vikings from Byglandsfjord in southern Norway, said, 'Why don't we build a Viking boat and sail it across from Norway to the Isle of Man, as our forefathers used to do?'

That was in July 1978. As BBC TV producer Ray Sutcliffe wrote in *Popular Archaeology* (August 1979 – 'The Bigland Boat'), for most people the conversation would have become airborne with the smoke of the after-dinner cigars. Not so where Robin Bigland was concerned, however; within one month of that conversation the keel of the proposed Viking ship was being laid, on August 29, 1978, by the President of the Norwegian Storting (Parliament)!

It was built at a small Norwegian boatyard, the Rød Batbyggeri at Frederikstad on the east side of Oslofjord; here, a small family of master shipwrights was commissioned to build a two-thirds scale replica of the most famous Viking ship ever found – the Gokstad ship, which was built around 850 AD and excavated from its funeral mound more than a thousand years later in 1880. It was launched on Saturday, April 28, 1979, at a delightful ceremony performed by Lady Paul, wife of His Excellency the Lieutenant Governor of the Isle of Man, Sir John Paul. There followed several weeks of sea-trials, and eventually, on May 27, 1979, 'The Bigland Boat', as I always think of it, set out from Trondheim in northern Norway on its voyage across the North Sea to rendezvous with the Millennium celebrations on the Isle of Man on July 5. From conception to completion, from idea to fulfilment, from brainchild to reality, the whole remarkable operation had only taken twelve months.

In retrospect, it was a truly astonishing achievement. Much had been written about it in various books and periodicals. It was the subject of a television documentary by BBC Scotland. It was the theme of a major book by the academic consultant on the project, Alan L. Binns of Hull University (*Viking Voyagers*, Heinemann, 1980). It delighted the media of many countries, and raised the pride of Manxmen all over the world. It was a triumph.

It was not the first time that someone had had the idea of building a replica of the Gokstad ship and sailing it from its homeland. As long ago as 1893 a Norwegian called Magnus Andersen, the editor of a Norwegian shipping journal, built a full-scale replica of Gokstad and sailed it across the North Sea and the Atlantic in 28 days to take by storm the Chicago World Fair of that year. Magnus Andersen called his replica Viking; 'The Bigland Boat' was named *Odin's Raven* as a result of a competition held in schools throughout the Isle of Man. Not everybody liked the name at first, but everyone got used to it in the end.

I had the pleasure of making the acquaintance of *Odin's Raven* on several occasions, while I was filming for the TV series *Vikings*! In the spring of 1979 I met her when she was still being built by young Magnar Hanson at Frederikstad. I was there when she was launched, to the accompaniment of an enchanting local band. I tried my hand at rowing her in Oslofjord at the start of her sea-trials. After her epic voyage was completed, I was a member of the crew that took her out from hibernation at Peel, on the Isle of Man. I saluted her in the forecourt of the British Museum in London, where she was a star of the Viking Exhibition in the spring of 1980. I paid my respects to her in New York, where she was the harbinger of the same great Viking Exhibition at the Metropolitan Museum in the autumn of 1980.

The building of *Odin's Raven* and its voyage across the North Sea may well have started as a spectacular gimmick to draw attention to the Isle of Man Millennium. But it became far more than that. In the first place, under the eagle eye of Alan Binns, it became an authentic and important exercise in experimental archaeology. All the Viking ships that have been recovered by archaeology have been little more than hulls, which are easy enough to reconstruct; but no evidence of how they were rigged is available – and it is the kind of rigging, the height of the mast, the area and consistency of the sail, that really determine how Viking ships may have handled. Building and sailing a replica can only add to the store of our knowledge about the original ships themselves, even though it may raise more questions than answers. But that is what all scholarship is about.

In the second place, it became an experiment in the *living* of the past. What was it actually like to sail on a Viking ship 1,000 years ago? We have the words of the poets who exulted in the speed and beauty of their boats, who described in elaborate figures of speech how their 'ocean-striding bison' or 'fjord-elk' clove the 'whale-path'.

But what was it like in reality to live on one of these poetic fantasies? In this book, marine biologist Michael Ingram, one of the crew-members who was eventually selected from the scores of volunteers, describes how it actually was, stripped of romanticism and glamour. He makes no claim to scholarship or seamanship. He was one of the self-styled Bilge-Rats who saw the voyage from the equivalent of the scuppers, often with a jaundiced eye. From his own diary, and diaries of his colleagues, there emerges a sea-log that is as uninhibited as it is refreshing. He makes no attempt to ennoble the feelings of the crew members when they were beset by apprehension or boredom; nor does he attempt to gloss over the very human reactions to despair or disappointment.

It is a plain, unvarnished tale. The voyage of the *Odin's Raven* was a remarkable occasion, and it had a remarkable effect on the men who were privileged to take part in it. Through it, and about it, there reverberates the sheer physical exhilaration of taking part in the adventure of the past, or being at one for a time with our hardy ancestors. I am not sure if I would have enjoyed it myself; but sometimes, now, I regret that I missed out on it.

Magnus Magnusson

PREFACE

About a thousand years ago, the Vikings landed on the Isle of Man and remained in control for a span of 400 years. During that time the law-giving assembly known as Tynwald was created, which has evolved into the present day Manx parliament; a parliament which is considered to have the largest unbroken tradition of any similar institution in the world.

To celebrate this record, 1979 was designated Millennium Year on the Isle of Man. Various jubilee events were planned, some obviously aimed at boosting the tourist industry, others directed towards re-living the Viking heritage which is so much treasured by the native Manx people.

Without a doubt the most memorable event of the year was that planned by a local businessman, Robin Bigland. He proposed that a replica Viking longship should be built in Norway and sailed to the Isle of Man, retracing the route taken by the original Vikings and reforging the links that used to exist between the Isle of Man, the Scottish Isles and Norway. Thus the Manx Millennium Viking Voyage was conceived and created. Robin Bigland not only suggested the idea but, with total dedication, guided the whole event through to the triumphant arrival on schedule in Peel, one of the havens where the first Vikings made their landings.

The project was announced early in 1978, and the inevitable money-raising campaign began. An estimated total of £95,000 would be required for the trip, and this was largely obtained from the Government of the Isle of Man (£25,000) and from business and private sponsorships, both on the Island and in Norway.

A Norwegian boat-yard was found, the Rød Batbyggeri of Frederikstad, to whom the challenge was irresistible, and within a few months the keel was laid. The longship was to be a two-thirds scale replica of the famous Gokstad ship, with a length of 50 feet and a beam of 11 feet.

A competition to find a name for her was organised among the schools on the Isle of Man, and an independent committee decided that *Odin's Raven*, suggested by Simon Gulliver of Onchan, was the winner.

This book concerns the voyage of *Odin's Raven* from her birth-place in Frederikstad to her arrival in Peel on the Isle of Man. It is a story of the crew and of the places visited on this historic trip and, as such, the technical details have been kept to a minimum.

CHAPTER ONE
Prelude

'... This Winter twenty-five Island residents are being trained for the 1,500 mile Millennium Voyage, of whom eleven will be selected to join five Norwegians in the final crew. Their training is being supervised by Major Shane Lucas ... who says, "Throughout this winter, the people in training are going to find themselves tired, fed-up, wet and freezing cold – frequently all at once." He is going to make them swim in the sea, trek on the mountains at night, learn First Aid, with particular attention to the effects of exposure and hypothermia ...'

(Excerpt from *Manx Life*)

Fleshwick Bay on the Isle of Man is a well-known beauty spot much frequented by tourists during the summer season. In winter, however, it is renowned for being one of the bleakest beaches on the Island, facing, as it does, directly into the cold blast of the northerly winds.

On a bitterly cold January Saturday in 1979, with a blizzard of snow sweeping horizontally across the sea towards them, twenty men stood in a semi-circle and stared in horrified amazement at the figure in front of them.

'What do you mean, walk into the sea fully clothed?' came a muffled voice emanating from a shapeless mass of wet-weather clothes, out of which a pair of eyes could just be discerned. In fact, most of those present were so wrapped up against the elements that there were, undoubtedly, many other unheard comments being directed at the recipient of the question.

Totally unperturbed by the obvious lack of enthusiasm, Shane Lucas, a 40-year-old retired Army Major who had been appointed training officer for the Manx Millennium Viking Voyage, repeated his order. 'I'll walk in up to my armpits and then you will all wade out to me, go around my back and out again. Then, when we've done that, we will climb the hill behind us four times and then have another little dip!'

So saying, he turned, walked into the sea and waited expectantly, his arms held high above the water.

With despairing glances at one another and many not so silent curses, the assembled group plunged into the water. The volume of noise increased in direct proportion to the depth of the icy water as it pierced the layers of clothing and reached the skin, and the bay echoed to tortured cries of anguish.

I don't think that there can be a more uncomfortable feeling than freezing water creeping up one's body when fully clothed. Soaking garments seem to enhance the effect and allow the bitter wind to cut straight through to the skin. In the few minutes that it took me to wade out to Shane Lucas I was chilled to the bone, my teeth chattering to such an extent that it was a physical impossibility for me to reply to his cheerful, 'Fun, isn't it?'

By the time we had all staggered back to the beach, I was just about ready to call it a day. When I had applied for a place as a crewman in the proposed replica longship, I had naively imagined that all it would involve would be a pleasant summer boat trip through the Scottish Isles; lazy days spent sunning oneself on deck as we sailed from island to island, returning home as bronzed Viking heroes. How wrong one can be!

For the previous two months we had spent every weekend clambering over hillsides in drenching rain, staggering through every stream that crossed our path. Shane Lucas appeared to have some kind of homing instinct for the wettest, most uncomfortable hikes on the Island, and, if he didn't think we were soaked enough, he would make a beeline for the nearest waterfall and suggest we all took a shower! All very pleasant on a hot summer's day, but in the depths of winter, with the ice crackling beneath our feet, our enthusiasm for water rapidly vanished.

Nevertheless the training was beginning to have a noticeable effect. The original short-list of twenty-five prospective crew members had gradually been whittled down, as, one by one, people began to recollect that they had other more pressing engagements on Saturday afternoons.

Perhaps the most obvious effect of the training was that a team of men who could get on with one another was slowly being created. Sixteen men living cheek-by-jowl in an open 50-foot boat for eight weeks could be a recipe for clashes of character that would jeopardise an otherwise well-organised voyage – unless they have already been together in extreme situations. And, slowly, as the weeks of training passed, a regular contingent of fifteen trainee Vikings had formed into a loose but definable group. The sense of rivalry was still very much in evidence, because it was known that at least five of the final crew were to be Norwegians; and of the eleven places left on the voyage, two were obviously already spoken for: the organiser of the whole project, Robin Bigland, was leading the voyage as Chieftain, and all of us had already cast Eddie Kaighan, the harbourmaster of Castletown, as the obvious choice for Skipper. So as we toiled up an down the snow-covered slopes of the hills surrounding Fleshwick Bay that bitter afternoon in January, we all knew that our chances of being chosen were no better than 2 to 1.

With this thought in mind I studied my companions closely – or as closely as was possible when the visibility through the snow was only about five yards – as I pulled myself up the slippery slope, with sodden clothes clinging to my shivering body.

After two trips to the top of the 1,500-foot hill, the group had become well spaced-out, and some of my fitter rivals were already on their way down!

In a flurry of snow the lanky figure of Ian Coulson appeared out of the murk as he practically raced down the steep incline. A photographer for one of the local papers, he was a keen sportsman and undoubtedly the fittest man among us. 'That's one certainty for the trip,' I thought to myself.

A few seconds later another figure shot past me, tobogganing downhill on his bottom – certainly the most logical if not the most comfortable method of travel under the circumstances. This was Brian Cousins, a schoolteacher and highly experienced yachtsman. Mentally I ticked off another definite place in the crew.

As I sat down for a few moments rest on a convenient rock, two of the youngest potential crew-members, both keen yachtsmen, almost galloped past me – going uphill! – and I wrote off two more places.

With growing dismay, as the afternoon wore on and the hill seemed to grow higher and higher and the water colder and colder, I began to realise that my chances of getting on the trip were virtually zero. Everybody was either younger, or fitter, or far better qualified in other ways for a 1,500-mile voyage in an open boat than I. There did not seem much hope for a 34-year-old unfit marine biologist. My only qualification for the voyage appeared to have boiled down to the fact that I might perhaps be able to identify the type of whale which would undoubtedly overturn us!

By the end of the afternoon, as we sat steaming in front of the fire in the local pub, I think I had convinced myself that I had better start getting prepared for the disappointment of not being chosen for the voyage.

If I were totally unselfish, I could console myself with the knowledge that I had already travelled the world a fair amount and enjoyed a few exotic trips; but deep inside I ached for the chance of adventure again. Since my marriage seven years earlier I had managed to curb my nomadic tendencies and had settled down to a very satisfying and enjoyable married life as a family man. But when the suggestion of the Viking voyage had first been mooted, the urge to roam had returned with a vengeance.

With some trepidation I had suggested to my wife, Wendy, that the chance of such a trip comes only once in a lifetime and that if I managed to get on it, my urge for adventure would probably be satisfied for ever.

Despite my total lack of seagoing experience and the fact that in my work as a Marine Biologist I was regularly sea-sick even when just taking samples from a research trawler, Wendy did not try to stop me from applying. But I think it came as much a shock to her as it did to me when we received a letter from Robin Bigland saying that I had been short-listed. Even so she clung to the perfectly realistic hope that I would still not be chosen for the actual trip, but would be a member of the reserve crew.

I learned later that there had been no fewer than 400 applications from would-be adventurers like myself. Word of the proposed voyage had flown far and wide, and there were applications from as far away as New Zealand, Rhodesia, South Africa, the United States and, of course, Norway.

Robin Bigland had decided, however, that only volunteers from the Isle of Man itself would be eligible. In the end I was one of the 25 men short-listed from 50 Island applicants. When I asked Robin why I had been lucky enough to be chosen he replied, rather crushingly, 'Oh, I suppose you seemed mad enough!'

As the time drew nearer to the date appointed for the final crew selection (the end of March), our training intensified. In addition to night-long treks across the mountains, we also had mid-week swimming training (including practice on a liferaft) and evening lectures on seamanship.

By the beginning of March, we were taking most things in our stride; Shane Lucas no longer had to force us to clamber up waterfalls or sit down in icy puddles – we were inured to misery by then!

As a training programme it was an undoubted success. Those who survived it had found that a great comradeship had been formed, based mainly on the good-natured humour that permeated all our activities. We had all accepted at an early stage that we had to be a little mad to consider immersing ourselves in icy water at every opportunity, and that the best tonic was to laugh and enjoy it.

It wasn't always easy. In Dhoon Glen one morning, a photographer from the *Daily Mirror* asked us to run into the sea stark naked, in mid-February, presumably in an attempt to compete with Page Three of *The Sun*. There was a Force 7 gale blowing, and the breakers were awe-inspiring. Nevertheless, we dutifully waded out into the icy water and waited patiently for him to remove his fur-lined gloves so that he could press the shutter on his camer. After he had been fiddling about for a couple of minutes our language became a little abusive and when, after another delay, he decided that he had fitted the wrong lens, we were having difficulty keeping our tempers. Finally, when he had organised himself to his satisfaction, he called out to us to face out to sea, in order that the readership would not be offended. Whereupon someone yelled back that we had been standing for so long in icy sea-water that it didn't matter which way we were facing!

During the course of our training, and with increasing regularity as the date of the voyage approached, we had been using an ex-naval cutter, loaned to us by King William's College, the Public School on the Island, to gain experience in seamanship and, in particular, learning how to row as a team. Although we knew that the Viking ship would be rigged in a different manner, we all gained valuable experience which was to stand us in good stead in the weeks to come.

The hours spent rowing out to the bell-buoy at the entrance to Castletown harbour in the cold winter dawns will long remain in my memory – as will the night sail in a rough sea, when my clothing got soaked by the first wave and I spent the rest of the night thinking of all manner of excuses to try to persuade Eddie Kaighin to turn back to harbour. But at least he agreed to put into Port St. Mary for a warming glass of rum before heading out again into the choppy sea. I must admit that the internal warming effect of alcohol did brighten my outlook on life a little.

By now the crew-selection time was drawing close. All our 'after-training' (more like 'post-mortem') discussions returned again and again to whom we thought were the obvious choices; and it came as a sad blow to all of us when one of our gallant band was injured in a car accident. Mick Kneale, whom we had all thought was a certainty due to his extensive seagoing experience, had to retire from the prospective crew only a week or two before the selection. After six months of training together, we all felt for him and it brought home to us the fact that at least half of the training crew were soon going to have to face up to that disappointment themselves.

In Norway the longship was nearing completion and events were beginning to move rapidly. The chosen crew were due to fly out to Oslo in mid-April; and suddenly, before we expected it, the time was upon us. Robin Bigland had decided that the uncertainty of waiting and not knowing could become demoralising, and advanced the crew-selection day. And so, on the evening of Friday, March 9, all the modern-day Viking aspirants gathered in Robin Bigland's office in Athol Street, Douglas, and to help the nerves, drank copious draughts of beer as the hour approached.

Finally Robin announced his crew. Excluding himself, six members had been chosen for their particular skills; and the choices were such that the remainder agreed unanimously with the decision (not that we could do anything about it, anyway).

As expected Eddie Kaighin was to be the Skipper, or 'Helmsman' in Viking parlance. He was undoubtedly the obvious candidate not only because of his experience on Merchant ships, but also because of his love of older sailing vessels and knowledge of their different types of rigging.

Brian Cousins, an accomplished 'deep-water' yachtsman, who exuded an aura of quiet confidence, was to be the 'Bosun' and second-in-command.

David Eames, who although only 21 years old, had more experience of inshore sailing, navigational expertise and knowledge of both radio and marine engines than most of the remainder of the crew combined, was chosen as one of the watch-keepers.

Nigel Wood and Rick Tomlinson, both very proficient sailors, completed the nucleus of the experienced sailors.

Georgie Kneale had all the necessary qualifications required for him to be elected as the ship's fitter, carpenter, blacksmith, etc.

As to the remaining four places, the committee which Robin had formed to oversee the organisation of the voyage had been unable to choose between the eleven other contenders. So these four places were to be chosen by lottery. Each man was to draw out of a hat a table-tennis ball, four of which had been marked with a large spot.

I was one of the lucky ones, as were Major Shane Lucas, Colin Bowen and Richard Young.

It must be admitted that our excitement was difficult to contain, but the faces of those who were not to make the trip, brave as they tried to be, dampened our enthusiasm for a short time. Nevertheless, we had all known that some had to be disappointed, and the thought of the weeks ahead soon dominated our minds.

Within the hour I had phoned my wife, who had by now become enthusiastic about the trip and would have been equally disappointed if I had not made it.

From that night on the pace was hectic. The ship was still not completely sponsored, and various methods of raising money were put into operation. Each of the shields carried by *Odin's Raven*, as she was to be named, cost £1,000 for sponsorship, and the oars cost £500 each. The Isle of Man Government had put up money for the voyage, as had the Den norske Creditbank in Norway.

Our sea-going waterproof clothing had to be fitted and our private lives organised to cater for the fact that we would be away from home for at least two months.

The evening spent at Robin Bigland's office 'kitting-out' turned out to be an extremely humorous occasion. The mounds of Viking costumes and survival clothing scattered around the room reminded one of a jumble sale; especially as bodies in various states of undress dived from one pile to another liberating the more exotic or warmer apparel!

Damart had sponsored the voyage to the extent that none of us would be short of warm underclothing (a fact for which we were to be very grateful a few weeks later on) and with both Tog and Helly-Hansen over-clothing we were well protected against the cold.

Unfortunately the oil-skins, we were soon to discover, leaked like sieves but, with so little time left we resigned ourselves to a damp few weeks.

Although the ship was not due to sail from Trondheim until May 27, arriving in Peel for July 4, at least four weeks' sea-trials were essential in Oslofjord. The expertise necessary to sail a Viking longship could only be obtained from practical experience and we had the task of learning how to handle one in a matter of only a few weeks.

Five of us were unable to take off the full time required away from our work, and therefore the first batch of the crew flew out three weeks before us, leaving on April 26 to arrive in time for the scheduled launching ceremony on Saturday, April 28.

The day after they arrived I sat at home listening to the commentary on the launching of the longship (relayed by a remarkably clear link-up between the local Manx Radio and the Norwegian National Service), envious that I was unable to be present. Robin Bigland, Eddie Kaighin (the skipper), Brian Cousins, Rick Tomlinson, Nigel Wood and David Eames were the members of the first contingent, with Richard Young, Shane Lucas, George Kneale, Colin Bowen and myself having to curb our impatience and wait a further three weeks.

The time passed rapidly though, and it was not long before I found myself at the airport saying farewell to my family. Our departure was chaotic, with press photographers insisting that we wore Viking helmets with ridiculous rubber horns. These drooped to such an extent that it must have looked as if we had just completed an exhausting session of looting and pillaging, or whatever else Vikings were supposed to have done!

All too soon the farewells were over. The hullabaloo was left behind us as we climbed aboard the aeroplane carrying our shields and wearing what was to become virtually our crew uniform when not dressed as Vikings – red Tog Jacket, *Odin's Raven* T-shirt, and jeans.

As we slumped exhausted into our seats and the plane lifted away from the Island, the memories of those cold winter training sessions faded from our minds. Ahead lay the Viking longship, and the adventure of a voyage about which one could normally only dream. One man had not only had the imagination to conceive such a method of celebrating the Millennium of the Isle of Man, but also the drive and determination to carry it through! Robin Bigland, christened 'Biggles' by the crew, had already proved himself to be as ready to rough it with the rest of us – even if his sandwiches happened to contain breast of pheasant compared to our cheese butties! In the weeks to come, not only was he to prove himself a brilliant organiser, but also a redoubtable leader capable of controlling fifteen rampaging Vikings of differing temperaments. He also had the spirit to withstand (and return with interest) the constant leg-pulling about his high style of living: the cry of 'Your bird, Robin!', accompanied by a barrage of make-believe shot-gun blasts, each time a seagull ventured near us, could be heard from Oslo to Peel.

Sitting in the aeroplane as we headed towards Heathrow Airport and our connection with the flight for Norway, I went over the crew in my mind, wondering how each would turn out.

Eddie Kaighin, the skipper of the longship, had already proved to us all that he knew his business, although some people thought that at times he tended to be a little reckless. Time would tell. As a non-sailor I could do no more than trust in him and his experience. Of the others I knew relatively little, even though I had seen a great deal of them during the previous six months.

Brian Cousins, the yachting schoolteacher, seemed a quiet studious person, completely at home in a boat; I little guessed that he would turn out to be one of the most humorous men on board.

Richard Young, director of a freight company, had impressed me as an organiser and a person who managed to get things done.

Colin Bowen, a manager of a company involved in the production of shaving brushes, (although as the whole crew had grown beards suitable for the occasion, a Viking ship was not an ideal advertising platform), gave me the impression of quiet confidence in his own ability. I already knew that he was an experienced sub-aqua diver. He and I had brought our diving gear in the hope that we might have time to dive during the course of the voyage. Little did we realise what surprises lay in store for us.

Of George Kneale (who worked for the Highway Board), Rick Tomlinson (an Estate Agent), and Nigel Wood (a trainee accountant), I knew virtually nothing, except that they were pleasant company.

Shane Lucas had proved himself adept at climbing mountains and waterfalls, but I had yet to see him looking really at home in a boat.

With David Eames (an electrical fitter at a power station), I had formed an immediate friendship during the training, and we were to find ourselves equally compatible for the rest of the voyage. For a young man of 21, he had already impressed me with his sensible outlook on life as well as his excellent knowledge of the sea.

Finally, myself. How was I going to face up to the voyage? Frankly, I had no idea. I was certainly not a great seaman, and have always had a very healthy respect for the sea – which is another way of saying that I found the prospect of crossing the North Sea in an open boat not a little frightening. Perhaps that was my basic motivation, as I suspect it was for a number of the others. How would we ourselves face any dangers that might present themselves? This was the basis of the challenge, in my opinion: not knowing how one would react to either danger or just plain boredom, crammed together in a relatively small boat.

In fact, I found that by the end of the voyage most of my questions concerning my own abilities had been answered and I still have a very healthy respect for the sea!

Of our five Norwegian companions-to-be I knew nothing, although I would be meeting them within a few hours; but I had little doubt that

Robin Bigland had chosen them very carefully, bearing in mind that any expedition or protracted journey involving men of more than one nationality can often cause special problems.

At midday on Wednesday, May 9, we landed at Heathrow Airport. As we wandered through the terminal carrying our emblazoned shields, a number of eyebrows were raised in our direction. In fact, the shields were a bit of a nuisance, as we discovered on the onward flight to Norway, when we had to sit with them wedged between our knees; and it was with relief that we watched the snow-capped mountains of Norway slide beneath the wings as we descended towards Oslo Airport and the real beginning of our adventure. In a few hours time we would be viewing for the first time, the vessel that would carry us across nearly 2,000 miles of sea — a return journey in a style that could not be further removed from the manner of our arrival in the homeland of the Vikings.

CHAPTER TWO

Oslofjord

The Rød Batbyggeri boatyard at Frederikstad nestles beneath the pine forests at the head of Elingaardskilen, a small inlet near the entrance to Oslofjord. It can only be reached by means of a precipitous, mud-slurried track, down which it is far easier to toboggan than it is to walk!

The yard itself is small, consisting of one main building housing the slipway and a few scattered storerooms but, as the saying goes, big is not necessarily beautiful; the Yard Manager Magnar Hansen, and his family team of shipwrights, had managed to build a most beautiful replica of a Viking longship in an environment which has changed little in a thousand years.

The morning after our arrival in Norway the whole crew assembled for the first time on the jetty beside *Odin's Raven*.

In the early morning sunlight she stirred restlessly on the sparkling water; behind her, the dark forest carpeted the steep hillsides on both sides of the inlet. My first impression was one of surprise. She was much bigger than I had anticipated. Having undergone all our sea-training packed like sardines into the small cutter we had used in Castletown Bay, the broad beam of the longship seemed incredibly roomy; I was to change that opinion radically after a few days at sea!

The *Raven*, as she came to be known among the crew during the course of the trip, looked as if she had been recently polished; her rakish lines gleamed from stem to stern with the curving, red tongue of the dragon figurehead, carved by David Swinton, sticking out contemptuously over the water. The healthy glow of the oaken woodwork had been obtained, I was later to learn, by liberal applications of a wood-preserver known as Trekkfast. As David Eames had been given this onerous task and had been up to his ears in it for the previous week, he was quickly christened 'The Trekkfast Kid.'

In fact, by the time the final contingent arrived on board, all the major fitting-out work had been completed, and after a morning spent familiarising ourselves with the various sheets and ropes, we were ready to set sail; not on the voyage itself, but to begin the Public Relations work which was an integral part of the whole trip. It is as well to emphasise at this stage in the narrative, that the Millennium Viking Voyage was essentially to publicise the Isle of Man to the world, and was to play a significant part of the Millennium celebrations that year. Scholars like Alan L. Binns, of Hull University, who was the academic consultant on the project, have emphasised the tremendous importance of the voyage from the point of view of experimental archaeology: it is only by building replicas and actually sailing them that scholars will be able to work out precisely how a Viking ship handled and performed. Alan L. Binns has already published his full account of the design, building and sailing of *Odin's Raven* (*Viking Voyagers*, Heinemann, 1980).

For the rest of us in the crew, our main concern was to learn to sail the boat, as competently as possible from A to B, without mishap, and to carry out the primary aim of crossing the North Sea from Norway to the Isle of Man with the maximum publicity benefit for the Island in its Millennium year.

One question we were frequently asked was – why was the *Raven* fitted with a 20 h.p. inboard engine? Didn't that in some way invalidate the whole project?

There were two main reasons for it. The most important was the question of insurance. In order to obtain the necessary insurance, both for the crew and the hull and contents of the vessel, an engine *had* to be fitted. The Norwegian Board of Trade carried out an extensive examination of our equipment before we embarked on the voyage. Insurance cover was largely conditional on a satisfactory report. No underwriter would have touched us without an engine – the chance of a collision in heavy fog between an oil-tanker and a wooden boat relying solely on oar-power would have been a very real one.

Secondly, it was very important that we kept to a very tight schedule throughout the voyage. In every port of call the arrival of the longship had been advertised well in advance and, quite apart from the receptions arranged for the crew, the ship herself was an undoubted tourist attraction. Thus the publicity to be gained suited our various hosts as well as the Isle of Man. However, the engine was to be utilised as little as possible and was only used in times of dire necessity in order that we could stay as much within our schedule as possible.

This public relations aspect of the voyage was rather distasteful to most of the crew, because we had never been involved in it before; but it did not detract from the challenge of having to sail a 50-foot open boat, whose design was a thousand years old, across 1,500 miles of some of the most treacherous waters surrounding the British Isles. It was in any event tacitly accepted by everyone that there would have been a voyage at all if it had not been for the publicity value.

And so, on a fine May morning, we slipped our moorings and quietly sailed away from the boatyard. For the first time I head the magic cry from Eddie Kaighin of 'Get the sail up, boys!' With much heaving and grunting, the 50 square metres of canvas was hauled up the mast.

The *Raven* rapidly picked up speed and we were soon slipping through the water at a steady six knots. Not being too sure of how my stomach would react when at sea, I had taken the precaution of investing in enough Dramamine sea-sickness pills to last me to America, in case our navigation went awry! Consequently, I was never troubled by the very lively motion of the boat; although my shipmates suggested that this was because my intake of pills at four-hourly intervals kept me in a state of permanent torpor!

In fact, during the early days of the voyage, I was so convinced that we were going to capsize at any minute that I have never been more alert in my life! This morbid fear was no reflection on the seamanship of the rest of the crew, but rather my own total inexperience of deep-sea sailing. Crewing a Viking ship was very different from crewing a Firefly dinghy in Chichester Harbour!

On our arrival on board we had organised ourselves into rowing positions and had placed our sea-chests, or 'kists', in the appropriate places for use as rowing benches. There were seventeen such kists on board and with an equal number of men (Alan Binns was the extra man), space was very limited. My original impression of there being a large area of spare deck was quickly dispelled as I experimented in an effort to find the most comfortable method of relaxing. As the afternoon wore on I discovered that the Viking vocabulary obviously had not included any words for 'comfort', and it became a question of determining how double-jointed one could be!

Robin and Eddie had decreed that all personal gear had to be stowed in our kists, leaving the small area beneath the deck-boards free for essentials such as food, water and sailing tackle. Trying to cram clothing, cameras, films, books, sea-boots and various other paraphernalia into a box measuring 2 feet by 2 feet by 2 feet was virtually impossible, and secret hoards were very quickly hidden away in the various 'rooms', as the areas below the deck planking were optimistically called. Our skipper Eddie Kaighin is not particularly tall (he was nicknamed 'The Demented Dwarf' after one or two hair-raising escapades) but even he could not make himself comfortable in a 2-feet-high 'room'.

This salting away of various items of personal equipment resulted in constant searches for missing sleeping-bags or oil-skins – not that it made much difference, because anything placed beneath the deck was soon saturated; for example, I stowed my sleeping-bag beneath my kist on that first trip into Oslofjord and was unable to use it for the rest of the voyage!

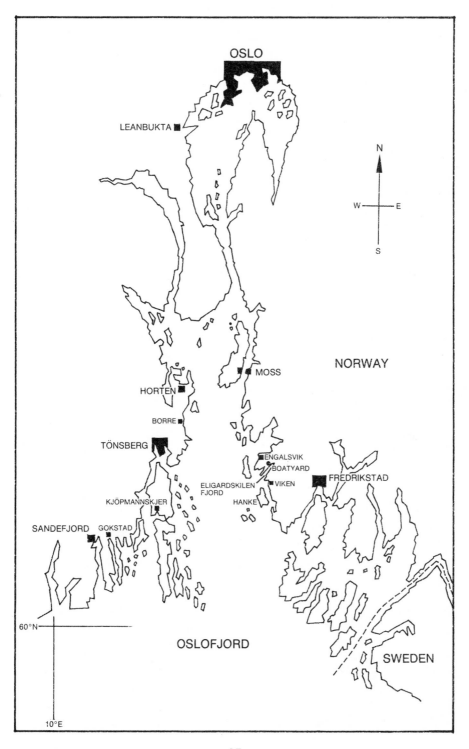

By lunchtime on that first day we had sorted ourselves into some sort of order as we approached the small harbour of Engelsvik and my first experience with the media, (the boat and some of the crew had already been exposed to the media at the launching, of course).

The last lap of the voyage from Trondheim to Peel through Scottish waters was to be covered for television by a film crew from BBC Scotland, but during the trials in Oslofjord, we were to be filmed in action by a team from BBC2 in London, directed by Ray Sutcliffe. They were in the process of making a ten-part series on the Vikings, written and presented by Magnus Magnusson, in which *Odin's Raven* was to be featured. During these early days the presence of a film crew on board was a novel experience for all of us and, no doubt, we 'hammed it up' to some extent. Even so I don't think we made it at all easy for any of the various television teams throughout the trip with our constant use of salty 'nautical' language.

In addition to taking endless shots of the ship being sailed, rowed, tacked and worn, Ray Sutcliffe wanted Magnus Magnusson to do what they called a 'sync piece' – television jargon for 'synchronised sound', when the presenter addresses the camera with a prepared piece. For this, Magnus took over the stroke position, and uttered (or rather, gasped) a few well-chosen words as he laboured at his oar. We couldn't properly hear what he was saying; but as 'stroke oar', he would never have made the Oxford and Cambridge Boat Race. (Actually, when we saw the completed sequence in the second episode of the TV Series *VIKINGS!*, it looked rather good – and they say the camera never lies!).

This important rowing position, from which the rest of the oarsmen take their rhythm, had been allotted at a very early stage to George Kneale, our resident blacksmith. His strong, even strokes allowed us to row with no great discomfort for hours at a stretch, which stood us in good stead on a number of occasions.

Although the experience of being film stars may have gone to our heads initially, we soon became irked by the ever-present lens prying into our every action – without exception! By the time we had reached the Western Isles of Scotland, where we attracted the interest of ITV film cameras as well, we had devised a number of ploys to discourage their less acceptable attentions.

On that first afternoon, however, having picked up the BBC2 crew from the pleasant harbour of Engelsvik, we sailed erratically across the fjord, manoeuvring into the best positions for the camera which was based on an accompanying boat called Sunshine IV. At various times during the afternoon, mid-water transfers took place when shots of the interior of the boat were required, which gave some of us the opportunity to change vessels as well, in order to take photographs of the *Raven* under sail ourselves.

In the early evening we said farewell for the day to the 'Beeb' and rowed unheralded into the small harbour of Horton. We had not yet begun our P.R. trip in earnest and were therefore unexpected, but within an hour the news of our arrival had spread and the first sightseers arrived.

We were due to stage a 'raid' on the Norwegian car-ferry *King Olaf* the following morning, and with an early start ahead, the evening festivities were not prolonged. Most of the crew walked into town to sample the local night-life, while Colin Bowen and I remained on watch. It was the first night that the whole crew were together on board, but most elected to sleep on the jetty. I remember my amazement in watching Alan Binns, the technical adviser on the longship, who was to travel with us on the first stage of the voyage to Lerwick, negotiating his way into the cavernous tent that he called a sleeping bag. Having first divested himself of a number of garments, he wriggled into a wet-suit and then caterpillared across the jetty, working his way deeper and deeper into his overnight accommodation. When this writhing mass had finally settled down, all that could be seen was a protruding nose, which then proceeded to emulate the Mersey foghorn!

Rick Tomlinson, the youngest member of the crew, also kept me amused for a time, as he attempted to launch himself into a hammock which he had slung between the mast and one of the yokes carrying the furled sail. After a number of unsuccessful attempts resulting in spectacular falls on to the deck, he finally achieved a precarious sitting position, with the hammock swaying dizzily out over the water. There followed a further 20 minutes of furious activity, interspersed with curses, before he was securely cocooned in his sleeping bag. I then had the pleasure of informing him, just before he settled down for the night, that we were due to sail in an hour and perhaps, as he had taken so long getting into the hammock, he should now begin to extricate himself. His reply was indecipherable, but I did get the gist of it!

At 3 o'clock in the morning a cold and drowsy crew rowed out of Horton to keep our appointment with the *King Olaf* car ferry. But 'the best-laid schemes of mice and men gang aft agley'. What followed can only be described as a fiasco, and a new phrase was coined by the crew: 'Typical Norwegian Cock-up', or TNCU for short.

Our five Norwegian crew members – Arne Wisth (photographer of international reputation). Odd Børstad (whom Robin Bigland had elected to be ship's cook), Rolf Hansen (one of the original members of the Brendan Voyage and a highly experienced 'squaresail' sailor, Knut Hoff (an international journalist), and Knut Skogøy (an architect), – were con- stantly appearing and disappearing at irregular intervals during our stay in Norway, as they were in charge of organising transport, accommoda- tion, food and P.R. On this particular occasion, Knut Skogøy (later to be nicknamed 'Action-Man') was on board the ferry co-ordinating the 'attack'. The general idea was for us to board the ship, 'kidnap' the

Captain and ransom him for a case of whisky; the whole event was planned as a stunt to be covered by Norwegian television.

The physical problem of stopping a massive Townsend-Thoresen ferry with a 50-foot boat had been solved by arranging for the ship to heave-to at a convenient spot in the fjord. Similarly, to avoid the problem of having to scale a forty-foot hull of vertical steel, Knut Skogøy was standing by to make sure that one of the boarding-doors, near the waterline, was opened for us. Such is the advantage of being a modern Viking!

Initially, all went smoothly. We rowed towards the ferry as it reduced speed and, for the first time, heard the vibrant notes of Knut's Viking horn echoing across the water. Then the plans began to go awry. As we neared our target a small launch unexpectedly shot in front of us and tied up at the open port which had been opened to facilitate our boarding. Not to be outdone, we came alongside the launch, all shouting various war-cries as requested by the television team, and the raiding party leapt on board.

Four of us had been awarded this dubious honour: Robin Bigland, Arne Wisth, Shane Lucas and myself. Dressed to kill in our Viking costumes, we attempted to storm our way across the launch and thus gain access to the ferry.

Robin Bigland, our Chieftain, was grandly arrayed in his costume and the original helmet worn by Kirk Douglas in the film *The Vikings*, but found himself baulked by the diminutive skipper of the launch. With much pushing and shoving and a torrent of Norwegian invective, the four of us were prevented from going any further; Robin's helmet had been twisted around to the extent that he was unable to see, and as he groped his way back towards the *Raven* one could hear his muffled voice telling Arne to 'Get this bloody fool off my back', and 'If he pushes me again, I'll knock him down!' Unfortunately, Arne was leaning against the side of the boat by this time, helpless with laughter!

During all this chaos, Shane Lucas (one of the few of us who really enjoyed dressing up as a Viking) had somehow gained entry into the ship and was now employed in terrorising one of the ship's officers. With an evil grin on his face he had gripped his chosen prey by the throat and was brandishing a lethal Viking battle-axe over his head. Mercifully, Knut Skogøy appeared a few seconds later with a rather bewildered-looking Captain, and we all returned to the *Raven*, along with an assortment of Norwegian and Danish reporters.

What had actually caused the confusion was that no-one had seen fit to warn the skipper of the Customs launch, (for such it turned out to be) about the planned raid. It must therefore have come as quite a shock, especially at 6 o'clock in the morning, to experience such an event, and no doubt his spirited resistance was on the assumption that we were attempting a novel method of smuggling contraband!

Still smarting over our defeat we hoisted sail and headed back towards

Horton to land our newly-acquired guests. The ransom had degenerated into a case of lager but our spirits were soon lifted when one of the reporters produced a bottle of Danish akvavit. This fiery liquor is a powerful pick-me-up and should only be drunk with due caution. Luckily we had been warned to treat it with respect, because a little later we needed all our concentration.

The *Raven* banner (named *Land-Waster* after the famous banner carried by King Harold Hardradi of Norway when he was defeated by the English at the Battle of Stamford Bridge in 1066), was accidentally knocked over the side and Eddie Kaighin immediately seized the opportunity to practice our 'man-overboard' drill. By the time the banner had been retrieved, all of us were uncomfortably aware of how long it took to manoeuvre the ship in a complete circle, even on a relatively calm sea. It didn't need much imagination to picture the problems which would be presented if somebody went over the side in the middle of the North Sea.

This was an ever-present hazard, considering that the gunwale of the longship was only two feet above the waterline. It was a constant worry to Robin Bigland that the success of the voyage might be marred by such an accident. The danger was always present, especially when one bears in mind the ablution techniques required on board a boat totally lacking any modern methods of sanitation: relieving oneself over the side of a corkscrewing longship constitutes quite a challenge.

It was tacitly accepted by all of us that if we did go overboard our chances of being picked up alive were very slim indeed. Under full sail with a good wind on the quarter, the *Raven* had already showed that she could achieve 10 knots easily, and at one stage we had logged 14! At any speed over 6 knots, depending on the state of the sea and the direction of the wind, it was highly unlikely that the boat could be turned around in under 15 minutes. One would be extremely fortunate to find a man in the cold North Sea after such a time, even assuming that it was relatively calm – a rarity in itself.

In the event the problem never arose, although on many occasions when the yard was being lowered so that a reef could be taken in during foul weather, the violent motion of the boat sent a number of us sliding helplessly across the deck clutching desperately at any available hand-hold. The cramped conditions, coupled with the weight of the yard and the vicious flapping of the huge mass of canvas, made any sail-changes in rough weather extremely hazardous operations.

In the relatively calm waters of Oslofjord, when the North Sea seemed far away, nobody was morbid enough to dwell on the prospects of what 'might' happen. Those few days spent 'showing the flag' at the various towns along the side of the fjord were considered by many of the crew to be the highlight of the voyage: after six months of constant training we were at last enjoying the fruits of our labour.

Between our various social engagements on land, we learnt to handle our vessel as well as time would allow. The weather assisted our endeavours by remaining totally unpredictable and we were constantly tacking, reefing, rowing or skimming along under full sail. With only a single square-rig the *Raven* could only just beat to windward, and, with virtually no keel, the amount of leeway produced was quite extraordinary. When tacking a Viking ship it is necessary to use two bow oars and row the head around; as soon as the vessel comes into the wind, the sail 'backs', and she then moves astern very rapidly. This caused much confusion on a number of occasions when small sightseeing boats ventured too close to our stern while we were tacking.

Eddie Kaighin realised at an early stage that by raising or lowering the sail by only a few feet, the speed of the boat could be altered quite radically. Similarly, the weight and position of those on board was an integral part of the trimming when under full sail.

The importance of this effect was only discovered by chance when we were sailing in the strongest wind that we had experienced up-to-date in the fjord. I was on the 'steering oar' for the first time and we were virtually planing before an estimated Force 6 wind, the knowledgeable sailors among us waxing lyrical about the performance of the longship. All of a sudden the wind veered and the *Raven* heeled over to such an extent that the oar-ports were nearly under water. Desperately I heaved at the steering oar in an effort to 'bear away', but to no effect. As the sea began to lap at the 'ports', I yelled to Eddie to come and take over. Quickly we exchanged places and he rapidly ordered the sheets 'let-go' to relieve the pressure on the sail. Even this made no immediate difference until he noticed that most of the crew were forward of the mast and quickly ordered them aft. Within seconds, the *Raven* came under control again, and the danger of a capsize was averted.

Two valuable lessons were learnt from this occurrence. One was that the trim was critical in order that as much of the steering-oar as possible was in the water. With such a shallow draft, and a virtually flat hull, the longship literally floated on top of the water, rarely cutting into waves but tending to ride the top of them.

The second lesson was one of basic seamanship. When Eddie had ordered the sheets 'let-go', the crew member on the starboard side had tied his sheet 'off' and it required a number of valuable seconds to loosen it. From that moment on they were always held under tension, so that they could be instantly released.

Quite apart from learning how to sail our vessel, the time spent in Oslofjord enabled the crew to get used to living in extremely close proximity with one another and, as on any ship, various small groups began to form. Not to the extent that they became cliques, separating themselves from the rest, but enough to provide a kind of on-board rivalry.

The formation of the 'Bilge Rats' was a good example. Colin Bowen,

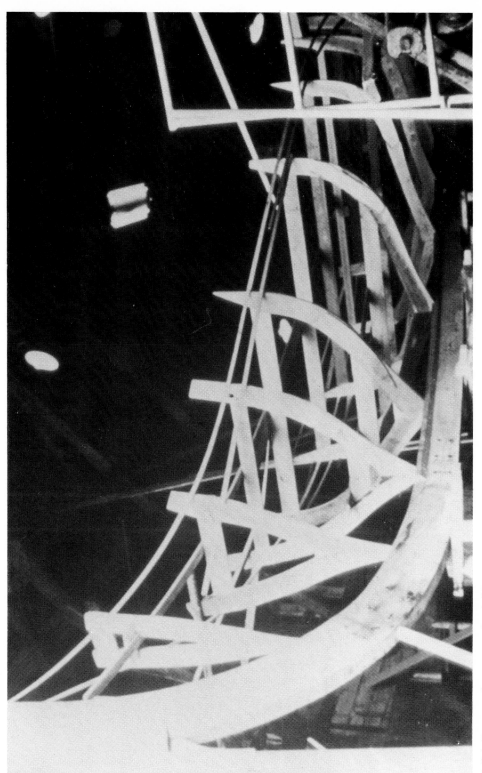

Odin's Raven under construction in Norway.

Robin Bigland

The Author

Eddie Kaighin

Colin Bowen

The
Crew of
*ODIN'S
RAVEN*

Brian Cousins

David Eames

George Kneale

Shane Lucas

Rick Tomlinson   Nigel Wood   Richard Young

Alan Binns   Odd Børstad   Rolf Hansen

Knut Hoff   Knut Skøgoy   Arne Wisth

Magnus Magnusson on board the *Raven* in Oslofjord.

The Chieftain and Standard Bearer with local Viking in Tønsberg, Oslofjord.

Odin's Raven leaving Trondheim at the start of the voyage.

A 'Femboring' in Trondheim Fjord. Note 'Topsail' and stern rudder.

Cramped sailing positions at sea!

Richard Young and myself were the least experienced sailors among the whole crew. We were therefore expected to carry out the more menial on-board tasks, such as pumping out the bilges. Due to our lack of experience we often made basic nautical mistakes in the early days, and were constantly being reprimanded by the skipper. We therefore decided to form our elite 'society' and, by committee decision, elect to it any other crew-member who also felt the lash of Eddie's tongue. Needless to say, by the time that the voyage was completed most of the crew had become honorary Bilge Rats, including the skipper himself!

The first person to be so honoured, to the extent that he was immediately voted President of the Society, was the bosun, Brian Cousins, known on board as B.C. He was in charge of all activities involving the use of the sail and, on one occasion during the sailing trials, he ordered the sail hoisted with no 'sheets' attached. The skipper's use of the vernacular was quite remarkable to hear as the sail billowed out virtually parallel to the deck!

Although the Bilge Rats were mainly utilised for the 'unskilled' sailing work (such as rowing the boat around during tacking and hauling up the yard), on land, our ability in other fields was very much in demand. Led by Richard Young, who was a natural 'fixer', we were in charge of procuring whatever the rest of the crew desired, up to a point! For example, we would make a point of convincing the local hoteliers, disco managers and so on that a free supply of their T-shirts for the crew would gain them free publicity if we wore them during some of the filming sequences. On our arrival in Peel we had each accumulated at least 15 such shirts.

Richard Young had also arranged, through one of his contacts in the Isle of Man, that each of the crew at the start of the voyage was issued with a special *Odin's Raven* T-shirt, over-printed with the word 'Crew' or 'Navigator'; Eddie Kaighin and Robin Bigland had special T-shirts over-printed with 'Helmsman' and 'Chieftain' respectively. During the following weeks, as the various small groups were formed, or memorable events occurred, the 'Crew' T-shirts were supplemented by others bearing such memorabilia as 'Survivor', 'Bilge-Rat No. 2' and 'Gobshite'. The latter were issued to those who earned them through a literal translation of the word!

The final four days of the time set aside for P.R. work and training in Oslofjord were both the busiest and the most relaxing of the whole trip. If this appears to be a contradiction in terms then such a phrase exactly describes our activities over that period, for we were either working very hard on the boat or relaxing just as hard with our hosts in the various towns on our way up to Oslo.

Following the fiasco of our 'raid' on the car-ferry and our return to Horton to disembark our guests, we set sail again for Borre, where a number of Viking Age royal burial mounds overlook the fjord. Here we met up again with Ray Sutcliffe and the BBC2 team (who had wisely wanted no part of the car-ferry stunt) and, for a couple of hours, we rowed up and down the coast while they filmed the mounds; the silhouette of the *Raven* moving slowly across the background of the burial mounds provided a very romantic scene.

The filming completed to the Beeb's satisfaction, we hoisted sail and, on a glorious sunny afternoon, made our way back to the Rød Batbyggeri for the last time. As we approached the boatyard Eddie Kaighin produced an inspired piece of seamanship and sailed us between the jetty and a moored fishing boat with literally inches to spare.

In the early evening it was a very weary crew who clambered ashore and boarded the mini-bus for the shore-base near Frederikstad. This was a converted warehouse in which the last contingent to arrive had only spent one night, but which had been home for the rest for the previous three weeks – all, that is, except Rick Tomlinson and Nigel Wood who had been on permanent watch at the boatyard. It doesn't sound an enviable task, but, in fact it had enabled them to obtain more sleep than the rest of the crew combined, due to the yard being so far off the beaten track.

For our last night in Frederikstad we decided to sample the local discotheques, after first viewing our day's exploits on Norwegian television. The car-ferry stunt apparently merited a 2-minute sequence at the end of the News – a commonplace occurrence over the following weeks.

Norway has not only the most expensive beer in Europe (and the stiffest penalties for driving under the influence), but it also has very stringent rules concerning the 'portage' of spirits in public, and, for this reason, it is often the rule in many 'discos' that all jackets must be removed at the door. But in common with most of the locals around us, we managed to achieve a reasonably lively evening, so lively, indeed, that our Chieftain eventually emerged from his room, dressed only in a pair of long thermal underpants (a sight guaranteed to sober anybody up) and reminded us in no uncertain terms that we were due to set sail early in the morning. Somewhat chastened we crawled into our sleeping bags, and within a few minutes the warehouse was silent.

Sandefjord lies near the mouth of Oslofjord on the western coast. The local people proudly claim it to be one of the major Viking settlements, from which many of the original longships set out on their voyages of conquest and discovery. Our reception was to set the scene for the next few days.

The morning after our carousing we cleared all our gear from the warehouse and transferred everything on board the *Raven*. Here we said farewell to the BBC2 crew, with whom we had all become good friends, as well as to Alan Binns, who was to rejoin us in Trondheim for the North Sea crossing.

At ten o'clock *Odin's Raven* slipped her moorings and, watched by the man who had created her, sailed quietly away from the jetty for the last time. As we rounded the point at the mouth of Elingaardskilen the boatyard merged into the trees and was lost to view.

The day was overcast and windy, with the occasional shower of rain testing our waterproof clothing. Unfortunately these garments turned out to be a major disaster and from that moment on, non of us was ever really dry at sea. With the prospect of 1,500 miles ahead of us, we felt distinctly bitter about the manufacturers of the so-called 'oil-skins'; but it was too late to do anything about it, and so we soon became resigned to being permanently we through.

But any gloom we felt was soon dispelled by the exhilaration of the sail across the Sandefjord. In a choppy sea the longship was put through her paces at speeds of up to 10 knots, her narrow stem slicing into the waves then lifting high as she skimmed over the surface. With the sail un-reefed the *Raven* heeled over with each gust, foam creaming past the open oar-ports. Bearing in mind that there were no scuppers, Eddie ordered Georgie Kneale to fit the covers (called poppets) over the ports on the leeward side to reduce the risk of shipping too much water. The shields were also repositioned for extra protection until we neared our destination, when the oar-ports would have to be cleared for rowing.

Even after these precautions had been taken, the spray from the bow regularly showered across the boat, soaking the foredeck team. During this trip many of those who were not actively engaged in sailing duties took the opportunity of finding the driest place on board – with little success! Robin Bigland and Eddie Kaighin had staked a claim as far aft as was practicable and were the most sheltered, mainly by the bodies in front of them; such are the privileges of rank!

I found that by sitting between two of the kists leaning against the stacked oars with my feet braced against the foot of the mast, I was sheltered from all but the largest of the waves. Comfort did not really enter into the problem as there was never room enough to stretch out, except along the oars themselves, a position which was even more open to the elements.

Towards midday the wind began to slacken, and as we neared the entrance to Sandefjord the motion of the boat eased. None of us really knew what to expect as regards the forthcoming reception, and Robin Bigland took the opportunity of giving us a pep-talk. He explained that we were likely to be inundated by press-men and photographers at all our ports-of-call, and reminded us of our function as ambassadors for the Island. I don't think that, even then, we really had any firm idea of what was in store for us, but within the hour we were to find out.

As we neared Sandefjord harbour the wind died on us completely and it became obvious that we would have to row in. This was unfortunate because, to the waiting spectators, the sight of a Viking ship bearing down on them under full sail would have looked much more dramatic. On all our arrivals during the course of the voyage we tried to sail up to the reception committee whenever possible; if not, we would row, but on no occasion did we have to arrive under engine.

Before unlashing the oars, there was one more chore to be undertaken – the dressing-up session. This was never particularly pleasant, because our Viking costumes were stowed in the bilges when not in use, so they became a little smelly, to put it mildly. The costumes themselves ranged from the Chieftain's immaculate jerkin and kirtle (hemmed to the 'in' length for the season) to Colin Bowen's unbelievably baggy 'trews' whose crotch extended down to his knees. Only a few of us wore helmets (hornless, of course, in deference to modern scholarship), but this detracted not at all from the war-like appearance of the crew because of our unshaven and windswept appearance. The carrying of weapons was voluntary, but most of us usually brandished either a sword or an axe. In addition, Robin Bigland had put our battle-standard *Land-Waster* in my charge for the voyage, so I had my hands full.

Once fully attired we moved the 'kists' into our rowing positions and unshipped the oars. This was quite a tricky operation, for they were each 16 feet long and, although well balanced when in use, extremely heavy to lift. It was to be a few days before we developed a proper drill for handling such unwieldy objects on a cramped ship.

With a fine drizzle adding to the dampness of our sheepskin cloaks we rowed into the confines of the harbour. While still a couple of hundred metres away from the quayside we heard a low murmur of noise, and looking over our shoulders we beheld an astonishing sight: the entire harbour was black with people! As this was our first 'official' landing, we took extra-special care and moored neatly alongside the designated jetty. While Robin Bigland, Eddie Kaighin and myself (as standard-bearer) climbed ashore, the rest of the crew stowed the oars, made the boat shipshape and then followed us on to the pier.

After the speeches of welcome and an appropriate reply from our Chieftain, we were escorted to a nearby restaurant for lunch amidst a blizzard of flash-bulbs. It had been just outside Sandefjord that the original Gokstad Ship had been discovered and excavated, and after lunch we were driven out to see the burial mound, which was carefully rebuilt after the excavation. Standing on top of the mound with our swords stuck in the soil for the benefit of the local press, we all felt a strong emotional link with the spot. The fjord, sullen and grey below us, could have change little since the days of the original Vikings, and with our own vessel soon to begin its epic voyage, we felt a real kinship with those adventurers of old. I know that on many occasions, especially when hove-to in some lovely cove in the Western Isles, we all felt the same feeling of time having flicked back a thousand years.

In the late afternoon we rowed the *Raven* out of Sandefjord, the cheers of the spectators and the hooting of ships' sirens ringing in our ears, and remained at the oars for the following two hours. Our next port-of-call was Tønsberg, and we moored for the night beneath an impressive suspension bridge linking the mainland with the string of islands which terminated in the aptly-named village of World's End.

Colin Bowen and I were again on watch and, while the rest of the crew were taken off to sleep in a nearby school for the night, we set about making ourselves comfortable.

In the absence of our shipmates we were able to arrange reasonable accommodation by utilising the sail as a tent and with so much available space we could at least stretch out full length on deck. It still made a hard, unyielding mattress, but our bodies were becoming accustomed to it.

During the three days following our reception in Sandefjord we landed at Tønsberg, Moss and Horton for similar civic receptions. Everywhere we went we were right royally entertained at dinners and lunches, and went on visits to places of local interest laid on for us by our Norwegian sponsors, Den Norske Credit Bank. At the Naval Museum at Horton, for instance, we were shown a remarkable collection of models of ships, old and new, and given an exhaustive account of the history of sea-faring.

During all the P.R. trips, people were allowed on board in harbour and, at Robin's discretion, also at sea, since the distances between our ports-of-call was only a matter of 20 or 30 miles. It always gave us pleasure to see the thrill that people got out of sailing on a Viking longship. Unfortunately the numbers had to be severely restricted; when fully crewed, the *Raven* had very little room to spare.

By Wednesday evening, May 16, the *Raven* was moored alongside a converted fishing boat which was to be our accommodation for the evening, in a small fjord just outside Oslo. The next day was the Norwegian National Day and our arrival in the city was timed to coincide with that. To celebrate the successful completion of the first lap of the voyage, we all drove into the outskirts of Oslo to a huge restaurant/disco. From what we saw, National Day in Oslo appeared to be a rumbustious display of rivalry between two groups of students, the 'Reds' (who had just graduated in Economics) and the 'Blues' (the Arts graduates).

The whole city was alive with young people wearing favours of either colour and our red Tog jackets blended in well with one of the factions – the right one too, because the 'Blues' appeared to be outnumbered by at least 4 to 1!

The holiday was due to begin at midnight and the place was a riot of noise – car-horns blaring, hooters braying, whistles shrilling, and everybody singing either the 'Reds' chant or that of the 'Blues'.

The evening was a resounding success, even though the final bill must have made a sizeable dent in the budget, with beer at £1.50 a pint. But psychologically it was very well worth it. The crew had now molded into a unit, morale was high, *Odin's Raven* had exceeded all expectations, and everyone was looking forward eagerly to the main voyage. Our stay in

Oslo was to be a bit of a holiday, subject to our numerous official engagements; because however much we tried to hide it, a certain amount of nervous tension was bound to start building up as the departure date approached. Crossing the North Sea in an open boat was not going to be a joy-ride; it was a challenge that we had accepted blithely enough, an epic never-to-be-repeated voyage.

That happy evening in Oslo we all felt ready for it – but not without an inward tremor of apprehension.

CHAPTER THREE

Oslo Interlude

Norwegian National Day itself in Oslo was a riot! In the morning we rowed the *Raven* to the central jetty of the ferry terminal, practically in the centre of the city. There we were besieged by hundreds of spectators, and throughout the three days of our stay we were never given a moment's respite.

From the social point of view, the highlights of our visit to Norway came on our second day in Oslo, when we were presented to the King – King Olaf V of Norway. As a former Olympic yachtsman, he showed great interest in the technical details of the *Raven* and the way she handled. Not for nothing do the Norwegians affectionately regard King Olaf as a true descendent of the Viking Sea-Kings of old.

The audience with the King was followed by a superb farewell banquet hosted by Den Norske Credit Bank, and we were all touched by the mementoes that were heaped on us.

Saturday was to be our last day moored in Oslo – and our first real experience of the hardships that could be involved in our forthcoming voyage.

In the afternoon we took the *Raven* out into the fjord for the benefit of one of Norway's most experienced 'square-rigger' sailors, Erik Rudstrom. He is an electrical engineer to trade, but his all-consuming enthusiasm is for sailing the old North Norwegian type of nineteenth-century fishing-boat known as a *Fembøring*. It is an open boat with a single squaresail, supplemented by a small topsail; in it, Erik Rudstrom goes sailing into the Arctic every year to the cod fisheries off the Lofoten Islands, catching cod in the traditional hand-line way. The BBC *VIKINGS* team went filming with him, and the series was liberally sprinkled with shots of his boat pitching and tossing in the icy wastes. Both he and his boat are true Viking descendants, and we felt proud to have him on board. He had shown intense interest in our project since its inception, and certainly he knew more about sailing our type of vessel than all the crew combined.

The weather was overcast and wet, the squally showers sweeping up the fjord with monotonous regularity, but the conditions were ideal for some exhilarating sailing. Eddie Kaighin handed over the helm to Erik Rudstrom as soon as we had cleared the harbour, and he was hard-pressed to wrest it from him again!

To all sailors, handling the longship was a unique experience, regardless of their ability with modern sailing-boats. The steering oar (as the tiller was known) is positioned towards the stern on the starboard side, held against the strakes by a leather strap. Due to the 'drag effect' there was always the tendency to 'port the helm', which took a little time to get used to.

The wind was gusting between Force 4 and 6 and the longship creamed along at a steady 9 knots, the spray cascading over the deck as she plunged into the waves. For the first time we experienced the difficulties associated with tacking in a relatively heavy sea. The angle at which the sail was held was critical at any time, because if the yard was allowed to swing around, the sail would suddenly 'back', and with such a spread of canvas the vessel would very quickly be in trouble. Unlike a modern Bermudan-rigged yacht when everything can be 'let go', when the sail was 'set' on the *Raven* it involved the use of a minimum of seven sheets and braces to hold the canvas in the correct contour. Consequently, when a tack was required, there appeared to be ropes whistling about all over the deck; anyone who was not 'au fait' with what was happening could very easily be flicked overboard as the sail filled and the ropes sprung taut.

In rough weather, with the slip pitching and rolling, great gouts of spray crashing inboard and the decks awash, any alterations to the set of the sail became hazardous.

That afternoon in the fjord, with Erik Rudstrom gleefully testing the longship to the limit, we began to get an inkling of what conditions were going to be like at sea. On three occasions when attempting to back, we were unable to pull her head round into the wind, the pressure on the sail being too great; in the end it required two men on each of the bow oars.

Richard Young and myself had, at an early stage in the trials, been detailed as the oarsmen for tacking. It was our job to pull the bow round until the yard could be swung over to catch the wind on the opposite tack. Now, for the first time, we were attempting to manoeuvre in rough weather. While the bow party stood by the sheets, ready to pull the leading edge of the sail around, we slid from one side of the deck to the other, trying to arrange two kists into the rowing position. Actually pushing the oars outboard through the oar-ports was extremely difficult as we required both hands to hold them; with the boat corkscrewing beneath us we were repeatedly flung against the side, frantically grabbing hold of any available rope to save ourselves from going over.

When finally we were in position and the order to 'give way together' was given, we found that the oars either disappeared under-water or waved about in the air. Nevertheless, we soon developed a rhythm that was relatively successful, and gradually began to turn the boat into the wind. Our positions for rowing under those conditions meant that we were in the midst of a number of ropes whose free-running was vital to the successful completion of the tack. It was a little nerve-wracking to experience these various ropes suddenly stretching taut at neck height, and we had to keep our wits about us.

When the ship was 'in irons' (heading directly into the wind) the sail would fill and we would begin travelling backwards. Our problem in a strong wind was to provide the physical power required to get the ship into this position, but with extra help on the oars we succeeded in the end.

Once round, in readiness for the new tack, the helm would be put 'hard-over' as we were travelling astern, thus helping to turn the ship, and then the order to 'bring the sail round' would be given. With Richard and myself still rowing, the bow party of three would swing the 'tack' across the boat, desperately hanging on to it as the wind filled the sail threatening to pull them over, until the slack was taken up on the cleats in the stern of the boat. The whole operation was fraught with hazard, and any close-hauled sailing coupled with a lot of tacking always left the crew exhausted.

As we sailed back to Oslo, Robin Bigland asked Erik Rudstrom what he thought of our chances now that he'd had a chance of sailing in the *Raven*. His words cheered us up immensely. 'Until this afternoon', he said, 'I would have said that your chances were very slim indeed. Sailing a craft of such an old design, with no protection whatsoever, across what is regarded as one of the most treacherous seas in the world, is going to require a great deal of skill and more than a fair share of luck; but with such a well-trained and cheerful crew your chances are enormously improved'.

Such praise from an acknowledged expert was extremely gratifying, and provided a fitting note on which to finish the sailing trials. As if to prove the point, Eddie Kaighin produced a superb bit of seamanship as we approached Oslo jetty for the last time, bringing the *Raven* in under sail until the last possible moment and then stopping the boat dead in the water alongside, using the oars as brakes while the sail was lowered in record time.

That evening we moored alongside the tender to the King of Norway's yacht at the Royal Yacht Club and celebrated the completion of the trials in true Viking style. By the early hours of the morning the *Raven* was awash with discarded prawn shells and beer cans.

Sunday dawned with a cloudless sky and at an early hour we motored across the harbour to the commercial docks. The longship was to be shipped up to Tondheim by freighter where the final preparations for the actual voyage would be made.

Beneath the hot sun, which made a welcome change from the weather we had experienced up until then, we stripped the boat bare in readiness for the trip north. All the deckboards were removed, and everything which had been stowed below was lifted on to the quayside. Then she was scrubbed out from stem to stern, the mast lowered and finally, she was craned out of the water. Magnar Hansen and his men had travelled up from Frederikstad, and they constructed a cradle on the quayside. Seeing her out of water for the first time was a fantastic sight. She really was a beautiful boat, her graceful lines shown off to perfection. Many sailing boats, when high and dry, tend to look very dumpy and inelegant, mainly due to the size and weight of the keel. The longship didn't have a separate keel and consequently her lines were classically symmetrical.

During the course of the sailing trials there had been much discussion concerning various aspects of the design of the longship. The hull itself had been scaled down from the original, but was otherwise a replica of the Gokstad. Due to this scaling-down the oar-ports had been raised as high as possible, because men cannot be reduced in size. If they had been left in the same position as on the original, they would have been on the water line.

The rigging, on the other hand, was a matter for scholarly and technical discussion, as were the relative sizes of the mast and the steering oar. Alan Binns was the expert chosen to design these unknown quantities and he had carried out a great deal of research in this respect. In the early days of the trials he kept bounding around the deck checking and altering the rigging – a hazardous operation at that time because a number of the deck-boards had still to be fitted. His sudden cries of 'Rakke, Rakke!', followed by a headlong gallop to the mast, were not an old Viking war-cry, but simply his way of drawing attention to the fact that the coupling which held the yard against the mast was caught and required releasing! 'Rakke', it transpired, was the Norwegian name for this particular piece of equipment.

Several of the original names were used on board, as there was no modern equivalent – such as the *Seglstikke*, whose purpose was to hold the 'tack' forward, and *Priare*, which was a system of ropes designed to hold the foot of the sail down, near the deck. It had originally been intended that all the rigging would be referred to in Norwegian, but when it came down to the practicalities of sailing, modern terms such as bowline, brace and sheet ensured less likelihood of misunderstanding.

Our Norwegian crew-members felt quite strongly that there were too many ropes involved in the rigging, and never agreed with Alan Binns on this subject. Although none of them could claim to have the same

42

technical experience, Rolf Hansen had been a crew member on the voyage of the Brendan leather curragh from Ireland to North America and was well used to the problems involved in handling a square-sail.

Eddie also felt that one or two changes would make for easier handling, and with Magnar Hansen at hand and the boat out of the water, he took the opportunity to make some alterations.

The shrouds with their *Jomfru* purchases (the main lateral supports for the mast) had originally been attached inboard. It was felt that by moving them outside the gunwale they would provide greater support as well as increase the stacking space for the oars.

Eddie Kaighin also made some drastic changes to the steering oar. It had always seemed heavy and cumbersome and the *Raven* had certainly been very sluggish in turning to port, but we had assumed this to be a basic fault of the original design. However, after Eddie had visited the museum and seen the Gokstad ship at first hand, he felt that our steering-oar required considerable reshaping. Magnar Hansen was hesitant at first, but after he too had visited the ship museum at Bygdøy, the power-planes were produced and long strips of oak soon littered the dockside. Within a short space of time our new slim-line steering-oar was completed, and the longship was ready for her journey.

By midday she had been loaded on to the freighter *Slettner*, along with a container into which were packed all the kists and loose gear. Eddie Kaighin was to travel with her, while the rest of us were to make our own way north to Trondheim, with orders to arrive no later than Thursday, May 24. Our sailing date was to be Sunday, May 27.

We had decided to travel up to Trondheim by various methods, some by train, others either hitch-hiking or by car; Richard Young and I chose to go by car.

The road from Oslo to Trondheim passes through some of the most dramatic scenery, the terrain gradually becoming more mountainous as one travels north. With time in hand we ambled sedately along the side roads, exploring the country as much as possible, and it was late on the Thursday evening when we finally drove into Trondheim.

The view of the fjord below us was magnificent as we came over the last mountain, and it was with a real feeling of sadness that we realised our time in Norway was drawing to a close. The holiday was over, and the real test was now about to begin. The huge expanse of Trondheim Fjord lay like a map in front of us, and the leaden grey water, flecked with the white of breaking waves, looked extremely cold and unfriendly.

'If it's like that 90 miles inland', said Richard, 'What's it going to be like in the North Sea?'

'Cold and wet', I replied. Although we had experienced some dangerous moments during the trials, we had always been in sight of land; and, more often than not, there had been a vessel of some description in fairly close proximity. Once we set sail from Trondheim we would be on our own, at the mercy of the elements, exactly as were the Vikings of old. Contrary to rumour, there was not going to be, and nor had it ever been envisaged that there should be, a support ship travelling with us.

That evening the crew were reunited in the Landlord Pub close to the waterfront. The change in the mood was immediately obvious, regardless of the outward signs of joviality. Everybody felt their fears and doubts building up again, and there was an underlying aura of nervousness in the conversation as we discussed what the future held in store for us.

Outside, *Odin's Raven* lay rocking gently at her moorings, having been unloaded from the freighter earlier that afternoon. Her mast swung lazily against the backdrop of the snow-covered mountains, while around her the chilly water of the fjord lapped hungrily at the wooden hull.

In the cold light of an early summer evening I stared out across the water towards the mouth of the fjord some 80 miles away. In three days time our little Viking ship (for in her true setting she seemed to have shrunk in size) would venture forth as her sister ships had done centuries before, to face whatever the sea chose to offer her. How many longships had set out from virtually this same spot, dwarfed by the mountains which rose up on either side, white-faced monoliths towering contemptuously over the tiny matchstick vessels? More to the point, how many had failed to make the crossing safely to the Shetland Islands?

With a final glance at the 'white-horses' which scudded across the harbour entrance, I clambered down on to the deck of the *Raven* and quickly huddled down into my sleeping bag. After the last few days of sleeping rough in the car, the unyielding surface of the deck was almost comfortable, and within a few minutes the gentle rocking of the boat had lulled me to sleep.

CHAPTER FOUR

Departure

The two days spent in Trondheim were hectic. The victualling and stowing of gear on board occupied all the crew for the whole of Friday. When we surveyed the huge pile of stores on the quayside and then looked down at the longship, it seemed an impossible task to cram everything below decks. Space was so limited that the deck working-area had to be kept free of extraneous matter at all times.

For the first time everybody took a great deal of care in not only stowing their own effects, but also noting in which 'room' they were stored. With at least a week at sea ahead of us there were unlikely to be many opportunities to move the kists around in order to find a sleeping bag. Every 'room' below the deck was covered by a kist in any case, and the fewer that had to be moved the better. Heaving a weighty sea chest around when the *Raven* was sailing under any conditions was no easy matter.

The Bosun, Brian Cousins, jealously guarded his sail locker, the only-below deck area on the ship which could be easily opened, as it was located amidships, just in front of the mast. Nevertheless, however hard he tried to keep it free of non-essentials, whenever he had cause to open it there was always a sleeping-bag or other form of bric-a-brac which had been quietly stowed when his back was turned!

Arne Wisth, the official photographer, was one of the main culprits, tidiness not being his forte, and we were forever coming across various pieces of photographic equipment scattered all over the ship.

Loading the food stores created some amusement as well as some nervous stomachs, especially when some bags of dried fish and reindeer meat began to fill up one of the lockers. We had already tried some of the reindeer and the reactions had been very mixed. Personally, I found it too strong for my taste, and had made sure that my own kist covered the locker containing the cheeses; at least I knew that was edible!

The position of each kist on board was to become a relatively important factor, due to our overcrowded conditions. Each man, theoretically, was to have a small area on board which he could call his own. This 'psychological space' was intended to create some form of normal privacy; but in the event, the constant movement on board when at sea made it impracticable. As it turned out, where possible most of the crew chose to place their kist in the position in which they rowed, and tended to remain in the vicinity when under sail, if conditions permitted. The most common cause for irritation was when an off-watch member of the crew tried to sleep full-length along two or three kists. It was always at such a time that someone would require an essential piece of clothing from his kist; but sleep was usually so difficult to come by that to wake a fellow shipmate was regarded as extremely bad form.

But for one member of our company we showed no such decency and regard – our ever-genial Norwegian ship's cook, Odd Børstad. I'm sure it is the fate of all ship's cooks to become the butt of the 'real' sailors – and Odd, bless his heart, was no exception.

Odd Børstad was the most Viking of all the Vikings. He stood over six feet tall, weighed at least 18 stone and sported an unkempt, windswept beard which reached half way down his chest. In his exalted position as cook he was not required to stand watches, and therefore took the opportunity to rest as much as possible between meals – in particular from eight in the evening until breakfast! None of us would have had any cause for complaint if he had not chosen to stretch out over the galley! It required three of the watch to lift him bodily across the boat, in order that the deck-boards could be lifted and the small cooker utilised.

This gas cooker which has been fitted in one of the 'rooms' was largely intended for use when in port or hove-to for the night in a cove, exactly as the Vikings had done before us: it is generally accepted that, whenever possible, they would moor overnight and cook on land over a camp fire. It was not expected that we would be able to use the stove a great deal while at sea, due to the motion of the boat, but hot black Norwegian coffee at 4.00 a.m. whenever conditions allowed worked wonders on a cold body.

When we saw Odd Børstad in Trondheim, while we were loading the boat, sitting on the deck with his feet in the galley and a broad grin on his face, surrounded by a mountain of cooking utensils, Eddie Kaighin nearly had a fit.

'Where the hell do you think you're going to stow all that?' he enquired.

'Do not worry, Eddie', replied Odd, clasping an enormous saucepan to his ample stomach, 'All will fit, you will see'.

It very nearly did, but time and again his efforts to close the deckboards were thwarted by an extremely large kettle which refused to fit neatly into its appointed position. For nearly an hour Odd tried every possible combination of pans and ladles, to no avail; it always ended up with the deckboards resting unevenly on the ribs which supported them.

'We can't leave it like that, Odd', said Eddie. 'Somebody's bound to trip over it.'

'I know, I know,' said Odd, quite unperturbed. 'But do not worry, I am having the answer.'

So saying, he leapt into the air and landed with his full weight on the offending planking. Needless to say, an 18-stone Norwegian landing from a great height solved the problem, and from that time on we had a smooth deck but a very badly dented kettle!

In the event most of the cooking equipment proved surplus to our requirements, as we fed almost perpetually out of one saucepan, one frying pan and one kettle; but that did nothing to dispel Odd's culinary enthusiasm.

As more and more equipment was stowed away on board the longship settled deeper into the water, and some of us eyed the decreasing distance between the gunwale and the surface of the water with a certain amount of trepidation. The position of certain items was critical, as the heavier ones were the only means of ballast available to us. The heavy bags containing the fresh water, for example, aft and amidships. Having experienced the effect of weight on the trim of the ship in Oslofjord, most of the heavier items were stowed as far aft as space would allow. This included the cumbersome liferaft which we were required to carry, but its position beneath the steering oar made it necessary for the helmsman to stand or balance precariously on the sheerstrake.

It was in Trondheim that the Norwegian shipping inspection was carried out.

We were about to find out how well a Viking ship would in reality face up to the crossing our forebears were known to have made. It was the ship and its environment that was to be tested, in exactly the same manner that other epic sea-voyages had been attempted. But there was a new and strictly modern hazard – we were intending to cross some of the busiest shipping lanes in the world. The Vikings of old, while tackling the elements themselves, did not have to worry about other ships, or oil-rigs, or oil-tankers that now accompany the operations in the North Sea. That was why the Norwegians insisted that we carried an engine as well.

An oil-tanker requires a massive area of sea room in which to stop or turn; even if they saw a small wooden vessel on their radar it would be highly unlikely that they would be able to avoid us. The sailing ability of the *Raven* was such that her manoeuvrability in even the most sympathetic wind was sluggish and, in any kind of sea, oar-power was virtually useless. It was therefore an unavoidable safety regulation that we were equipped with some form of power to enable us to decrease the chances of collision.

In any event it was the sea-worthiness of the longship, and our ability to cope with the lack of weather protection, which formed our main concern.

47

To meet the stringent safety regulations we were also equipped with the necessary distress-flares and life-jackets (although I can only bring to mind one occasion when some of the crew actually put these on for any length of time; most of us found that they restricted our movements too much). The skipper had ordered these life-jackets to be placed at the top of our kists, ready for any emergency, but as the trip progressed they gradually sank lower and lower as the more regularly required personal items, such as plates, mugs, books and warm clothing, submerged them.

By the early evening of Friday, May 25, the longship was fully laden, neat and tidy and had been passed by the Safety Officer as fit for the sea.

The following morning we were joined by the BBC Scotland film crew who were to film the start and end of the voyage for a documentary. By now we had become fairly blase about our role as 'film-stars' and their arrival on board created no more than a ripple of interest. We were to get to know the producer Bill Hook, narrator David Scott and production assistant Jan Riddell quite well by the time we reached home waters, due mainly to their uncanny habit of arriving at the most inopportune moments as far as we were concerned – although presumably the most opportune moments for them as regards good documentary material.

On board that day we also had the pleasure of the company of Kathy Lewis, Robin Bigland's personal secretary and the one person (other than Robin and his family) whose constant endeavour had enabled the voyage to reach this stage. From the moment that Robin had first mooted his plans, Kathy Lewis had been the prime co-ordinator of virtually every aspect of them, and we were all pleased to be able to take her out for a sail in the boat which had been her sole project for the previous year.

I have often wondered how Robin Bigland first broached the subject to her, but I am now convinced that he simply walked into his office one day and said, 'Kathy, I'm thinking of building a Viking longship and sailing it from Norway to the Isle of Man. Organise it will you, please?'

She had arrived the day before and brought with her a stack of mail and for once, there had been absolute quite on board as everyone read their letters. It was the first contact with home that most of us had had for the past three weeks, and even the most mundane reports of how our loved ones were faring were eagerly devoured. Naturally, we had all been writing home at regular intervals, but because we had been on the move all the time in Norway, our wives and girl-friends had waited until Kathy came over to give her their letters by hand. Consequently, each of us received quite a number of letters – the bachelors in the crew each collecting more than the rest of us put together!

The sail on the day before our departure was memorable for one particular event. I have already described the difficulties encountered when tacking the longship and the necessity to use the oars to turn the bow into the wind. With such a light breeze blowing, Eddie Kaighin decided to try it without the oars. Slowly but surely she came round, and to an exultant cheer, the sail backed, cracked loudly and then bellied out again, carrying us easily away on the opposite tack. Just to prove that it was no fluke, we repeated the operation twice more; each time it was touch and go whether she would make it, but slowly, agonisingly slowly, she clawed her way around.

Not being a sailor of experience I did not really understand what all the fuss was about and nor, I could see, did Bill Hook.

'What's all the fuss about, Eddie?' he asked.

'It's the first time that a square-sail design like this has been known to do it, Bill; that's what!' replied the skipper.

Robin Bigland, realising that this was a moment of great significance, delved into his kist and produced a bottle of gin as a celebratory offering to Odin. The Bilge Rats co-operated so enthusiastically that when the Chieftain requested the return of the bottle, we realised that the fountain had run dry. To cover up this inconvenient fact we surreptitiously put in a little sea-water and handed it back. Robin Bigland obviously wasn't born yesterday; seeing the gleam of mischief in our eyes he nonchalantly handed the bottle to Eddie Kaighin, who was still waxing lyrical about the 'tacking'.

With a cheerful toast to us all, the Skipper downed the remains of the 'gin' in one gulp. The effect was electrifying. The BBC sound recordist snatched his headphones with a yelp of pain; and the Bilge Rats spent the rest of the morning carrying out the most onerous tasks on board that the skipper could dream up.

By the time we returned to our mooring everything was back to normal, even to the extent that the morning sunshine had disappeared and drizzle had set in again. Having forgiven us for the gin episode, Eddie Kaighin requested Colin Bowen and me to dive and fit the 'strawkeel' on to the *Raven*. This was a device used by the Norwegian Fembørings, and would give us a keel depth of nine inches. It was hoped that this would enable the longship to head closer to the wind; but even after it was added, our keel depth was still so small that we were to average 15 degrees leeway in a Force 4, and the closest that the *Raven* could make was still 70 degrees off the wind.

It was the general consensus of opinion that the Vikings rarely used the sail unless they were running before the wind. If caught on a lee shore they would have had very little chance of sailing clear.

Both Colin and I were a little dubious about the job, if for no other reason than the First Law of Diving, which is never to go under water if one has consumed any alcohol in the previous 12 hours. But as it was a shallow dive and essential to the ship, we agreed to do it. While Colin Bowin went hunting for some air-bottles (we only carried our basic equipment on board), the BBC reporter, David Scott, asked for details of the planned dive for filming purposes.

49

'How are you going in?' he asked, 'We want to set up the camera to get the best angle.'

'Well,' I replied, 'we'll be doing a shallow water jump from the floating jetty, legs astride to prevent us going too deep in case there is some obstruction. Then we'll surface and collect the keel, bolt it on underneath and be out as quickly as possible. It looks bloody cold in there!'

Armed with this information the 'Beeb' spent the next few minutes carefully positioning themselves. They needn't have bothered. Before they were ready, Colin returned with the bottles, changed into his wet-suit in a flash (he is a much more experienced diver than I am and had a special quick zip suit) and was under water checking the existing keel. By the time I was fully kitted-up the camera was running and I was obviously going to have to stand in for both of us. Unfortunately, as I walked to the edge of the platform, still groping for my mouthpiece, I tripped over my fins and fell flat on my face in the water!

We were underwater for an hour and twenty minutes, and it was the most uncomfortable dive that I have ever experienced. Apart from the cold, which quickly numbed all feeling, the presence of rusty ironwork and thick sediment immediately below the ship made it a hazardous operation. The 'strawkeel' had to be bolted on to the existing one, necessitating the hand drilling of four holes through solid oak. Then the unwieldy new addition had to be manhandled into position and bolted into place. As so often happens when one is in a hurry, there is always one recalcitrant bolt that refuses to slide in easily, and it was two very cold and exhausted divers who finally surfaced on completion of the task.

What an extraordinary welcome awaited us. Kathy Lewis, who was anxious that we didn't suffer any ill effects from the cold, had dispatched Richard Young (Bilge-Rat No. 1) to obtain 'something warming' for us on our return to the surface. Not content with just buying something, Richard arrived back on the quayside ahead of two waiters, resplendent in white jackets and bow-ties, both laden with trays of Viking sustenance. A masterly feat in any event, but even more noteworthy when one remembers that it is illegal to carry or consume liquor openly in Norway.

It was an interesting psychological fact that as our days progressed as Vikings, the normally accepted protocol concerning the self-imposed rules by which most of us live was stretched to a great extent. I don't mean to imply that our manners or behaviour towards one another suffered in any way; rather, we began to experience a greater freedom of initiative and action which the constraints of a repetitive existence tend to smother.

Our growing ability to obtain virtually anything we required was reinforced by the generosity of the local people, wherever we went; they cheerfully accepted the fact that since a shipload of Vikings was in town, events were likely to be lively and unconventional. It was almost as if we were expected to act like Vikings – although the rape and pillage had to be kept to a minimum!

The air-bottles for the dive, for example, were conjured up by knocking at the door of the local fire-brigade, which is something that few diving-clubs would do except in a case of dire emergency.

For what was confidently expected to be our final evening in Norway, Robin treated us all to a meal in the local steak-house, followed by some drinks in the Landlord Pub. The evening was dominated by a Norwegian boxer who insisted on paying for every drink after he had failed in a challenge match with Richard Young – not in the boxing ring, I hasten to add, but to see who could drink a pint of beer fastest.

The evening ended on a high note and I took a certain pleasure in occupying Eddie Kaighin's bed in the hotel, leaving him to sleep on the floor. It was sweet revenge for sending me into that cold harbour!

It was perhaps to be expected that the night before setting out on such a voyage, we would lie awake thinking of what the future held in store. But with the crew morale at its zenith and the months of concentrated training and sea-trials behind us, we were all of the same mind. Nobody was going to back out now and therefore it was just a question of nervous anticipation. The next morning would see us sailing down Trondheim Fjord and, for the first time, out into the open sea. The forecast was in our favour; a north-westerly wind, Force 4 to 5, with the usual rain-showers expected along the coast. It appeared that a 'weather-window' was in the offing, and we were determined to make the most of it.

A 'weather-window', I was to discover, is a term used by sailors in the North Sea for a break of 2 or 3 days in the dominant inclement conditions. This relatively small area of sea has the reputation of being one of the most hostile stretches of water in the world. Robin Bigland had been dined, earlier in the week, by the skipper of one of the rare Colin Archer boats which was in port at the same time. He was not greatly cheered to be informed by this well-travelled man that every skipper dreams of accomplishing three major crossings in his life: the Atlantic, the Pacific and the North Sea! The fact that we were going to attempt it in an untried, open, Viking longship did nothing to shorten the odds on our chances of success.

The day of our departure dawned as dismally as had been forecast. A steady shower of rain put paid to our plans to take our leave of Norway in Viking costume. If we had to stow sopping wet sheepskins below deck for a week, they would not have been in a fit state to wear on our arrival in the Shetland Islands.

Our advertised departure time was 1300 hours and, as I suppose is usual in such cases, the morning seemed to pass very slowly. Apart from taking on some extra diesel to top-up our tank, the longship had been fully prepared for sailing the previous evening. As the minutes slowly ticked by, the crew sat around the deck in small groups talking quietly together, our

51

nervousness hidden behind the banter and the final packing and repacking of kists.

Since our arrival on the quay at nine o'clock, when there were few spectators around, the crowd on the quayside had gradually swelled in number until, an hour before our appointed time of departure, the whole area overlooking the *Raven* was packed with people. A school band played in the background as Bill Hook arranged some last-minute interviews, while others of the crew scribbled last-minute letters to go back to the Isle of Man with Kathy Lewis.

Before the farewell speeches we had one final act to perform, apparently in accordance with ancient Norse tradition. The sagas described the hammering of a nail by each crew member into the prow of the longship as an offering to the gods – a request for a safe voyage. These were referred to as 'God-nails' or 'mighty-nails' and one by one, in the order of rowing positions on board, we each clambered up to the figure-head and solemnly hammered a nail in the appointed place.

As the sailing time drew closer, the yard was lowered across the gunwales (it was slung across the two 'yokes' midships when not in use) and the sail prepared for hoisting. The aft four oars were made ready so that we could row away from the quay before raising the sail. The day was relatively calm, but there was a light breeze which, if it held its direction and strengthened in force, would enable us to sail away down the fjord on our first leg to the open sea.

Now it was time for the farewell speeches. The Bishop of Trondheim presented the longship with a stone from his Cathedral with the hope that it would be carried safely to rest in the new Cathedral at Peel. Then he said a prayer for the *Raven* and her crew in excellent English. We all found it deeply touching.

A succession of dignitaries followed him on board. The harbour-master presented us with the Trondheim coat-of-arms, to join the many other plaques we had already received from the towns along the shores of Oslo-fjord; the ship inspectors who had given us a clean 'bill-of-health' to sail came to wish us all the best. Finally the Lady Mayoress, clad in all her finery and not wearing the most suitable shoes for the occasion, was helped across the floating pier from the jetty to the boat by two of our gallants, wading knee-deep in water on either side like latter-day Walter Raleighs. To their credit, the Mayoress was deposited back on the jetty completely dry-shod.

At 12.55 on Sunday, May 27, the *Raven* cast off her mooring ropes and moved slowly away from the quay while the band played 'God Save the Queen'. The aft four oarsmen pulled her steadily out into the fjord, while the crowd clapped and cheered, and the surrounding boats rent the still air with a veritable barrage of siren blasts. In farewell, the crew struck up with the Manx National Anthem 'Ellan Vannin'.

It was a profoundly moving scene. Against the lowering backdrop of the massive Norwegian mountains the little longship slowly pulled away from the shore and headed out into the open water. As she cleared the end of the harbour wall Eddie Kaighin ordered 'Get the sail up, boys; quick as you can now!' The yard went racing up the mast and the great square of canvas impatiently shook itself free. For the hundreds of well-wishers lining the harbour, it was a sight which must have brought back pagan ancestral memories; we heard afterwards that many of the spectators found this historic moment as affecting as did all of us on the *Raven*.

For the first half-an-hour we remained quite close to the land, the gentle breeze pushing us along at a sedate two or three knots. The road along the shore was packed with slow-moving cars as they tried to match our speed, and we noticed that several others were speeding ahead to the point where a headland jutted far out into the fjord.

Around us an armada of small boats jockeyed for the closest position. Bill Hook and his film crew were desperately trying to obtain a shot of us alone against a classic Norwegian fjord background, but in the end they had to give up; they shouted their good-byes and good wishes and with cheery waves and cries of 'See you at the oil-rigs', they veered away and headed back to Trondheim. We had an appointment with them in the Ninian Oil Field where they hoped to film the contrast of the ancient and modern. Their confidence in our ability to navigate the longship to pinpoint a particular oil-rig (Ninian Central) in the middle of the North Sea was flattering, but not necessarily shared by our own watch navigators.

Our accompanying escort of small boats gradually dwindled as we reached out further into the fjord and began to pick up the stronger breeze. The longship, as if revelling in her freedom, rapidly picked up speed and was soon forging towards the mouth of the fjord at a brisk 8 knots.

For sometime we had noticed two brown squaresails far behind, which had been slowly closing on us while we remained close to the shore. Rumours had been rife before our departure that the Fembørings *Munin* (Memory) and *Siste Viking* (Last Viking) were going to attempt to board us, possibly in an effort to prove that Norwegians could sail Viking ships better than a Manx crew. Whatever their intentions, we had no wish to become involved in a sea-battle however light-hearted, which might result in damage to our longship.

We had known for some time that some of the Fembøring sailors were a little peeved that our ship had been named *Odin's Raven*. According to Norse mythology, Odin had two ravens called *Hugin* (Mind) and *Munin* (Memory) which sat on his shoulders, and which he sent out before breakfast every day to the far ends of the earth to bring him back news of what was happening all over the world (this was in the days before Reuters, of course!). The skipper of the Fembøring called *Munin* had apparently vowed to race us to the Isle of Man, thereby stealing our thunder by arriving first. The Vikings of old, as we know, were addicted to making reckless pledges of this nature. Even so, the sight of the two Fembørings bearing down upon us was indeed spectacular. We felt proud of the fact that we had led them for so long, but the fitful wind was more in their favour than ours. Being lighter boats and having extremely useful small topsails, they were able to take advantage of us when the wind dropped a little, although whenever it strengthened it gave us a useful unexpected turn of speed. Inevitably though, they caught up with us and a very fine pair they made as they raced down on either side of the *Raven*. The wind increased again and they were hard pressed to stay with us, the *Munin* twice coming dangerously close as she attempted to land a boarding party. Their avowed intention was to cover our dragon figure-head with a sack and remove the shields from their positions on the sheerstrake, but with our speed increasing to six knots the attempt had to be abandoned. Instead, the *Munin* pulled away to windward on our port side and suddenly turned to starboard, cutting across our bows. It was a brilliantly executed manoeuvre requiring tremendous skill and seamanship, but at the time we were incensed at the riskiness of it. Until that moment we had greeted their presence alongside with cheerful waves and pleasantries, our enthusiasm fired by the fact that most of the crew of the *Munin* were strapping blond-haired Valkyries. But now the atmosphere changed. To a man we were furious as we visualised the catastrophe that could result from a mid-water collision. But that wasn't the end of it. The *Munin* came at us again. It was obvious that one of the crew, poised on top of the small cabin at the stern, was going to attempt to throw a sack over our figure head. On seeing this, Robin Bigland charged down the full length of the *Raven*, leaping sure-footedly from kist to kist, shouting at Rolf Hansen in the bow to 'Keep those bloody idiots away from the figure-head. If they touch my ship I'll, I'll . . .'. He then jumped up and entwined himself protectively around the dragon-head.

Eddie Kaighin, realising that a collision was unavoidable, swung the steering oar over in a desperate attempt to lessen the impact; but a sudden freshening of the breeze filled our mainsail and with a sickening crunch the prow of the *Raven* struck the *Munin's* rudder. The *Munin* sheared off to leeward and hove-to, while the crew inspected the damage and effected temporary repairs; as good luck would have it we were able to continue on our way unscathed.

A slightly dishevelled Robin Bigland returned aft and sat down on his kist, muttering imprecations at our disabled adversaries. He was not at all amused when somebody pointed out that the *Siste Viking* appeared to be making a similar run at us. In this instance, our attacker attempted to close with us from astern and, with her full-bellied sail towering over us, she drew to within a few feet of our side, her crew poised to leap across the intervening gap.

Odin was obviously on our side that day, for as the Fambøring took our wind, the *Raven* suddenly lost way and the large spiked dragon's tail on our stern gashed a great hole in our adversary's mainsail. With exultant satisfaction we watched her drop rapidly astern, the rent in the sail visibly widening; accepting defeat, she broke off the engagement and turned in towards the shore and the town of Statbygd.

The *Munin* by this time had again caught up with us, the crew having jury-rigged their damaged rudder. Side-by-side we sailed down the fjord before a gradually strengthening breeze. As a result of a Norwegian parley, conducted by Knut Skøgoy and the skipper of the Fembøring, a truce was called. Tempers had cooled somewhat by then, and our erstwhile rival was invited on board for lunch.

It was only then that we realised what it had all been about. According to ancient Viking law, any ship on a peaceful mission was required to remove or cover the dragon-head and shields in foreign waters, especially when entering or leaving port. It was a gesture to the land-spirits of the place, an indication that the ship had no hostile intent. Any vessel that flaunted her dragon-head was assumed to be a marauder, and could thus be legitimately attacked as a potential pirate. All that the Fembørings had been trying to do was to teach us a lesson in the niceties of Viking law.

It taught us another lesson, too. We had been somewhat light-heartedly playing at Vikings in the homeland of the Vikings, putting on stunts to capture the attention of the media. In Trondheim fjord that day, we learned a little of the real thing – and that there were Viking descendants who were not prepared to see their cherished heritage traduced by anybody – even Manxmen!

When the skipper of the *Munin* now requested formal permission to cover the figure-head and remove the shields, Robin Bigland agreed without hesitation. As the shields were taken off, the crew of the *Munin* applauded – and so, this time, did we.

But there was another lesson we learned that day – how incredibly difficult it must have been for pirate Viking vessels to board and capture their prey at sea. It must have called for seamanship of the highest order and nerves of steel. Admittedly the Fembørings had approached us with all due care, in order not to damage us at the outset of our voyage (even though we hadn't thought so at the time); a real attacker would have crashed into us, and through our oars, regardless of risk. But there must always have been the danger that the attacking boat would have disabled itself, as the *Siste Viking* had done. A great deal must have depended on the skill of the helmsman.

The longship literally floated 'on' the water due to her shallow draft, as did the Fembørings, and consequently the motion of the boat followed the contours of the waves. In any conditions therefore, apart from a flat calm, the deck was always on the move, exaggerated to a much greater extent than in modern sailing ships due to the ribs being 'tied' to the keel, rather than rigidly bolted. This resulted in a serpentine twisting movement, complicated by the natural lateral roll, the whole culminating in a feeling that the ship was a living entity, completely at one with the sea.

With the departure of the *Munin* we were at long last truly alone for the first time since the longship had been launched. As we neared the end of Trondheim Fjord the wind freshened again, and sailing close to our windward limit we were still able to achieve a steady 8 knots.

The weather, which until then had remained cool but sunny, deteriorated to a universal overtone of grey skies and we began to feel the chill of the evening creeping upon us. The snow covering the mountains on either side extended down to the shore line and the uninviting water reflected the coldness of the grey skies as our vessel surged along beneath those majestic, silent spectators.

As I sat on my kist wrapped in the warmest clothes I had, feet braced against the mast and my back leaning uncomfortably against the stacked oars, I gazed up at the massive white sentinels towering above. Not for the first time I allowed my mind to wander back into the romantic past, lost in a dream world of fleets of vessels of identical design crewed by bearded adventurers as they set out along this same path on voyages of discovery, conquest or disaster.

The scenery had remained unchanged for thousands of years, its grandeur more eloquently impressive than words could describe. This was the Norway that every travel brochure attempts to portray, but they never really succeed in reproducing the overwhelming, almost oppressive, aura of history which pervades these dramatic vistas.

I felt at the time, although glad at last to be on our own, that a head-on picture of the longship flying over the grey, white-capped waves, with the mountains stretching up on either side and disappearing, range upon range, into the distant haze behind us, would have made a dream shot for any photographer.

As the light gradually faded in the late evening (at that time of the year it never becomes totally dark at that latitude) the cold intensified and I greeted the change of watch with relief. It was a pleasure simply to be able to move around a little and restore the circulation to my limbs.

The watches had been in force since our trials in Oslofjord and by this time we were well into the routine of four hours on and eight hours off. To make the system fair (so that the midnight to 4.00 a.m. stint did not always fall to the same crew-members) Eddie had introduced the two hour dog-watch from 4.00 to 6.00 and 6.00 to 8.00 in the evening. This effectively rotated the crew but it meant that on every third day, each particular watch was on hand for three 4-hour sessions; to make for that, there was also a day when one was only on duty for a total of 6 hours.

The watch leaders were those members of the crew who were trained in navigation, and Eddie Kaighin had allocated the remainder with a great deal of careful thought.

My own watch consisted of Knut Hoff, Shane Lucas and myself – the three most inexperienced deck-hands – under young David Eames. Any misgivings we might have had about the appalling responsibility that this placed on David were quickly dispelled. He soon proved himself more than capable of handling three inexperienced landlubbers, while still finding the time and patience to teach us the basics of seamanship and navigation. And this despite the fact that Knut Hoff was the only one of our five Norwegians whose grasp of the English language was extremely limited. In times of crisis it could have led to difficulties if, for example, the helmsman ordered the rapid release of the sheet or brace held by Knut, for his understanding of the Manx accent was virtually non-existent. In fact his stock English phrases seemed to consist of 'Hello, my old buccaneer', and 'Merry Christmas!' Not a great deal of help when discussing the finer techniques of sailing! Having said this, he was a truly likeable character and, when given time during periods off watch, we had many a painfully slow but fascinating conversation about life in his home town in the north of Norway.

The other two watches were led by Brian Cousins, with Richard Tomlinson, George Kneale and Colin Bowen, and Rolf Hansen with Richard Young, Nigel Wood and Knut Skøgoy. Arne Wisth as photographer and Odd Børstad as cook were both excused the extra duties of keeping watch, while Robin Bigland as Chieftain and Alan Binns as technical adviser had over-riding responsibilities not compatible with keeping watch. Eddie Kaighin, as skipper, was of course on hand at all times, and as befitted his position he took over command when making a landfall or departure, or when other conditions demanded.

With Trondheim Fjord fading into the distance behind us, the combination of twilight and an ever-thickening haze forced us to search for a suitable anchorage in which to heave-to for the few hours before dawn.

Kjorsvik is a small hamlet nestling among the snow-covered pines at the foot of the mountains. There was no visible sign of a jetty so, at 2 o'clock in the morning, we eased our way gently through the mist into the middle of the tiny bay; with a clatter that echoed around the sleeping foothills, the anchor chain rattled over the side.

As quickly as possible the yard was lowered on the yokes and the sail stretched across the boat forward of the mast. The kists were then carried aft and stacked, leaving an area of clear deck for sleeping accommodation. It was only possible to create this kind of space when we were moored, and as the sail was usually our motive power it was also the only time that we were able to have some form of cover. Even so, with seventeen bodies crammed into such a small space like a carelessly-stacked pile of firewood, sleep did not come easily, even to men who just experienced such a physically and emotionally exhausting day.

Our watch was on duty again by this time and, for once, I was extremely glad. To have watched the dawn rise over an idyllic Norwegian landscape is a memory which will remain with me for a long time. With my sketch-book on my knee and a scalding cup of thick black coffee beside me, I revelled in the silence and the timeless feeling that surrounded me. The rhythmic slap of water against the hull only added to the peacefulness of the scene. It was with a twinge of regret that, at six o'clock in the morning, I had to waken the sleeping crew and broke the magic spell.

CHAPTER FIVE

The Storm

At 6.30 a.m. on Monday, May 28, *Odin's Raven* slipped out of Kjorsvik cove as unheralded as she had entered it four and a half hours earlier. We had not observed any sign of life on shore during our brief stay and the local inhabitants are probably unaware to this day of the longship's visit.

The morning was fine and sunny and a gentle north-easterly breeze nudged the *Raven* along at a sedate 3 knots. Our first breakfast at sea proved to be excellent; Odd Børstad was able to take advantage of the relatively calm sea to produce a welcome hot meal of fried eggs, cooking a dozen at a time in an enormous frying pan. We did not, at that early stage of the voyage, fully appreciate how difficult it was to cook anything other than soup when we were under way, due to the lively motion of the boat; it was to be some time before we would enjoy another hot breakfast at sea.

Our normal Viking breakfast in the days that followed was a combination of Norwegian and English preferences. The kettle was so grotesquely disfigured that it could now be jammed over the gaz, wedged beneath the deck-planking; consequently it was only in very rough weather that we were unable to brew up some coffee. Odd's Norwegian coffee was incredibly strong, the beans being stirred in the kettle as it came to the boil, with the result that you were more than likely to get a mouthful of sediment along with the coffee. Nevertheless it was hot and sweet (for those who took sugar) and an ideal defence against the chill of the early mornings.

Norwegians have unusual tastes for breakfast. Not for them the familiar cornflakes and toast of home. Arranged on the deck every morning would be cheese, sardines, bread, jam, reindeer meat and dried fish. The more cautious among us initially restricted ourselves to jam or cheese sandwiches, but within a short space of time the sea-air had its effect on our appetites and we thought nothing of combining everything visible into one gigantic sandwich.

Although we had all equipped ourselves with the necessary mess tins and eating utensils, for most of our meals our seaman's knives became as indispensible for eating as for boat work. Every crew member carried a razor-sharp knife, always worn outside whatever clothing the conditions forced us to put on, so that we were always in a position to cut a rope quickly if the necessity arose. It would have wasted valuable seconds if, during a brief rain squall, we had put on our oil-skins over our knives and then had recourse to use them in an emergency.

By the time we had completed our breakfast, the wind had increased and the *Raven* was making a steady 5 knots towards the open sea. Estimates vary as to how long it probably took the original Vikings to cross to the Shetland Isles, but it is generally accepted that, given fair weather and an average speed of 6 knots (from our experience a realistic figure), the distance could probably be covered in 48 hours.

It was not surprising therefore that the morale of the crew lifted appreciably when, after consulting a passing coaster about the latest weather forecast, Eddie Kaighin and Robin Bigland agreed that we should head out to sea without further ado. It had been intended to call in at Kristiansund to buy a transistor radio so that we could pick up the BBC weather forecasts, as the radio fitted beneath the deck-planks was already suffering from a surfeit of salt-water. It was still capable of transmitting and receiving over a range of a mile or so and had been our source of contact with the coaster; what we did not know at the time was that the forecast we were given was not a general one, but referred only to the local area.

So at 8 o'clock the proud serpent-head of the *Raven* swung away from the coastline and pointed out towards the western horizon. The general atmosphere on board was a mixture of anticipation, eagerness and nervousness: anticipation at the thought of taking our craft out into the open sea; an eagerness that stemmed from the real possibility that we could make the crossing with only one night spent out in the North Sea; and always that element of nervousness with regard to whatever dangers might be lurking ahead of us.

Spirits were high, though, and there was an air of excitement about the ship. The *Raven* was making a steady six knots towards Grip lighthouse, which would be our last visual navigational reference point until we sighted the oil-rigs. The weather was still fair, but cold, and all the crew were wearing oil-skins as a protection against the constant showers of spray which swept the deck.

Huddled between two kists with my feet braced against the mast-fish (a beautifully carved piece of oak which formed the main support for the mast), I attempted to sleep for a few hours. This was a virtual impossibility as far as I was concerned and I was never able to do more than snatch an hour or two at various intervals throughout the voyage. In contrast, some of my shipmates were able to sleep for 10 hours at a stretch, even when the longship was cavorting at its liveliest.

Lunch on our first day in the North Sea consisted of soup and coffee (or cold reindeer meat and fish for those so inclined), and this was to be our staple diet until we reached the oil rigs. The seas off Grip, surrounded as it is by small skerries of rock, were a seething turmoil of white water and the longship corkscrewed her way past in an exceedingly uncomfortable manner. Holding on to a scalding hot cup of Odd's soup with one hand while gripping some form of support with the other was not the most restful way of eating one's food; every few minutes an extra large cascade of spray would crash onto us, and my appetite soon disappeared.

Odd's soups became a legend on board and it was suggested that he should publish the recipes. The only problem was that since everything available was thrown into the huge saucepan, he had no real idea of the final composition! The three witches in *Macbeth* could have learnt a thing or two if they had been present. His only real disaster was a concoction which came to be known as 'Harpic' soup. It was a lethally unpalatable brew due to a mammoth injection of cayenne pepper (apparently added by mistake, we were to learn afterwards); but what was even more disconcerting was the way it was gulped down with obvious relish by Shane Lucas!

As the afternoon wore on, the sky gradually darkened until it was a uniform, threatening grey colour and the wind swung remorselessly around to the west. This unfortunately was the direction in which we wished to travel and slowly but surely we were forced to bear away from our intended course, heading more northerly by the hour. Coupled with the worsening of the weather, the sea began to build up into a long, heavy swell, causing the ship to roll wickedly as she swooped up and down with a sickening motion. It became obvious to us as we wedged ourselves tightly against the side to avoid sliding across the deck that the early morning forecast had either been wrong or only referred to the local area in which it had been received.

By the early evening the conditions had not altered to a great extent but our progress had slowed down considerably. The *Raven* was making little headway, her violent corkscrew movement continually spilling the wind out of the sail. We were nearing the edge of the continental shelf, where the comparatively shallow bottom (80 to 90 fathoms) drops sharply away to over 400 fathoms, when we sighted three Norwegian trawlers. As was usual in such meetings they closed on us for a better view, and as soon as they were within range the skipper made contact using the V.H.F. radio. He learnt that a south-westerly gale had been forecast for the area between our present position and the Shetland Isles and was advised by the skipper of one of the trawlers to head for shelter, as he and his two companions were in the process of doing. We thanked them for their advice, and for a gift of freshly caught Pollack, and then watched the trawlers slowly draw away from us as they headed towards the distant coast.

There was a long discussion between Eddie, Robin and Alan Binns on the advisability of our running for shelter as well, and I think everyone was secretly relieved when they decided to turn back. In our view any sensible Viking would have done the same, rather than knowingly face a North Sea gale. The change of course would not upset our plans too much, as the Norwegian coast runs in a south-westerly direction down to Stad, from which point we could again turn west towards Shetland. Nevertheless it was a profound disappointment having to turn back after a full day's sail out from the Norwegian coast, and our spirits drooped as the *Raven* slowly came round onto her new course to the south-east.

The excitement of the morning had waned throughout the day as the constant buffeting and soaking had sapped our stamina. We were all physically and mentally exhausted as we watched the coastline draw nearer, becoming more and more indistinct as darkness fell. We had all wound ourselves up mentally for the crossing, with the adrenalin pumping through our bodies as we sailed broadside on to the heavy swell, the top of the mast describing dizzy arcs across the sky; now the pressure was off for a time, and we reacted in the only possible way: in the nearest available free space, those who were off watch sealed their oil-skins as much as they could, and curled up on the deck to sleep. With the change in direction the motion of the longship became less violent; even so it was, as always, lively enough, and for some of the crew sleep was difficult to come by.

We were heading back towards the more sheltered channel from which we had sailed so enthusiastically earlier in the day, and the plan was to make for the town of Aalesund where we would ride out the storm and at the same time purchase a transistor radio. Judging by the days events it was obviously essential to be able to receive more general weather forecasts.

For those of the crew who were either on watch or couldn't sleep, the sail back to the Norwegian coast did not allow for much relaxation. The wind, having freshened from the south west, sent the *Raven* scudding towards the chain of islands and islets which marked the seaward side of the channel and the waves were now regularly breaking over the starboard bow – sheets of spray soaking the sleeping bodies which lay heaped around the deck. A misty rain added to the navigational difficulties as the boat threaded her way between the dark sinister rocks which littered the lead into the channel, and it was with some relief that Brian Cousins at the helm picked up the stern light of a coaster travelling, it was hoped, on our intended course.

Unknown to us at the time, the forecast Force 9 gale had indeed swept the area through which the *Raven* was supposed to be sailing and, that night, two other ships were lost, both of them larger than the longship.

We were glad to hear later that the crew of one were rescued by helicopter, but apparently the other vessel simply vanished. As far as our own families and other interested parties knew, we were supposedly in the middle of the North Sea, and but for the chance encounter with the Norwegian trawlers, there was no reason to suppose that our plans would have changed. Such are the ways of Fate, or Lady Luck, call it what you will: for all the advantages of modern technology our escape from what turned out to be a major gale depended entirely on a sharp-sighted Norwegian fisherman whose curiosity brought his ship close enough for the longship to contact him.

The imminent gale was forecast that evening on British television and how our wives and girlfriends must have felt can only be imagined. I was told afterwards that Kathy Lewis, as mindful as ever of her duties, had telephoned our various homes and reassured everybody that the Coast Guard was keeping a lookout for us. Nevertheless it must have been a very worrying time for them and it emphasises that the pressures imposed by such a voyage are not all directed upon the participants themselves. It takes considerable courage to accept that your loved one has decided to attempt an undertaking which would certainly be hazardous and could, in the extreme, end very suddenly and very finally. This is not an overstatement of the facts, as any sailor knows, but I think most would agree that the thought of such an event always remains in the background: it never happens to oneself, it only happens to others.

However, this did not alter the fact that, as far as the people at home knew, *Odin's Raven* was out there somewhere in the middle of the storm. Perhaps the ones who stayed behind required a greater strength of character than those who were at sea.

Kipling, in his *Harp Song of the Dane Women*, described it all so evocatively:

> *What is a woman that you forsake her,*
> *And the hearth-fire and the home-acre,*
> *To go with the old grey widow-maker?*
>
> *She has no house to lay a guest in —*
> *But one chill bed for all to rest in,*
> *That the pale sun and the stray bergs nest in.*
>
> *She has no strong white arms to fold you,*
> *But the ten-times-fingering weed to hold you —*
> *Out on the rocks where the tide has rolled you.*
>
> *Yet when the signs of summer thicken,*
> *And the ice breaks, and the birch-buds quicken,*
> *Yearly you turn from our side and sicken —*

Sicken again for the shouts and the slaughters.
You steal away to the lapping waters,
And look at your ship in her winter-quarters.

You forget our mirth, and the talk at the tables,
The kine in the shed and the horse in the stables —
to pitch her sides and go over her cables.

Then you drive out where the storm-clouds swallow,
And the sound of your oar-blades, falling hollow,
Is all we have left through the months to follow.

Ah, What is Woman that you forsake her,
And the hearth-fire and the home-acre,
To go with the old grey widow-maker?

It was a tired and dejected crew who climbed stiffly on to the quayside at Aalesund at 5 o'clock in the morning, welcomed by a single lonely figure who stood waving ecstatically at the harbour entrance. The town was shuttered against the wind which whistled over the roof-tops as if emphasising our prudence in running for shelter. While the Norwegians dispersed to find an early morning cafe, other crew members arranged themselves more comfortably for sleep, rigging the sail over the yard as a tent and organising the kists accordingly.

Robin Bigland and I walked around the town hunting for a radio shop — at 5.30 a.m. we were being rather optimistic, but it was more of an excuse to stretch cramped limbs. And as we walked we discussed the effect on morale of the events of the previous 24 hours. It was a measure of his qualities as a leader that whenever the opportunity presented itself he would be only too pleased to discuss any problems or worries with any member of the crew. He was always open to suggestions or critical comment, and this led to a very easy relationship between us all.

On our return to the longship we discovered that all of the crew except George Kneale, who was on watch, had repaired to a cafe at the far end of the harbour. Robin's arrival at the breakfast table was greeted with enthusiastic cheers for we knew that he at least, had retained some Norwegian money! Most of us had changed ours back to English in Trondheim, Assuming that Lerwick would be our next port of call. Nevertheless, with a confidence born of our Viking role the rest of us had blithely ordered up food before Robin's arrival, with little thought to the problem of paying. That breakfast can only be described as manna from Heaven when one considers that we had only managed to snatch a couple of quick mugs of soup and bread since leaving the cove at Kjorsvik the previous morning.

That day in Aalesund was one of restless waiting. Originally it had been intended simply to call in, buy a radio (in which Robin was finally successful), snatch a few hours sleep, and then continue on our way towards

64

Stad. But the worsening weather and the reports coming in of ships experiencing difficulties (it was there that we learnt of the loss of the two yachts) were to keep us tied to the quayside until the following day.

Most of us had already, at the first opportunity, telephoned home to reassure everyone that we were safely in harbour, but nobody remembered to contact the BBC TV documentary team. This was an unfortunate oversight as they were apparently scouring the seas for us and, as they were to hear no word from us for the five days following our departure from Trondheim, it was doubly regrettable that they were left so ill-informed.

Aalesund was not a lively town, to put it mildly, and with squally showers and high winds sweeping across the harbour, few of us ventured far from the longhip. The spare sail had also been rigged as an awning along with the mainsail (the only occasion we were ever able to cover the ship completely) and the tent thus formed, although very cramped, was at least relatively dry. The available deck space was even further reduced by the presence of a spare sail-yard, which had been the cause of much grumbling over the previous two days. It had been placed along the deck-planking between the mast-fish and the kists and due to its cumbersome weight and length had proved to be exceedingly irksome. At one stage, after yet another member of the crew had tripped headlong over it, Robin Bigland was overheard to say 'That yard has got to go!'

In Aalesund, therefore, the Bilge Rats decided to remove the offending article from the ship, as it had been agreed by all that the chances of the mainyard breaking were very slim; the continued presence of the spare yard would only increase the chances of somebody breaking a limb, or worse. So while Robin was away shopping for the radio, Colin Bowen, Richard Young and I started out on a round of the local ships-chandlers, with the aim of negotiating some sort of exchange deal. In this we were initally unsuccessful, but after an hour we ended up on a nearby building site where we had learned that one of the directors was in the process of constructing his own yacht. With a sales-patter born of experience, Richard Young came to a very satisfactory arrangement, the deal being, to use his own characteristic style, 'boxed-off!'

In exchange for the yard we were to receive three cases of lager. Bearing in mind the exorbitant cost of alcohol in Norway, we reckoned that we had done remarkably well. It was, however, a condition of the agreement that we must first purchase the lager; only then would we be reimbursed for the cost, on producing a receipt. Normally this would not have presented us with a problem, but Aalesund was a virtually 'dry' town and it was to be another hour before we tracked down the only brewery which sold off-licence ales. Even then our troubles were not over, because of the strictly-enforced law against carrying alcoholic beverages publicly through the streets. By this time our patience was beginning to wear a little thin, so, casting caution to the winds, the three of us shouldered a case each right through the middle of the town, arriving exhausted but triumphant back on the quayside, to be welcomed by a thirsty and very grateful crew. We omitted to mention to Robin the fact that it was the spare yard that had gained us the refreshment, and it was not until we were at sea the following day that he even noticed its absence – only to be told that, as he had drunk his share, he had unwittingly condoned the exchange!

On our return to the longship we were introduced to a portly gentleman visitor who turned out to be the owner of a circus which was in town for the week. He generously offered free tickets for the evening performance to the whole crew and, for those who accepted, it was apparently a highly entertaining evening. Some of us declined, preferring to sleep as much as possible while our floating mattress was in a pleasantly stable position.

During the afternoon the original Colin Archer sailing lifeboat entered the harbour and tied up near to the *Raven*. Some of our more knowledge-able sailors were invited on board where they learnt that the seas to the south (our projected route) had been very wild indeed. The newly arrived crew agreed emphatically that we had made the right decision in running for shelter, because, as Eddie himself so succinctly put it to a local reporter, 'Not even the Vikings were daft enough to try and ride out a storm, on a lee shore, with a safe anchorage only 25 miles away!'

The high winds continued gusting across the town throughout the day. Frequently we glanced up to the top of a nearby hill, on which the Norwegian flag was flying, only to see it standing stiffly out to the north-east, the strength of the gale such that it appeared to be fixed permanently to the mast like a cardboard cut-out.

At midnight, those members of the crew who had been to the circus returned in time to hear the forecast for the following day. The gale was apparently decreasing and it was hoped that we would be able to attempt the crossing again at first light. There was little need for a watch to be kept that night, so the whole crew crammed together beneath our makeshift tent, and, to the sound of Odd's sonorous snores and the howl of the wind overhead, we fell into a restless sleep.

The early morning forecast was consistent with the one we had heard at midnight and the wind was expected to drop to a Force 5. Therefore, at 6 o'clock on the morning of May 30, the longship quietly pulled out of Aalesund harbour with only a few early-risers in the vicinity to wish us 'bon-voyage'.

Our route took us southwards in the shelter of the islands until, at midday, we came out of the lee of Stadland. The wind may well have been only a Force 5 (although it was generally reckoned among the crew to be a minimum of Force 6), but the innumerable islets and generally wild nature of the coast served to create an extremely troublesome sea. The massive headland of Stad had sheltered us from the worst effects up until that point, but as it was essential that we rounded this point before heading out towards Shetland, the *Raven* now faced the full brunt of some very rough water.

As we soared up over the streaming crests and crashed down into the troughs, corkscrewing wildly away from the threatening cliffs which looked far too close for comfort, I enquired generally of the assembled company as to why we had to get round Stad rather than head straight out to sea – not that I particularly fancied turning beam-on to the sea in its present temper in any case!

It was Alan Binns, our resident expert on the Vikings and their history, who not only answered my question, but also told us of the strategic importance of the headland since people first sailed down this length of coastline. Once round Stadland we would be in a position to head directly due west towards Shetland, but the lee shore under those conditions was totally untenable. By heading out to sea we would not only experience far worse conditions, but we would still have to change course to the south-west directly into the prevailing winds. Apparently the headland jutted out across the channel down which we had travelled and which continued further south. Stadland provided a very solid barrier to vessels travelling in either direction and had to be weathered before the journey could continue. Throughout the centuries, Alan explained, the sea conditions at this point had often been the deciding factor in the speed at which certain leaders had been able either to return to troubled kingdoms, or, conversely, escape from invaders.

This was all very interesting and increased one's store of general knowledge but the plain fact remained that this particular Viking ship was getting nowhere, very uncomfortably! Eddie Kaighin, who had been on the helm since the early morning, estimated the sea state to be the equivalent of the Force 8 gale we had so narrowly avoided. Fate was obviously determined to test our little vessel, which now felt very small and frail as she was constantly battered by the short but vicious waves. As we were heading directly into the not inconsiderable wind the engine had been switched on in a desperate attempt to get around the headland. There was no possible way that we could row in such seas and if the sail had been hoisted we would have capsized in no time at all. By 4 o'clock in the afternoon we were making no headway and barely managing to keep the ship head-on to the seas.

The vista was magnificently awe-inspiring if viewed in a detached manner. If not so viewed, then it became a very frightening seascape, a turmoil of white-water with the breakers crashing against the menacing headland, which appeared uncomfortably close to my inexperienced eye. The sky was a mass of threatening storm-clouds and the blanket of mist which rolled incessantly down the slopes of the brooding mountains gave the impression of a line of ancient sentinels, frowning at our arrogance in attempting to defy the storm.

On board we were far from comfortable. For the first and only time most of the crew had put on their lifejackets. We sat huddled as far aft as possible not only to keep away from the drenching spray but also to keep as much weight as possible over the propeller to keep it in the water. The gyrations of the ship were such that she was either slipping backwards down the side of a steep wave, her figure-head rearing up against the murky sky, or sliding forwards at an acute angle, the helmsman staring down the length of the ship into the uninviting blackness at the bottom of a trough, with white-capped surf rising up on all sides.

It was at times like this that one fully appreciated the genius involved in the classic design of the longship. The continual soaring motion of the *Raven*, though forcing us to wedge ourselves tightly wherever we could, carried her over the waves rather than through them, even with the engine tending to force us into the water. Consequently the sheer line of the bow threw the water aside and it was only the spray that showered inboard, rather than a far more dangerous inrush of 'green' water.

As if to prove the point, during the course of the afternoon two small coasters thudded slowly past us, the water streaming back against their superstructure as they butted their way into the seas. Very ungainly, but at least they succeeded in weathering the headland.

Sitting wedged between the mast and a couple of kists, the spray regularly crashing down on to my soaking oilskins, I pictured the scene as it might have been a thousand years earlier. I would imagine that most of the crew were probably engaged in a similar form of mental stimulation, as it did not do morale any good at all to think of our own problems at such a time!

The Vikings often carried live animals on board to provide themselves with fresh meat, and one could easily imagine the turmoil that such conditions at sea would produce. A small crowd of figures huddled in the stern, crouching in their soaking wet sheepskins or leather coats, the ship under bare-poles, pitching and rolling in front of the storm as it drove them ever nearer to the waiting shoreline. Probably one or two of the crew would be desperately trying to calm the terrified sheep or horses tied to the mast as wave after wave crashed over them. As the longships often voyaged in company, it was highly likely that this small area of sea could have been littered with anything up to twenty or thirty ships, all being driven virtually uncontrollably before the storm with the added danger of a collision.

Perhaps the helmsmen of old would have come earlier to the decision that at 5 o'clock in the evening a tired and frustrated Eddie Kaighin was finally forced to acknowledge. It was obvious that there was no way that we were going to get around the wild waters off Stadland, and a search for the nearest available anchorage was once again initiated. Turning our backs on the impenetrable mass of rock which had so successfully blocked our passage, the cold, tired, soaking crew prepared the sail for hoisting and the *Raven*, rolling wickedly, turned her prow towards the land.

Nestling beneath the over-shadowing mass of Stadland Point, lay the small hamlet of Honningsvag and it was towards this tiny refuge that a course was now laid. Even so there was no guarantee that the cove was in fact sheltered from the prevailing wind, but at the time we had little choice. With the wind now behind us, the sail was reefed and hoisted and the longship almost took off! With Eddie still at the helm (there was no way that he was going to relinquish his position under the prevailing conditions), but looking very tired indeed by now, the *Raven* surfed her way towards the hostile-looking shore-line. Now out of the maelstrom of white-water off the Point, the steep swell carried her rapidly shorewards, the ship alternately speeding along with the front third of the hull clear of the water and then sinking quickly down almost at a standstill, until the next massive roller caught her up to repeat the process. The pressure on the steering oar was tremendous and the sight of Eddie straining to hold the boat on a level keel, both arms gripped tightly on the tiller arm, his hair and beard blowing in the wind against the background of grey skies and distant shore-tossed waves remains imprinted on my memory; he looked the archetype of the Norsemen of old we were trying to emulate.

With unconcealed relief we noticed what was obviously a very new breakwater jutting out across the entrance to the cove as we neared our intended anchorage. We must have presented a dramatic sight viewed from the shore, as we surged around the marker buoy and into the sheltered waters behind it. Once inside, we moored the longship alongside two fishing boats which were tied to the tiny jetty.

For three long days (the expected time for the North Sea crossing itself, given fair weather) we had been trying to force our way out from the confines of the Norwegian coast, and here we were forced back into yet another anchorage for shelter. The morale which had been so high on our departure from Trondheim was now at its lowest ebb. It seemed that Fate was against us and that we were to remain penned against the hostile coastline.

The locals, as usual, were anything but hostile, and within half an hour of our arrival a small reception committee had formed to welcome us. Having prepared our minds to the problem of crossing to Shetland, the frustrations of the last two days had profoundly depressed us all, and it was a credit to these generous people that within a very short space of time our spirits were soon raised to their normal, cheerful level. The local shop (in fact the only shop) was quickly opened for our benefit and the purchase of assorted chocolate, lemonade, crisps and anything readily edible had the children staring at us wide-eyed. We had eaten very little during the day and the strength required to hold a position in the ship had sapped all our reserves of energy. Nevertheless, it was remarkable how quickly one recovered when safely moored with the enticements of a modern grocery store laid out so temptingly! Laden with most un-Viking-like stores we returned to the longship in a much more cheerful frame of mind.

Some of us obviously recovered more quickly than others. Shortly after our return on to the deck, Dave Eames gave a shout. 'Where the hell's Shane off to?' he cried, gazing up at the steep hillside which surrounded the little bay.

'Why, where is he?' asked Nigel Wood.

'Look, about half-way up, beside that grey boulder.'

And so he was. Bounding up the hillside like a gazelle, heading towards the distant summit.

'Probably left his helmet in Aalesund and he's going back for it,' suggested Georgie Kneale.

'More likely looking for a sheep,' mumbled Brian Cousins with his mouth full. 'You know what sailors are.'

We were all soon to follow Shane's sudden dash into the wild blue yonder. Within the hour the longship was deserted as the crew, either singly or in small groups, wandered away up the road and around the adjacent hills. It was as much a matter of winding-down mentally as taking the chance to stretch cramped limbs. For all of us, skilled and unskilled alike, the previous 12 hours had been spent experimenting with the unknown. Most modern yachts of a similar size to the longship would probably not have experienced too much difficulty in weathering the kind of seas in which we had been caught, but the difference was that the skippers would have known the capabilities of their vessels. Knowledge breeds confidence, which itself reduces fear and tension. Of course we all had confidence in the *Raven*, but on differing scales relative to our own separate experiences of the sea. The longship was untested under such conditions and bearing in mind the losses of Viking ships estimated by the historians, it is not surprising that, for most of us, it had been a nerve-wracking experience, regardless of the confidence exuded by our skipper. I have no doubt that, to him, there had never been any question of danger and that he had probably revelled in the way that the *Raven* coped with such a wild sea. I am equally sure that Alan Binns, as an experienced practical as well as a theoretical sailor, had viewed the day's events from a totally detached point of view, comparing the reaction of our ship with his own theories on the behaviour of the various types of Viking vessels. For the rest, however, regardless of experience, I am sure there had been a very real element of nervousness, if not actual fear. With relaxation of the tension we became aware how tired we were and plans for a barbecue on the beach faded rapidly. We had been invited by one of the locals up to his house to watch the European Cup Final on television; gratefully we sank into the luxurious comfort of soft-sprung chairs, or lounged back against piles of cushions. It is embarassing to record that on our arrival we naturally removed our sea-boots at the door out of deference to our host's carpets, but in retrospect it was not perhaps such a good idea. The aroma of twelve pairs of 3-day-old socks (only 12 pairs because five of the crew were watching the match in one of the fishing boats) is not a particularly pleasant gift to inflict upon a healthy Norwegian family! It was probably for this very reason that they declined to join us in front of the television set, preferring to talk quietly among themselves at the opposite end of the room! It is also unfortunate to relate that, due to a combination of a centrally heated, double-glazed sitting room and the tiring day behind us, we were all sound asleep before the half-time whistle! Nevertheless our host was the perfect gentleman, apologising for having to wake us up when the match finished, informing us of the score and seeing us out into the night with his best wishes for a successful voyage. The pleasurable warmth of that house in one of the wildest areas of Norway served to emphasise the discomforts we had wished upon ourselves, and it was a quiet, thoughtful crew who wandered slowly back around the bay to the longship.

During the course of the evening the wind had died down to virtually nothing and the looming hulk of Stad was silhouetted against a cloudless, moonlit sky. The air had grown very chilly and it was with grateful relief that we crawled into our sleeping bags. The crews of the fishing boats had offered us the use of their bunks for the night and not even the overpowering stink of fish could keep us awake for long, once we had clambered onto the luxury of real mattresses.

Our last view across the glittering water before going below had shown us that the churning waters of the headland appeared to have subsided and we knew that, barring a sudden change in the weather, the next day would see us heading out across the North Sea.

CHAPTER SIX

The North Sea

The Norwegian coastline which had taunted the *Raven* for so long, holding her close like an invisible magnetic force, finally faded into the misty horizon around midday on Wednesday, May 30.

We had awoken that morning to clear skies and an untroubled sea, and with the weather forecast predicting moderate winds from the south east, no time was wasted in preparing for sea. The air was crisp but clear and the sharp outline of Stadpoint stood etched against the blue, cloud-flecked sky – a startling change from the dreary, storm-battered coastline of the previous afternoon. It appeared that the longed-for break in the weather really had occurred at last and as such comparatively calm conditions are notoriously infrequent, it was decided to attempt the crossing to Shetland at once via our rendezvous with the oil-rigs. If the wind held, the longship could be among the oil-fields within two days, and what we all considered to be the most dangerous part of the voyage would be behind us. How wrong we were!

The *Raven* moved lithely across the choppy waters of the bay as she sailed out of the small harbour of Honningsvag with an easy grace that must have delighted the onlookers scattered around the surrounding hills. A party of local school children, obviously happy to be out of class on such a morning, waved excitedly when the longship hauled up her red and white striped storm-sail and stood out from the land towards the open sea.

Everyone had been surprised at the very small area of the spare storm-sail; and but for the expected short seas off the headland it would not normally have been used, for the wind was only in the region of Force 4 or 5. As soon as Stad had passed astern without trouble, the mainsail was hoisted instead.

Changing the sails was no easy task. With the main yard lowered diagonally across the deck, at least 6 feet of it protruded over the gunwale

72

on either side. In the choppy sea the motion of the boat was very wild indeed, as it was to remain for most of the journey across. The short, steep waves crashed into the side, shedding great sheets of spray across the foredeck on which the work was being carried out. The *Raven*, not content with see-sawing into the oncoming seas, sliding up and down in her typical corkscrew manner, also rolled wickedly – the movement accentuated by the heavy yard as it slid from side to side across the boat.

The first problem was how to hold this massive timber relatively steady while keeping our footing. Time and again we were flung to the deck, clutching frantically for a handhold. The sea was uncomfortably close, each roll bringing the gunwale almost level with the surface, the water spurting in through the cracks around the 'poppets' which covered the oarports.

When most of the storm-sail had been unlashed, we then had to untie the remaining lashings at either end of the yard, which dangled over the side. When each side was hauled in separately, Eddie Kaighin was able to stretch out along the yard-arm, two of us holding on to his legs while the remainder gripped the yard as tightly as possible to stop it sliding. The process had to be repeated when the mainsail was 'bent-on', and we were all exhausted by the time we finally hauled up the new sail.

Luckily it was only necessary to repeat a similar sail change (or sail removal as it turned out to be) once more under such conditions; hanging over the side of a gyrating longship is a hazardous operation.

These conditions remained much the same for the first twenty-four hours of the crossing. Movement on board was restricted to an ungainly clamber; the relentless rolling meant having to wedge one's body between kists or the side to avoid sliding all over the deck. For this reason alone it was to be an extremely uncomfortable sail even when the seas moderated slightly. The heavy swell that replaced the shorter, steeper seas did nothing to lessen the angle of the pitch and roll, but it did decrease the frequency of such movements. Also, with the storm sail removed it became available for use as a 'spray-shelter', rigged over the foredeck; this seems to have been what the original Vikings did, according to a number of historical sources.

The Iceland Sagas contain the only realistic reference to actual conditions on such ancient voyages; but even so, the details are sparse, for the writers tended to highlight the dramatic events rather than recount the every-day life of their heroes. The reconstructions of the ancient burial ships provide few insights into the precise uses of the perishable materials, such as sails and ropes, which were obviously an integral part of the handling of a ship.

Magnus Andersen, the Norwegian who made his historic voyage across the Atlantic in 1893 in a full-scale replica of the Gokstad ship called the *Viking*, had built a fixed waterproof shelter over the foredeck; this was not

73

necessarily true to the original, but a very sensible precaution when one takes into consideration the journey that he faced.

The temporary 'sail' shelter on the *Raven* could only be erected when the wind conditions were absolutely ideal and was, in fact, only in use for a few hours. The amount of working space required on the foredeck if any 'beating' was necessary made the presence of such an all-embracing covering a potential hazard. It was probable that the longships of old had a similar form of small hide-covered shelter across the narrowest part of the foredeck as a permanent structure; it is arrogant to assume that such masters of the seas had not designed some element of protection against the weather if at all possible. The problem of exposure must have been an equal if not greater hazard to these mariners, clad as they were in leather or sheepskin coats, although possibly their powers of resistance were greater than ours in view of their naturally robust existence.

After our sunny departure the rain very quickly caught up with us and with the final disappearance of the mountains of Norway as the misty horizon swallowed them up, a cold, drenching, heavy drizzle set in with a vengeance. The North Sea may have reluctantly withdrawn the awesome power of its storms, but it was obviously determined to make our voyage as uncomfortable as possible! But now that we were well and truly on our way, the morale of the crew had soared in a matter of hours and the disappointments and depression of the previous drawbacks were quickly forgotten. The possibility of having to run for shelter if the weather again turned foul on us was always present but, with the vast expanse of choppy, white-flecked sea around us, everybody settled into a routine in preparation for at least two nights at sea – if we were lucky.

When 'running' before the wind, or 'reaching' as was now the case, sailing the longship was a pleasant, unexacting task. The watch were able to relax and converse comfortably, with little fear of having to maintain total concentration on their particular job – except the helmsman who, naturally, had to keep a careful eye on the course and set of the sail. Under ideal conditions, such as we had on that first day out at sea, the longship moved easily with the waves. The lively motion of the deck was now natural to us, and the constant rhythm as she pitched and rolled in her individual serpentine manner was not at all unpleasant and we quickly adapted our positions accordingly.

The helmsman, half-seated on the starboard sheerstrake, one arm looped over the tiller, was in the most exposed position; the elegant rise in the line of the strakes meant that he was always fully exposed to wind, rain and the rogue waves which periodically broke against the hull, just below the steering position. It was always the coldest and wettest position in the ship and, under normal conditions, the position changed hands every hour. Thus, on a four-hour watch, each crew-member had a spell on the helm. This system was not always adhered to, however, as some members of the crew were not necessarily adept enough at holding a reasonable course. Although our aiming point (the oil-rigs) covered a relatively wide area of the North Sea, it was the intention to approach the Ninian Field as accurately as possible – in particular the main rig, Ninian Central. The 'feeling' of the steering-oar was very different to that of the stern-tiller of a modern yacht, and the longship could easily veer a few points off the intended course unnoticed by an inexperienced helmsman.

Of the three members of the watch crew, one was positioned on the brace controlling the yard and thus the angle of the sail to the wind (a critical position when sailing close to the wind, as any lack of concentration could result in the sail 'backing' with possibly disastrous results); another would be in control of the 'tack' line, the tension of which was important with regard to the manner in which the wind filled the sail; and the fourth member of the watch was normally occupied with navigation or was available to carry out the minor adjustments to the other ropes which decided the set of the sail. More often than not, during the day, any off-watch member of the crew who was nearest the particular rope in question would carry out the necessary alteration, but at night time there were few spare hands available.

The set of the sail was governed by a system of triple ropes attached to the foot of the canvas and the deck. These held the 'foot' down near the deck and assisted in altering the curvature to make full use of the available wind. The bowline (an endless rope) fixed half way up the leading edge of the sail was utilised in a similar fashion, the line extending to the prow of the ship, holding the middle of the sail out into the wind.

Apart from the helmsman, therefore, the positions of the rest of the watch often enabled them to sit on the deck below the level of the gunwale, thereby gaining some respite from the wind and rain. Although this protection was very limited they were no worse off than the rest of the crew and consequently there was rarely any advantage in being either 'on' or 'off' watch. The exception was when one was rudely awakened from a restless sleep to go on watch in the bitter cold of the hours before dawn.

This was always the time when the real effect of being at sea in northern latitudes in an open unprotected vessel was most forcefully brought home to one. Curled up on a hard wooden deck is not the most idyllic sleeping accommodation. In addition the lack of movement and consequent loss of body heat, coupled with the fact that the dampness inevitably penetrated all the protective layers of clothing, always resulted in a severe bout of shivering with no room available to exercise muscles properly, in order to get the blood circulating again.

For those who were not on watch during the day, recreational facilities were severely limited. We had become virtually immune to the relentless drizzle which was to remain with us until the middle of the third day of the crossing. Similarly, the frequent showers of spray which swept across the foredeck made that area particularly untenable, except for the small space (anchor locker) immediately beneath the figurehead. Due to the configuration of the hull the sheerstrake swept up with the simplicity of line that is the characteristic of all longships and their immediate descendants. The increased protection thus gained overrode the probability of the occasional drenching when a wave broke inboard. This position was regarded as the most comfortable on board, mainly because the spare sail which was normally stowed there provided a much softer mattress than the unyielding oak of the deck-planking.

Whenever a watch ended, those wishing to sleep would make a bee-line for the bow and attempt to wriggle their way amongst the incumbent bodies. Nearly always there would be a person already in residence who was due to take over the watch and I never actually saw anybody come to blows in their efforts to salvage a little comfort. At a very early stage in the voyage, Arne Wisth staked a claim to this anchor-locker and, unless he was actively involved in filming or eating, one gathered the impression that his body had been built into the ship in that position as a permanent fixture! Even in the roughest waters with the sea regularly cascading over the bow, the gnome-like features of a sodden Arne, water streaming down his face, would peer unblinking back at us out of the crumpled assortment of soaking oil-skins and a shaggy coat in which he was usually enveloped.

The lure of this position on board was so great that competition was fierce. On one occasion Robin Bigland had to rouse himself to answer a call of Nature; by the time he returned to resume his interrupted sleep he found that his place had been usurped: Rick Tomlinson, who had been waiting for just such an opportunity, feigning sleep but alert for any such movement, had made his move as soon as Robin's attention had been diverted. The actual process of relieving oneself over the side in a very choppy sea required total concentration, leaving one with no chance of defending a hard-won sleeping position!

The anchor locker was really only big enough for two people to occupy in comfort, but that meant nothing. Once when coming off watch I went forward to rouse Georgie Kneale to take my place and, although it was broad daylight, I literally could not find him on board.

'Don't be ridiculous,' said Nigel Wood, who was on the same watch. 'He can't have gone for a walk!'

'Well, I can't find him,' was my reply. Together, Nigel and I checked the sleeping figures, but again we could find no signs of Georgie.

'He's asleep up forward,' said Rick Tomlinson.

'He's not,' we replied. 'We've just been up for a look.'

'Well he can't be anywhere else,' Eddie Kaighin remarked. 'Shift them around a bit and see if you can find him.'

Once again Nigel and I clambered up to the bow and, sure enough, by prising apart a pair of occupied sleeping bags we unearthed the sleeping Georgie, who had either burrowed his way down beneath those above him or they had simply settled down on top!

Apart from this First Class accommodation in the bow which, even in extreme circumstances, could only house four recumbent bodies, the remaining sleeping positions were a matter of personal choice or, more often than not, the only space on deck left available. There was no room in which one could stretch out full-length except on the oars which were stacked along either side. By mentally convincing one's hips that they were in fact flat, this position at least allowed cramped limbs to be extended to their normal length. As always, however, there was a catch and, in this case it was the proximity of the gunwale, level with one's body and thus within easy reach of every playful wave. But as we were perpetually damp it didn't really matter and by lying on one's stomach, or facing inboard, most of the water tended to land on a fully protected back – protected, that is, by leaky oil-skins! The most common position of repose was on the deck itself. Covered as it was with kists and ropes this entailed a certain amount of athletic ability and a total blanking of the mind to the effect of various unyielding lumps of wood which projected into certain parts of the anatomy. It was a common occurrence to be awakened by somebody tripping over you, or to find an occupied sea boot comfortably tucked under your armpit!

At the start of the voyage we had all been issued with thin rubber 'Karrymats' for use as mattresses, but had quickly discovered that these were more trouble than they were worth. During the sea trials in Oslo-fjord one or two had been conveniently 'lost'. In one instance, Rick Tomlinson was moving a 'mat' from one position to another when a well-timed nudge from a lurking Bilge Rat sent it over the side. Robin Bigland, who noticed the bright yellow mattress floating rapidly astern, proceeded to scold the youngest Viking, thus enabling the Bilge Rats to announce that Rick had been elevated to the heights of an Honorary member of the Society. The fact that he had been powerless to stop the mat from going overboard made no difference, and he became the first person to receive this much sought-after accolade!

The problem with these 'Karrymats' was not that they were uncomfortable (they did at least soften the effect of lying on solid oak) but rather their awkward bulk, which caused constant difficulties when trying to stow them out of the way. In Trondheim, when the longship was being loaded, Brian Cousins was faced with this problem, when the available storage space had all been taken up. He recorded in his log:

'. . . Having carefully stowed all the necessary equipment and stores, and in doing so accounted for every conceivable space beneath the deckboards, I suddenly realised that no provision had been made for the Karrymats. With 16 of these items on board, whose dubious purpose was to make sleeping on the wooden deck more bearable, the problem assumed the proportions equivalent to about one cubic metre! Consultation with Bilge Rat No. 1 brought no solution short of towing them behind or tying them up the mast.

77

'What we really need to do is forget to put them on board,' suggested Richard; to which I readily agreed. 'Is that an order, Boss?' – I must have nodded. An hour later I caught sight of Bilge Rats 1 and 2 marching along the quay with a large trunk between them. Swiftly averting my gaze, I saw no more. The following day, half an hour before our departure, a breathless and obviously self-satisfied member of the Trondheim police force shouldered his way through the crowd and informed Eddie that he had found a trunk, which we had over-looked, behind a pile of timber on the quay. Two uniformed officers in procession, trunk of Karrymats between them, announced the return of a problem.'

By the time we finally ventured out into the North Sea, only three of these 'mats' were still on board; it must therefore be presumed that the Bilge Rats found an alternative and more successful method of disposing of them, somewhere between Trondheim and Honningsvag!

Although we did not make a habit of 'losing' or bartering the ships' equipment at every opportunity, space was so limited and our minds tuned to such an extent to the ease with which an accident could happen in such crowded and perpetually unstable conditions, that anything that was deemed to be useless or dangerous was removed at the earliest opportunity.

With an empty grey sea around us, sleeping was naturally a recom-mended method of passing the time, but during the daylight hours it was relatively unusual to find more than the previous 'watch' actually engaged in this pursuit – with the exception of Arne Wisth, who appeared to be catching up on about a year's lost sleep! On that first day's sailing across the North Sea, much of the time was spent talking in small constantly-changing groups, our bodies huddled together in a vain effort to shelter from the drizzle and spray.

The sea was to remain a cold, uninviting grey colour for the next fifty hours or so; the waves, capped with white spume, marched in an endless procession across our path, breaking into clouds of icy, windswept spray whenever the longship had the audacity to cut into their timeless rhythm. Overhead an unbroken blanket of murky cloud stretched from horizon to horizon. Visibility was poor due to the unpenetrable curtain of mist which occasionally turned into heavier showers, but never completely let up. Reputed to be one of the busiest shipping lanes in the world, the North Sea hid us in an all-enveloping shroud of moisture and we were to see no vessels or aircraft of any kind until our rendezvous with the oil-rigs.

At lunch time Odd Børstad succeeded in producing a hot reindeer-meat stew which took some of the chill out of our bodies. The pot was of such a size that the same stew was served for the next two consecutive meals, with the flavour tending to fade with the passage of time. Accompanied by hunks of cheese and bread, those first few meals depleted our stores more than had been anticipated, but our confidence in reaching Lerwick within three days meant that no one worried unduly about the food running out.

We had loaded an abundance of water in case a contrary wind swept us off our intended course and kept us at sea for longer than planned, but the taste was so tainted by the rubber of the water-bags that it was always boiled for use in the coffee. This problem remained with us for the whole voyage, and when occasions arose when it was impossible to use the gaz cooker the crew were reduced to bartering for the few bottles of lemonade which those with more foresight among us had stowed in their kists.

With a cup of strong, sweet coffee in hand I settled myself in my usual position, tucked down between two kists on a level with the mast. This was the 'smoking cabin', the domain of the Bilge Rats and other nicotine addicts.

During our months of training on the Isle of Man, Robin Bigland had warned us that he would not permit any smoking on board the longship. It had therefore seemed a heaven-sent opportunity to make a determined effort to give up the habit, and Richard Young, Brian Cousins and I had all vowed not to touch another cigarette once we had left the island.

Unfortunately, on our arrival in Norway we had been met by our Norwegian shipmates, four of whom smoked like the proverbial chimneys. When we informed them of Robin Bigland's diktat there was very nearly a mutiny and, I have to admit, our will-power crumbled and we sided with our smoking companions. Robin made no comment at the time and it was not until the final sail in Oslofjord that his irritation finally erupted. On that occasion he was in his usual place aft, sitting on his kist (which due to his eminent position as Chieftain was athwart the ship as far towards the stern as possible) and talking to Ray Sutcliffe, the BBC producer. During the course of the conversation, Ray heedlessly knocked the ash out of his pipe, to windward, and Robin received the cooling embers full in the face! He promptly decreed that smoking could only be carried out 'before the mast', no doubt taking grim pleasure in the knowledge that if anybody wanted to smoke they would also be in the prime position for a good soaking.

By this stage on the voyage our supply of cigarettes was in any case decreasing rapidly and the non-smokers in the crew, who had purchased their duty-free allowance at Oslo airport with a view to selling them off cheaply to the locals, found themselves increasingly more popular. As the stocks dwindled so the price rose, culminating in the cold of an early dawn when it cost me a Mars Bar for a match, let alone a cigarette! This bartering was naturally carried out in a jocular manner but, as any addict will confirm, as long as there is a single cigarette left in the packet the craving for it is minimal, in comparison with the desperate need when there are no cigarettes left and the nearest shop is 150 miles away across the sea!

The formation of the 'smoking cabin' became an 'on-board' joke, any non-smoker in the crew having to request permission to pass through it on their way forward. This developed into a natural progression of the 'members' also standing and saluting (or emulating a bosun's whistle) whenever Eddie Kaighin or the Chieftain passed through. There were, of course, no distinct boundaries to the 'cabin' simply the presence of the mast denoting the entrance to the 'lower decks'.

Such a heavy handed humour and adaptation to the circumstances played an important part in relieving the monotony of the longer passages undertaken on the journey and also, as the voyage progressed, the process of welding the crew into a single unit. Anyone who felt 'left out' became more noticeable as the separate groups coalesced, which undoubtedly encouraged them to join in to a greater extent – whether at sea or on land. In these early days at sea, a number of the crew remained somewhat aloof from those with more extrovert tendencies, in most cases because they were either naturally solitary (as were our Norwegian shipmates), or because this was their first experience of living in close proximity with a number of men whose characters were so different. This is not to suggest that any form of gulf separated us, but rather that the self-imposed or habitually imprinted barriers of 'decorum' were more quickly dissolved among the older crew members – with one or two exceptions. Anyone who has experienced an all-male outing, be it a Rugby Tour, Stag party or whatever, will be able to picture the quieter, younger members of the group who, initially, stand open-mouthed on the sideline as they listen to a highly respected local bank manager giving out with Eskimo Nell! (Not that I am suggesting we crossed the North Sea to the strains of uncensored Rugby songs).

It takes time to recapture the elusive vision of lost youth, but the older or more self-repressed one has become, the quicker the transition occurs. We were living our part as completely as we could. Our predecessors had left their wives and sweethearts to challenge the sea and find adventure, and although we had a better idea of what lay beyond the horizon I don't believe that the male mentality has changed a great deal in a thousand years. The difference was that once safely landed in Lerwick a telephone call would quickly allay any fears for our safety that our wives might be suffering. For the Viking women there was no such easy relief, and years could pass before the return of their men – if indeed they ever did come back.

The long hours of daylight and the unrelenting emptiness of the surrounding waters allowed the imagination to wander back into misty antiquity. As I sat staring out across the restless sea I could easily picture those longships of old, their great sails gleaming against the grey, rain-spattered sky. How many times had they crossed and recrossed those same waters, first in search of land or conquest and then as more peaceful traders?

'. . . King Magnus Bare-Legs of Norway came from the east with a powerful force . . . He took Earl Paul and Earl Erland and sent them east to Norway . . . King Magnus then proceeded to the Hebrides.' Such lines, taken at random from the *Orkneyinga Saga*, emphasised the familiarity with which the Vikings regarded these crossings.

In a similar vein, the *Faroese Saga* describes voyages back and forth across the hostile stretches of the North Sea with such comparative frequency and safety that one wonders why the design of ships ever altered from that of the longship! But, in the same *Saga* (as described by G. V. C. Young) the true perils of such crossings are placed in a better perspective when one reads '. . . In the summer, Sigmund set out with Thrand for Norway with the tribute for King Olaf, but the ship was wrecked and the tribute lost, although most of the people on board were saved, Thrand being rescued by Sigmund. Sigmund then prepared another ship, but Thrand said that the journey would be unlucky if he were forced to go. Sigmund, however, made Thrand come with him, but once again the ship was wrecked.'

My mind pictured the sight of a solitary Viking ship, virtually identical to our own, pitching its way towards the gaunt rocks of the Northern Isles, the crew hoping desperately that the weather would not turn against them and splinter their ship to matchwood on some forbidding coast.

Or again, through the curtain of rain, one could easily imagine a fleet of longships forging towards Lindisfarne on their way to mark the beginning of hostilities against Anglo-Saxon Britain. Alcuin, the great Yorkshire scholar, described the attack, writing from the Court of Charlemagne: '. . . never before has such a terror appeared in Britain as we have now suffered from a pagan race, nor was it thought that such an inroad from the sea could be made. Behold, the church of St. Cuthbert spattered with the blood of the priests of God, despoiled of all its ornaments; a place more venerable than all in Britain is given as prey to pagan people.'

My thoughts were brought back to the present by the sound of Odd Børstad clattering around in his tiny galley. The second-hand stew was on the menu yet again but, grateful for some hot food to combat the chill of the evening, we wolfed down the stringy reindeer meat and washed it down with another mug of steaming coffee.

To prepare for our first night at sea the soaking storm-sail was rigged low down, across part of the foredeck, allowing room for the mainsail to be handled if necessary; as the murky daylight faded, darkness closed around the ship, lightened only by the hissing white surf as the waves broke against our tossing prow.

With a great deal of grunting and various muttered imprecations, those who felt so inclined crawled beneath the shelter in an attempt to gain some warmth and, possibly, sleep. A few of us preferred to curl up in the open, rain or no rain, not relishing the thought of becoming enmeshed in that writhing tangle of bodies; a heaving mass, two deep in places, beneath the sagging canvas, that looked like an octopus suffering from insomnia!

Few of the crew bothered to climb into their sleeping bags mainly because, as the zips were positioned on the outside, there was very little chance of making an emergency exit if the occasion arose. Even if one succeeded in locating a sleeping-bag after heaving kists around the rolling deck it was almost certain to be soaking wet and consequently likely to provide little extra comfort. The waterproof Gortex covers for the bags were, however, utilised to a greater extent, as one could easily slip into them even wearing oil-skins. Unfortunately, they tended to produce large amounts of condensation and, although they kept out the external moisture, the internal dampness rather nullified their usefulness; nevertheless, they did protect one's body against the wind.

Our watch was due 'on' at midnight (the Graveyard watch) and I passed the intervening time curled up on the deck, half dozing and half listening to the comments from beneath the shelter.

'Move this bloody elbow, somebody!'

'Oh, yes please. Thank you very much.' This, obviously from Knut Hoff!

'Do you know, Georgie, you remind me of my wife!' There was a ripple of laughter because Georgie Kneale sported one of the bushiest beards on the ship.

'What on earth are you doing, B.C.?' Brian Cousins was caterpillaring across the massed bodies, working his way deeper into his sleeping-bag lair.

Gradually, a restless silence descended, soon to be broken, inevitably, by a plaintive cry of 'Oh, Christ, I need a pee!' and the whole rigmarole began again.

At midnight, I was awakened from a fitful sleep by the none too delicate pressure of a sea-boot on my ankle as one of the crew coming off watch groped his way forward in the forlorn hope of finding a space in which to lie down. In the dim glow of the torch used to light the chart-table, indistinct figures moved carefully across the lurching deck, picking their way between the sleeping figures, as the watch was changed.

Moving aft, I stepped over the recumbent form of Alan Binns who lay across the middle of the boat, his body completely shrouded by his huge tarpaulin sleeping bag. (When he left us in Lerwick the sleeping space on board seemed to increase dramatically).

Dave Eames looked up from the chart table, his face a ghostly white in the reflected torchlight.

'Can you take over the helm, Mike, while I work out our position?' he asked.

I clambered over yet another sleeping figure and moved up alongside Colin Bowen at the helm.

'What's our course?' I asked, teeth chattering in the bitter cold.

'West Sou-West,' he replied, staring into the faint green light of the bin-nacle compass. 'At least, I think that's what it is!' At night, with the rain and spray constantly showering down on to the glass of the binnacle, it was extremely difficult to keep to an accurate course and quite often, especially if no horizon were visible, one's eyes would soon tire from the constant effort of peering through the film of water which diffused the compass lettering.

Dr. David M. Wilson, in his book *The Vikings and their Origins*, describes the navigational practices of the Viking age. He states: 'To a large extent their ships were sailed within sight of land, but when ships crossed the seas to the Western Isles, . . . some form of navigational aid must have been used. Presumably the stars and the sun were used in such a context, and there is some evidence that bearing dials and azimuth tables were used as further aids. The Vikings seem to have had a fair idea of latitude, but none of longitude; they probably used a method of reckoning, known from later periods, by means of which they would sail to the latitude of their destination and then follow this parallel until land was sighted. On well-known passages, like that to the Faroes, they were probably able to sail by an almost direct route.'

As we saw neither stars nor sun during our crossing, we were grateful for the presence of our small but essential compass. With a number of the crew having to learn the art of steering by compass from scratch, it was a minor miracle that we ended up remarkably close to our intended destination.

Colin gratefully relinquished the helm into my care and made his way forward to sleep, blowing on his hands to restore the circulation.

Standing at the helm of a Viking longship as it plunges through the darkness towards the west must be one of the most exhilarating moments in life. The feel of the living deck beneath one's feet, with the great curving sail standing out from the yard and the cold salty spray on one's face, is something that cannot easily be described. Although the shadowy figures along the length of the deck provided the comfort of company, as did the quiet mumble of voices as Dave Eames and Eddie Kaighin discussed the course changes to be carried out during the watch, the impression of solitude was very real. On either side the breaking wave-tops rushed by in the darkness, brief flashes of white against the torpid blackness. The rhythmical rise and fall of the serpent-head in the bow, just discernible against the lighter hue of the cloud-covered sky, quickly lulled one into a sense of being one entity with the ship. The silhouetted forms of Knut Hoff sitting on the port gunwale in his position on the 'brace' and Shane Lucas on the opposite side holding the 'tack sheet', somehow served only to emphasise the utter aloneness one felt in such a setting. It was at times like these, with the cold wind and freezing rain driving into our faces, that we knew we were truly following in the wake of those who had gone before us. Maybe we were better equipped, but the fears, hopes and excitement of sailing such a vessel must have been very similar. The longship was a sheer delight to sail and the discomforts of the weather rapidly faded into insignificance.

Magnus Andersen, who sailed a replica Gokstad ship to America nearly 90 years before us, had obviously experienced the same exhilaration when he wrote, '. . . we often had the pleasure of dashing through the water at speeds of 10, and sometimes even 11 knots! This in spite of a primitive and relatively small rigging! Whether the old Norsemen used their ships in the same way as this is hard to say, but it does not seem unlikely that they used the ships for all they were worth. It seems absolutely certain that in those days too they wished to travel as fast as possible; why else should they have taken the trouble to improve the structure until it was so perfect that not even the shipbuilders of our time can do better as far as the ship's bottom is concerned. The fact is that the finest merchant ships of our day, those regarded as the best sailers, have practically the same type of bottom as the Viking ships.'

Small wonder that none of our crew ever baulked at the chance of helming the *Raven*, whenever the opportunity arose.

The early hours of the morning passed slowly – short snatches of conversation interspersed by long silences, each of us lost in our own thoughts. Night-watches seemed to have been specifically designed for meditation. With the remainder of the crew asleep, the hushed monotone of sporadic talk among the watch was the only sound to interrupt the perpetual song of the wind in the rigging and the sullen slop of the waves against the side of the ship. It was a time for reminiscences and future plans; discussions about the performance of the *Raven*; the exchange of stories and friendly arguments concerning the probable shipboard life of the old Vikings. Once we had become virtually immune to the rain and had recirculated some warmth into our bodies, those long hours of darkness seemed more peaceful and restful than sleep itself.

The dawn arrived almost unobserved; an imperceptible lightening of the sky which heralded the beginning of our second day at sea. The view remained unchanged: a limitless expanse of grey, rain-spattered waves, the wind occasionally whipping a crest into a shower of spray. The murky clouds still covered the sky in unbroken dreariness – a truly Wagnerian picture lacking ony the thunder and lightning.

Relieved from the 'watch' we usurped the positions of those who had taken over our responsibilities and fell into a deep sleep until, all too soon, the clatter of mugs and plates announced that Odd Børstad had surfaced to perform his morning chores. Along with David Eames, Arne Wisth and Rick Tomlinson he was one of the few men who obviously found no difficulty in sleeping while at sea – an ability which a number of us heartily envied.

For the whole of the day we sailed westward beneath the drab grey skies. The wind had veered slightly but not enough to affect our course, and it had also decreased a little. Consequently the amount of spray showering the foredeck was very much reduced which enabled the 'off-watch' crew to spread themselves more comfortably around the boat.

The major problem on long voyages, as many a sailor well knows, is that of boredom. With the lack of physical activity (subject to the prevailing conditions), surrounded by a seemingly limitless expanse of ocean devoid of any signs of life and none of the modern recreational facilities available to drug one's brain (such as television), a state of depressing apathy can be quickly attained. However, for whatever reason, no one appeared to suffer from this malady on board the *Raven* throughout the whole trip. A bored person becomes fractious and impatient for action, and such a person on the ship would have upset the natural easy-going balance that had materialised among us over the previous weeks.

Inured to the hardships of an open boat, most of the crew settled easily into the casual nature of ship-board life, occupying themselves as best they could. Colin Bowen recorded in his diary: '. . . the crossing of the North Sea seemed to be a never-ending cycle of sleeping, eating, going on watch, sleeping, eating and going on watch again.' This was a little over-simplified, but perhaps his zeal for sleep was to prepare himself for the reception we had been warned to expect in Lerwick. Robin Bigland had recounted to us a warning that he had received from a Scotsman, before the voyage had even begun. This had been to the effect that 'Those Islanders you know, they can't half put away some of the local product. They measure a man's manhood by the amount he can sink. You better have your drinking boots on or they'll not rate you as Vikings at all.'

Robin Bigland, as Chieftain, had perhaps the most difficult task of all during the longer sea passages, which was simply the need to keep mentally alert and cheerful. At first glance this might appear to be a ridiculous statement but, as a virtual Supercargo, he was under no obligation to assist in any of the everyday jobs that were necessary to maintain the smooth running of the ship. Alan Binns, our other Supercargo, at least had the stimulating mental exercise of studying the behaviour of the ship and her rigging from the academic point of view; but, as far as Robin was concerened, he was faced with three days of sitting on his kist or sleeping! The fact that he often offered to take over the helm for a spell must have relieved the monotony, but even more to his credit was his ability to initiate a lively conversation or discussion when he sensed any feelings of boredom beginning to set in. He did, however, on one occasion when the persistent drizzle had finally taxed even his patience to the limit, ask Rick Tomlinson and Nigel Wood 'how they could possibly enjoy sailing as a hobby when it was such an incredibly inefficient and remarkably uncomfortable method of travel?'

At the beginning of the voyage a number of books had been packed into various kists and their presence whiled away many an hour, the different novels being passed around in rotation. There were also a number of Playboy magazines on board, kindly donated to the crew by Sir John Paul, the Governor of the Isle of Man, whose wife, Lady Paul, had named the vessel at the launching. Sir John claimed to have found these magazines in a dustbin outside the back door of the Bristol Hotel in Oslo, but exactly what he was doing ferreting around in hotel dustbins was a question which was never satisfactorily answered!

To while away the daylight hours I occupied myself with writing poetry, sketching or, more often than not, surreptitiously studying my companions – mentally noting how their characters changed as the days passed by.

Eddie Kaighin, the skipper, seemed to be tied to the chart table as if by an elastic band. With no other method of navigation except the compass available to him, he was constantly checking and rechecking our supposed course; his repeated question to the helmsman of 'What course are you steering?' allowed the latter little chance of day-dreaming.

By this time, Eddie had gained the full confidence of the entire crew (the Norwegians have had differing views on his ability during the early days of the sea trials). One of his attributes was his readiness to discuss points of seamanship with the other sailors on board, thereby implying that he was not infallible. I noted however that we nearly always ended up carrying out his original intention. To the few of us who had begun the trip as virtual novices his patience in teaching us the basic skills required to sail such a vessel had borne dividends, and we were all confident that we could now carry out our allotted tasks a great deal more efficiently.

Robin Bigland had visibly relaxed since we had put to sea, the pressures of the organising behind him. All the planning of the previous twelve months was over and the problem was now simply one of keeping the crew in order when they reached land and being able to reach the Isle of Man without mishap. His major worry concerned the possiblility of an accident to one of the crew which would obviously detract considerably from the impact of the final landing at Peel, quite apart from his personal feelings if such an event did occur – although it has to be admitted that it would probably have been more in keeping with the actual happenings on the original longships; it was a fear which remained with him constantly until the actual moment when our prow touched the sand on the Isle of Man.

Apart from that nagging thought at the back of his mind he was, for the first time, beginning to enjoy himself. Not many men have the opportunity of sailing their own longship along the paths of history, through some of the most beautiful scenery in the world – not that the sulky waters of the North Sea were particularly thrilling at that moment.

David Eames had grown in my estimation. His knowledge of the sea and quiet confidence in his own ability belied his twenty one years. As my watch-leader, we had already spent many hours in conversation, he teaching me some of the finer points of technique with regard to sailing while I, in return, having had the luck to travel far more widely than he had, discussed a broader outlook on life. Of the two it was David, I think, who gained less from our discussions!

The Bosun, Brian Cousins, or B.C. as he was universally addressed, the second-in-command if anything should happen to Eddie Kaighin, was the ideal foil to the skipper: the one a fiery dominant character, ever ready to test the boat to her limit in situations where the difference between safety and danger was minimal, the other quieter, more careful, and possibly tending to err on the side of safety to a greater extent, while still revelling in the thrill of sailing such a unique vessel.

Rolf Hansen, the third watch leader, was nick-named 'Ganger' after a gigantic Viking called Hrolf the Ganger (Rollo) who founded the Duchy of Normandy and was so huge that no horse could bear his weight – hence he had to walk, or 'gang' as the Scots say, everywhere. Our 'Ganger' had spent some time on the *Brendan* and on the Norwegian fembørings, and his suggestions with reference to the general rigging and sailing of the *Raven* had resulted in both Alan Binns and Eddie Kaighin carrying out a number of modifications. On board he was perhaps the quietest member of the crew, constantly moving about the ship making small alterations to the ropes and sheets. This sometimes led to the only heated exchanges that were experienced and, even then, the temperature was never more than lukewarm. With seven highly experienced sailors on board there were bound to be differences of opinion, each watch leader preferring to experiment with his own setting of the sail.

David Eames, for example, never had much time for the *priares* (the system of ropes which held down the foot of the sail), claiming that in an emergency much valuable time would be lost in loosening them, apart from the fact that in his opinion they didn't greatly affect the performance of the ship. Consequently, when our watch was in charge, these particular ropes were always left loose. 'Ganger' argued to the contrary, but Dave was adamant:

'I don't give a damn how useful they are on a fembøring,' he would say, 'this isn't a fremøring in any case, and they're not going to be tied up while I'm on watch.'

The individualistic nature of our Norwegian shipmates was something which took the Manx crew by surprise. Knut Skøgoy, Ganger Hansen and Arne Wisth were the main offenders, suddenly altering some aspect of the rigging if they felt it was not fully effective. They may well have been correct in their assumption, but the one rule which had to work on board a ship whose safety had not been fully tested was that there was only one skipper, whose orders had to be obeyed, regardless of any personal theories.

This difference in temperament between the two nationalities could have caused difficulties; Ganger Hansen, for instance at one stage threatened to leave the ship while in Norway because he felt that it was unsafe, rigged in such a fashion, so Eddie tactfully accepted some of his suggested modifications which he agreed were for the better and harmony was restored. But the Norwegians quickly learnt to obey orders and, as the miles slipped away, so did the undercurrent of disagreement until, before half the voyage was completed, an amicable unity had been forged. Ganger still kept to himself while at sea, taking advantage of his ability to sleep in even the roughest waters; he was often to be found curled up INSIDE the roughly furled storm-sail! When awake he and Eddie Kaighin would discuss the relative merits of sailing ships and their various rigs, and Eddie freely acknowledged that he gained a great deal of knowledge about the handling of square-riggers from these conversations.

Knut Hoff, a Norwegian journalist, whose command of the English language did not enable him to converse easily, was a quiet but genial character. He spent most of the time sitting beside his kist, reading or writing or chatting to Knut Skøgoy. Most of the crew found Knut Skøgoy difficult to understand, not because his English was poor (quite the contrary), but because of his apparent unconcern about anything that happened on board. My own impression was that he strongly disagreed with a number of aspects concerning both the voyage itself and the long-ship, and the nick-name 'Action-Man' resulted from his apparent lack of enthusiasm for the on-board chores. Again, time was to alter things and gradually he too became more sociable, merging into the smooth running of the general team.

The position of Arne Wisth, as official photographer, meant that he was permanently on call, ready to film any event of note. When not so employed he would curl up in the bow to sleep. For a person who disliked sailing, finding little enjoyment in being thrown about for days on end, he always remained remarkably cheerful, his sense of humour relieving many a tense moment.

Odd Børstad can best be described as a very large, cuddly bear! Of all our Norwegian colleagues it was he who fitted in the easiest with the Manx crew. His strength was prodigious, and to see him heaving the kists around to gain entrance to the store lockers one would have thought they were empty. We had all taken to him instantly, on our first meeting, and he was to be a source of much amusement in the days to come. His only failing, if indeed it can be called that, was his insistence on smoking the foulest-smelling of cigars, especially when conditions were rough. It was a rare moment when one did not see Odd gnawing at a haunch of reindeer meat or tearing great lumps out of a piece of dried fish! (It is interesting to note that on no occasion did I ever see anybody sea-sick, although I was told that Rick Tomlinson and Nigel Wood had suffered this indignity during the early moments of their first sail in the *Raven*.)

The standard answer to the accusation, 'You're not eating again, Odd?' was always the same: 'When you see a thin cook, then he is no good. See me, I am not thin, am I?' This retort required no answer; the mound of fat which bulged out over his belt was ample proof. It was a point of fact that not one of the crew lost weight on the voyage.

As regards the remainder of the Manx crew, my original assessments of their character had changed little. Rick Tomlinson and Nigel Wood, close friends before the longship had been conceived, tended to remain together during these early days. Both of them were very keen sailors and to them the pleasure of handling such a vessel was their major recreation on board. With the knowledge gained from their sailing experiences in the Irish Sea and further afield, they knew that a relatively pleasant day's sailing could rapidly change and their expertise would then be urgently required. Consequently, when off-watch, if not reading a book, they would waste little time in getting their heads down, Rick Tomlinson having staked a claim on one of the oar-stacks as his mattress.

Colin Bowen, Richard Young and myself (the original Bilge Rats) spent much of our spare time in general conversation. Such was the gregarious nature of the boat that there was always a small group of the crew involved in some form of discussion while others joined in, or dropped off to sleep or read, depending on how the mood took them.

Richard Young had developed into the classic life-and-soul-of-the-party whose witticisms and wisecracks had the boat convulsed with laughter on many an occasion. Georgie Kneale, who had not previously ventured far from the shores of the Isle of Man, had suffered our only serious bout of homesickness during the weeks in Norway. Consequently he had remained quiet and withdrawn, unsure how best to settle into such a wild and differing company of men. Now with the prospect of the Scottish Isles in front of him, he began to 'come out of himself' and join in with the general activities with much greater enthusiasm.

Shane Lucas, who had been the instigator of our miserable ordeals during training the previous winter, was, quite simply, not at home in a boat. This fact he freely admitted himself, but he had worried all of us during the sea-trials by his inability to acknowledge the potential danger of certain situations – how the safety of the ship (and with it, ourselves) depended on each individual obeying an order instantly, without discussion. This may sound a harsh criticism and one which I am perhaps not justified in making, but Shane's transition from being in command for the six months of the training to becoming a lowly member of the crew was perhaps a more difficult psychological hurdle than any of us had to face. The fact that he did overcome it along with his fear of the sea speaks of a kind of courage which can only be admired.

The final member of the crew which traversed the North Sea was the Univeristy don, Alan Binns. He was to leave us in Lerwick and realising this he probably felt, to a certain extent, estranged from the rest of the crew. He obviously revelled in the voyage, but I would think from a technical point of view rather than a romantic one. Much of his time was spent in *sotto voce* discussion with Robin Bigland and Eddie Kaighin with regard to the sailing performance of the longship, especially the usefulness or otherwise of the rigging, which he himself had designed to a large extent. At night-time his habit of putting an a 'wet-suit' before entering the portals of his enormous sleeping bag always caused ripples of amusement among the rest of the crew. None of us, however, denied the fact that for a man in his fifties to undertake such a potentially hazardous and (from the exposure point of view) particularly dangerous voyage either required a singular type of courage or a compulsive desire for knowledge.

As the unrelenting rain continued to beat down upon her decks, the longship and her mixed assortment of individuals sailed westward into the evening of her second day on the North Sea. The waves had eased their constant battering against the hull and the waters now surged by in a typical heavy swell. The motion of the *Raven* changed into a more sluggish roll, the mast swinging lazily across the unchanging, impenetrable murk of the clouds. With the drop in the wind the spray no longer showered intermittently across the foredeck, which made life a little more pleasant for those of the crew who decided to wedge themselves against the kists to sleep.

The change in conditions, while decreasing the sharpness of the movement of the boat, had increased both the pitch and the roll. It was therefore of paramount importance to wedge oneself into a chosen position to avoid being thrown across the deck. The possibility of going overboard was an ever-present danger, especially as the gunwale, at times, was within a foot of the surface of the sea. In calmer situations it was common practice to sit on the gunwale, but nobody was going to tempt providence in such a manner in these conditions, unless a call of Nature so demanded. If such was the case it was a question of hanging on tightly to the mast stays or the gunwale itself, while fervently hoping that an extra strong roll would not immerse one's posterior in the icy water!

Eddie Kaighin estimated that if the wind held its speed and direction we should sight the first oil-rig around dawn. He immediately quashed the sudden surge of excitement by reminding us that along with the presence of the oil-rigs we could expect to find numerous boats, tankers, supply ships etc., and that everyone had better keep a sharp look out. The Vikings never had to cope with floating cities on their travels! The proximity of these mammoth structures filled us all with an increasing elation. Unless the weather changed drastically during the hours of darkness, completion of a successful North Sea crossing would be virtually ensured. For what was potentially the most dangerous part of the entire voyage, we had been incredibly lucky. It had certainly been an uncomfortable, choppy and exceedingly damp two days, with the dangers ever present, but at just the right time that hostile stretch of water had withheld most of its frightening powers. But then, as the darkness of the night merged with the grey of dawn it became apparent that we were not going to escape so easily after all. As the sky slowly lightened, so the mist descended, and within a few moments we were enveloped in a blanket of fog.

To have to sail through fog at any time is a dangerous pastime, but with no radar, fog-horn or other form of warning while entering one of the most technological areas of sea in the world, the hazard is potentially that much greater. With the exception of the watch who had just been relieved, the rest of the crew stared nervously out into the thick grey mist now surrounding the longship. Visibility was reduced to approximately a hundred yards and the only sounds to break the ghostly silence were the quiet murmur of voices and the slop of the swell against the wooden hull of the *Raven*.

'How far are we from the oil-rigs, Eddie?' asked somebody, as seven o'clock came and went.

'We should be seeing them shortly,' replied Eddie, 'if the bloody mist would only clear. A bottle of rum in Lerwick for the first man who sights a rig or a ship.'

What an incentive! Tired eyes brightened immediately and peered into the murk with renewed intensity.

Most of us had little idea how big an oil-rig really was. Not that it really mattered because there was no way that we could mistake one for something else. The real problem was how close would we be to them when we did make contact, figuratively speaking. We were just as likely to find the massive legs of a drilling platform suddenly appearing out of the mist in front of us as we were to see a vague shadow in the distance. In the same way, an oil-tanker could be upon us with no prior warning, and if it approached us travelling at a speed of 8 knots or thereabouts we would have approximately one minute in which to take avoiding action when the fog was at its densest. The manoeuvrability of the longship was certainly not that impressive!

To our universal relief, by eight o'clock the mist began to clear and the visibility gradually improved, thereby allowing us to relax our straining eyes. With the decrease in tension so the general excitement increased. We had nearly made it to the first outposts that marked our entry into home waters. Although we were only two-thirds of the way across, we knew that once contact had been established then, at least, people would know where we were.

Although the mist had retreated, visibility was still very poor and some of the crew began to have doubts about the accuracy of our navigation. A relatively small error in the course calculations could have quite easily directed us north of Shetland – in which case the next stop would be the Faroes or Iceland!

'Kaighin's navigation is up the spout,' said Richard Young. 'We're probably half way to Iceland!'

'I sincerely hope not; they've got prohibition there,' I replied. Richard's face paled at the thought.

'Are you sure we're on the right course, Eddie?' he enquired worriedly.

'Where's your confidence in me, lads?' was the cheerful reply. 'If I say the oil-rigs are here, then so they are.'

'And on the seventh day he rested,' came a blasphemous whisper from the foredeck.

As if on cue, Alan Binnes suddenly shouted, 'Oil-rig ahoy!' and pointed out across the starboard bow.

'Can't see a thing!'

'Figment of your imagination, Alan.'

'He's only after the rum.'

'Probably been at it already and is now having hallucinations.'

'No, Alan's right boys, thar she blows,' said the skipper.

Sure enough, away on the horizon, a tiny flame flickered in the mist, pinpointing the position of one of the rigs.

Most of us were a little disappointed, expecting to see a massive structure suddenly looming out of the haze. That tiny, insignificant-looking light, miles away, was about as undramatic as could possibly be imagined.

'Pipe spirits,' called Eddie Kaighin. 'Let's break the rules and celebrate.'

Normally 'spirits were piped' at six o'clock in the evening at which time the skipper would religiously pour out a measure of akvavit for each crew member; but as this was a special occasion we grabbed our mugs and gratefully accepted a generous libation of the stomach-warming liquor.

As we altered course towards our goal, the freshening wind drove away the last remnants of mist. Gradually the oil-rig grew in size as we approached it and, like a scene out of H. G. Wells' *War of the Worlds*, more and more of the huge drilling platforms appeared on the horizon, their vent pipes belching leaping tongues of flame into the sky.

The most immediate problem was to determine which oil-field we had come upon, but until we were close enough to contact the nearest rig by radio there was no way of finding out. It wasn't long before we were within range and Eddie Kaighin managed to raise the radio operator. Apparently we were at the southern end of the Brent field, twenty-five miles north of our aiming point, Ninian Central. Everyone was justifiably pleased on hearing this because, although it may have sounded a long way from the rendezvous point, after 170 miles of the North Sea using compass bearings only, and with half the helmsmen virtual amateurs at steering a ship in heavy seas, we had at least found an oil-field!

With communication established we circled around the rig to give them a view of our longship before heading south. Passing close to one of those monstrous towers was certainly an awe-inspiring experience. The gigantic legs which towered above us looked incredibly solid as they stood with the white water seething around them. Unfortunately recent history has shown that the power of the North Sea is often more than a match for them, however indestructible they might appear.

Whether or not the rig radio operator had alerted his crew to our presence we had no idea, but there was nobody visible on the platform. It amused me to imagine an insomniac rigger, who had noticed us while taking the early morning air, trying to convince his workmates that he really had seen a Viking longship sail out from east, circle the rig and then disappear to the south!

From that moment on, the day became a kaleidoscope of activity. Word of our presence had obviously travelled quickly and for the next few hours as we headed towards the Ninian Field, the crew-change helicopters (and there was an incredible number of them) thundered over our heads, detouring from the normal routes to give their passengers an opportunity of viewing a Viking ship under full sail.

News of our safe passage across the North Sea was flashed from the oil fields and, before midday, Kathy Lewis in the Isle of Man had already informed our families. To add to our enjoyment of the occasion, the miserable drizzling weather at long last abated and with the complex of the Ninian Oil rigs beginning to rise up in front of us the clouds finally dissipated to allow us our first glimpse of the sun since leaving Trondheim. Beneath a cloudless blue sky we sailed towards the huge monolithic structure of Ninian Central. We had obviously only just sighted the outermost rigs of the Brent Field earlier in the day because for the last two hours we had been sailing through a virtual forest of steel towers – their vent flames shooting skywards, looking like something out of Dante's Inferno. When the *Raven* finally penetrated to the centre of the Field we at last made contact with Bill Hook and his BBC camera team, as the helicopter carrying the film crew lifted off the rig and sliced through the air towards us. For the following couple of hours we sailed around the massive platform to enable the BBC to film the contrast between the past and the present. Tacking, beating and running before the wind we left Hooky deliriously happy, his excited voice crackling over the radio.

'Great, Eddie, fantastic! Can you do that again, please?'

Our mood was such that we would have been quite happy to sail around the rig all day if he had wanted us to. For a short time the pressures were completely removed; all our hidden fears and worries about what could so easily have happened during the last two days evaporated almost completely. But as so often happens, danger threatened when it was least expected.

'What the hell's that other chopper doing?' yelled an anxious Dave Eames, pointing towards a new arrival on the scene. With a growing feeling of horror we watched this second helicopter, presumably from one of the nearby rigs, start to descend and close in on us for a better view. The sea beneath flattened into a huge circle as the downdraught from the rotor blades caught the waves. Mesmerised we watched that ominous circle creep towards us.

'Christ, he'll have us over!' somebody yelled.

Eddie Kaighin sprang into action.

'Mike, on the main halyard. Rick, grab the Rakke downhaul. When I yell, drop that sail fast. Don't hold it, just let it go!'

As the wind hit us, the *Raven* keeled over sharply, the sail suddenly filling. The helicopter pilot must have realised what was happening (or so we thought) for at the last second he suddenly pulled away, allowing the longship to return to an upright position.

'Bloody hell, that was close!' exclaimed B.C.

'Oh, no, the idiot's going to try again,' said Nigel Wood in an amazed voice. Sure enough the helicopter was descending yet again and once more we heeled over dangerously close to a capsize as the downdraught cracked into the sail. For the second time the pilot pulled up just as we were about to drop the sail.

By now an irate skipper was frantically radioing the rig and within a few moments the offending helicopter had disappeared back to a neighbouring platform.

Still cursing and swearing – with relief – we sailed towards Ninian Central for a final pass.

'Bet you can't sail under that flame, Eddie!' somebody said, and the crew, as one, groaned aloud. If there was one thing that we had learnt it was that to dare Eddie to do anything was to court disaster!

'You can't anyway,' said Alan, 'there's a quarter of a mile safety limit around these rigs.'

'You just watch me,' replied the skipper, his eyes alight with the challenge.

"Now don't be silly, Eddie,' said Robin Bigland, visions of his beloved longship going up in flames no doubt filling his mind.

'Don't worry Robin, I know what I'm doing.'

This reply interested me at the time, because I was fairly certain that sailing a Viking ship beneath a flame of burning gas was not a feat that Eddie had practised to any great extent. Robin Bigland resigned himself to the inevitable and sat down on his kist, staring ahead at the rapidly approaching rig, and no doubt thinking how he was going to explain the loss to the underwriters.

Under full sail we moved in close to the single concrete pillar that supported the drilling platform. The oil-rigs either had a vertical vent or a side-vent, and in this case it was one of the latter beneath which we were attempting to pass. The catwalks along the side of the platform a hundred feet above us were black with spectators, all of whom were yelling and waving. At the time we thought they were cheering but we later learnt that, in reality, they were trying to warn us away – and we found out why a few moments later.

As we moved beneath the deafening roar of the flame, which was probably about one hundred and fifty feet above us, the heat struck us like a furnace and we were suddenly showered by a fine spray of boiling

94

droplets of water. This apparently was the end product of the sea water which was pumped in to cool the vapourising jet of burning gas.

All would have been well but for the basic physical law that hot air rises. In so doing, it created a vacuum beneath it; as a result, directly beneath that terrifying gout of fire, we were suddenly becalmed. Through the thunderous noise we heard Eddie yelling for the oars to be shipped and, with a fair amount of panic on board, we unlashed the nearest to us and thrust them into the oar ports.

'Put up your hoods,' Robin shouted, 'Cover your heads.'

'Damn, I could just do with a hot shower,' muttered a voice.

Slowly we rowed the *Raven* out of the updraught and the boiling droplets until the sail filled once again, and we thankfully left the spurting flame roaring angrily behind us.

'There, I told you it was no problem,' crowed a triumphant Eddie Kaighin, studiously ignoring Robin Bigland's baleful glare.

'*Odin's Raven*, *Odin's Raven*: This is Ninian Central, over,' crackled a voice from the radio.

'Ninian Central, Ninian Central, this is *Odin's Raven*, over,' replied Alan Binns.

'Ah, *Odin's Raven*, quite an impressive display that; thanks for the performance. Is there anything you require before you leave us?'

'Ninian Central, this *Odin's Raven*,' Alan replied, 'Thank you, yes. We would appreciate any food you may have spare, bread etc. and . . .' he looked around enquiringly.

'Marmite,' said Rick Tomlinson, hopefully.

'Beer,' came the request from a number of mouths.

Alan dutifully relayed the various items over the radio, receiving the affirmative answer to all our suggestions except, unfortunately, for the beer. Apparently most of the oil-rigs were 'dry' for obvious reasons. Having survived on thick, black Norwegian coffee since leaving Aalesund the thought of a long, cool glass of beer had become ever more alluring with each mile that had passed beneath our keel. Obviously we would now have to wait until Lerwick.

A quarter of an hour later a small boat roared out from beneath the shadow of the platform and came alongside. The oil-men had excelled themselves. The Norwegians on board looked on in amazement as Odd Børstad unpacked a veritable banquet with which to celebrate our safe crossing. Cold beef, bread still warm from the oven, home-made ice cream, cans of deliciously thirst-quenching Coca-Cola, cakes and, to Rick Tomlinson's delight, a large jar of Marmite. It may not have been true Viking fare, but at that moment nobody was going to complain.

Alan Binns conveyed our thanks over the radio and to a chorus of farewells the *Raven* turned her prow away from the oil rigs and headed westwards. The change in the weather was no temporary lull, and beneath a cloudless sky a gentle breeze carried us past a gigantic tanker in the process of filling her tanks, our last reminder of that amazing conglomeration of modern technology. The final picture of those spidery gantries silhouetted against the evening sky, their pencil thin spires of flame rising vertically into the air surmounted by long black tendrils of drifting smoke, remained etched on our minds for days to come.

The conversation flowed freely as we discussed our experiences of the previous twelve hours while the slowly reddening sky heralded a glorious sunset. We had learned from the rigs that the forecast for the next twenty-four hours was for gentle southerly winds and a cloudless sky. It appeared to us then that the worst was over. From now on it would be a summer cruise through the beautiful scenery of the Scottish Isles. How wrong we were to be proved.

The open sea for all its dangers has one big advantage over coastal, inter-island passages. The weather might be utterly hostile, extremely uncomfortable, or pleasantly genteel, but the changes in mood are relatively gradual, not sudden. In contrast, inshore waters can alter their temper with no warning; one minute a calm sea, the next a vicious squall funnelling down a glen or sweeping out from between islands. We were to learn only too soon that with only one third of our journey behind us the most difficult and dangerous sailing was yet to come.

At that time, though, most of us were convinced that our problems now lay behind us. Our vessel had brought us safely, albeit uncomfortably, across what was reputed to be one of the most dangerous stretches of water in the world. We had been lucky with the weather as we all appreciated, but then so also had many of the original longships – how else could they have made so many successful voyages across the same stretch of sea? We therefore allowed our minds to relax into complacency: an understandable reaction perhaps, but in retrospect one which we probably should have foreseen and taken steps to avoid.

That evening sail was enlivened by the reappearance of the camera team; now that they had re-established contact they were obviously making sure of filming us as much as possible in case we again carried out a disappearing act. This time they flew past in a twin-engined Beechcraft, with what seemed to be a potential Kamikaze pilot at the controls. I don't think that anybody on board had ever seen such an exhibition of low-level flying. With each pass the plane seemed to fly lower until on its final run all the crew agreed that the pilot had flown below the height of our 10 metre mast at very close range. Then with a waggle of its wings the plane said farewell to us and headed towards Shetland. Alone once more the longship glided across the gentle swell, heading in true Hollywood tradition into the blood-red glory of a northern sunset toward her first landfall.

Checking the rigging during sailing trials.

A seagull's view!

(l. to r.) David Eames, Shane Lucas, Brian Cousins (on helm), 'The Chieftain', Colin Bowen and Nigel Wood in Viking costume. Oslofjord.

Odin's Raven under full sail in Oslofjord.

Force eight storm off the Norwegian coast.

Approaching Ninian Central oil rig.

One of the more comfortable sleeping positions!

Enjoying the 'Fortnum's' hamper.

Rolf 'Ganger' Hansen trying to catch a dolphin.

The capsize.

The liferaft inflated a few minutes after the capsize.

The *Raven* being pumped out in the early hours.

The *Raven* under full oar power.

The past meets the present. *Odin's Raven* draws alongside HM Submarine *Odin*.

'Odd', the cook, carving the Sunday joint!

After the storm.

THE HITCH-HIKER

Long, lonely roads stretching endlessly away
Blue, hazy mountains, cities in decay
Dirty little cafes and smoke-filled bar-rooms
Hot, rumbling motorways choking in exhaust fumes.

See the Hitchhiker wander through the world far and wide
The soft earth beneath him, a girl by his side:
And you'll never find him crying or see him standing still
For he's a romany at heart and roam he always will.

You will find him in the woods in the fire's ruddy glow
Or cringing in a cave when the storm begins to blow;
Or sitting, heart contented, under foreign city lights
Or shivering with the cold in the snowy mountain heights.

You may meet him in the jungle in the sticky, sweaty heat
Or sitting by a crystal stream, cooling weary feet;
From Thailand to Morocco, New York to Katmandu
Always seeking, always searching, always hunting something new.

He hungers for the silence of the endless, rolling plains
As he stands in sodden misery in dirty, drenching rain.
The cry for more adventure echoes in his heart
As he waits, with aching urgency, the time to play his part.

And always there's the girl at home, the one he should have wed
Who waits with patient hopelessness beside the empty bed;
But even if he does return and take her eager hand
His heart will ever be elsewhere, in a foreign, distant land.

See the Hitchhiker wander through the world far and wide
The soft earth beneath him, a girl by his side:
And you'll never find him crying or see him standing still
For he's a romany at heart and roam he always will.

On board *Odin's Raven*
28.5.79

WORLD'S END

Soft, gentle rocks swell from the sea
Listless movements of ages past.
Cool, timeless mist envelopes me
And wraithe-like, you are there.
Beside the sea-worn harbour steps
Amid the ageless smell of life
The old mans' laughter wakes the gulls
And wrenches my memories to now;
Then you appear from empty dreams.
And as I sit and listen
To the kiss of the restless sea,
You take my mind and heart
And leave me breathless for a time.
Yet, even now, lifetimes apart
With naught around but sunkissed waves
My mind flies back to that ancient pool
Into which I threw my soul:
When, from the rippling eddies you called
Smiling, beckoning, reminding me
That love is life and life is love.
There, you took my dreams
And called me home, from World's End.

In the North Sea on board *Odin's Raven*
2.6.79

ODIN'S RAVEN

Out of the silent mist the dragon's head appears
Like a spectral vision form ancient times:
The mighty sail like a sepulchral shroud
Looms above, full-bellied, proud:
Reminding all of long-dead fears
Of rape and pillage and heinous crimes.

A thousand years have passed since Vikings ruled the seas
And timeworn warriors lie dusty, fleshless;
Vague memories mind in pageant plays
And homespun yarns call far-off days,
But time returns and history flees
Again a longship feels waters' caress.

Hewn from finest oak with adze and ancient skills
She glides across the timeless fold:
A breath of wind, a surge of life
The raking prow like a warrior's knife
Cuts through the straining tide and thrills
The hearts and minds of young and old.

The hiss of spray, sunkissed and crack of wind-racked sail
Drives her forth from ancient haven;
Her crew, adventure seekers all
Proud to be in history's thrall
In later years will tell the tale
Of the voyage made by Odin's Raven.

The Minches. On board *Odin's Raven*
10.6.79

SUNSHINE EYES

Deep, amber eyes that shine
Like sunlight
And light my heart
So cares
Decline.
Wide smile of beauty
Bantering
That lifts my life
To joyous heights.
Soft love I read in them
And care
For those who love you.
Even now upon the seas
Or quiet
In foreign bar
I picture you.
Eyes that haunt
Call my life
And aching heart.
In every girl I see
Your face
Your eyes
Your welcome smile.
So now I hurry
Homeward.
Then no longer
Need I remember.

On board *Odin's Raven*
Sule Skerry. 15.6.79

CHAPTER SEVEN

Landfall

The morning of Saturday, June 3, found *Odin's Raven* rocking gently in a virtually flat calm sea some five miles off Lerwick. Breakfast had been served at an early hour and the sun was already blazing down from a cloudless blue sky. The hazy shadow of the Shetland Isles had appeared on the horizon soon after the first pink flush of dawn crept into the eastern sky. The laconic report in the log read simply '0530, Shetland sighted.' All the drama expected from the first sight of land had already been exhausted with the misty view of that first oil-rig twenty-four hours earlier. Those massive steel sentinels, unknown of course in Viking times, had usurped the position of that first, faint smudge of land. No longer could North Sea mariners cry 'Land Ho!' Now it was 'Oil-rig Ho!' Not quite so romantic, somehow.

The final eighty miles from the oil-rigs had been completed under almost ideal sea conditions, in contrast to those experienced during the previous 150 miles from Trondheim. Those members of the crew who had been off-watch during the night had collapsed into an exhausted sleep, brought on no doubt by both the release of tension and the excitement generated by our activity in the oil-fields. Now we prepared for the reception which we had been warned would prove or disprove our claim to the Viking heritage!

The atmosphere on board was relaxed and the Viking clothes were hauled out of the bilges and reintroduced to the light of day. For the next sixty or so hours we would be on dry land; any worries concerning the problems which awaited us on the next leg of the journey were easily pushed into the background compared with the immediate prospect of comfortable beds and 'real' food.

At nine o'clock the first of what was to be an endless succession of floating welcome-committees arrived. This motor launch contained a reporter from the *Daily Mail*, who was immediately relieved of his packet of cigarettes! On learning of our need for liquid refreshment he generously agreed to return to Lerwick and purchase our requirements. We had been asked by the local harbour board if we could time our arrival at the quay-side as near to eleven o'clock as possible, and lying hove-to beneath the hot sun we were already parched with thirst.

Lerwick harbour could be entered down two channels – the North and the South. We had already been informed that those who arrived from the latter direction were known locally as 'South-mouthers' (pronounced Sooth-moothers) – apparently a derisory term. It had therefore been agreed that our entrance would be from the north, although it would entail us rowing in against a strong ebb-tide. The request for us to delay our arrival was to enable the welcoming committee to prepare themselves, for the speed of our passage from the Ninian Field had not been anticipated. It also gave time for the local radio station to acquaint the islanders of the presence of a Viking longship once again in local waters, so that any interested spectators would be able to travel in from the outlying districts.

The delay worked in our favour as well; not only did it allow time for the refreshments to arrive, but it also gave us a welcome opportunity to dry out our Viking costumes. Each plastic bag as it was manhandled on to the deck seemed to have doubled its weight, and by the time they were opened it was easy to discover the reason. The Viking costumes consisted, authentically enough, mainly of woollen garments which included heavy sheepskin cloaks. The constant battering of the seas against the hull, coupled with the gallons of water which had swept the decks throughout the previous six days, had made short work of even the most watertight seal. One after another, an assortment of sodden, reeking sheepskins was dragged out on to the kists, their proud owners recoiling in horror at the thought of having to wear them in close proximity to other people. But for the blessing of such perfect 'drying' weather there is little doubt that otherwise the crew would have been close to mutiny. The scorching sun soon had its effect, however, and by the time we were ready to start the last short lap of the North Sea crossing the worst of the smell had dissipated, along with the dampness.

Throughout the voyage all the various landfalls that were made remained as memorable events; but the romanticism and historical reminiscences associated with our arrival in Lerwick were so exceptional that it is worth describing the events of those $2\frac{1}{2}$ days in detail.

Two hours before our scheduled docking time, with the very light breeze coming directly on to our bow, Eddie Kaighin gave the order to prepare for rowing. Within minutes *Odin's Raven* was skimming across the wind-ruffled surface towards the entrance to the North channel, powered by her full complement of 14 oars. From a distance she must have looked quite a sight. We may not have had the polish of a University

Boat Race crew, but with long hours of practice in Oslofjord behind us we knew that our rhythm was consistent and tidy. Not for the first time I wished that I could have been an onlooker for a short period, watching from a distance. With the spray from the oar-blades glittering in the sunlight, the monotonous 'clunk' as the oars hit the oarports at the end of each stroke dictating the rhythm and our sheepskin-covered backs moving in unison, for the first time in a thousand years a Viking longship again entered the narrow channel which led to the capital of the Shetland Isles.

To the spectators who lined the low hillsides overlooking the channel we must surely have looked a truly romantic picture. The people of Shetland have always retained close links with Norway due to their geographical position relative to both the lands of the Norsemen and those of the United Kingdom, and most of them could boast direct links with Viking ancestors. In the past the sight of a longship forging across the water towards the beaches around which Lerwick was later to be built was the signal for panic, the rush for arms and the secreting away of wealth and womenfolk. The arrival of the *Raven* was probably just as dramatic, but this time our intentions were peaceful and if there was any panic at all it was to get down to the harbour in time to photograph us! In any case we had by this time formed our own considered opinion that if the Vikings of old had felt as tired both physically and mentally as we did, then they would have been in remarkably poor condition to carry out any strenuous pastimes, such as raping and pillaging.

The narrow entrance to the North Channel appeared to act as an accelerating force for the now strongly ebbing tide and the hitherto pleasant exercise of rowing quickly turned into a battle of mind over matter. With a score of small boats circling around us and innumerable people watching from the shoreline, it was a point of honour that we gained the harbour without having to pause for a rest. We were well aware that the cynics and critics would be delighted if we failed to show that a mixed Manx/Norse crew were capable of rowing the longship under adverse conditions for a long period. Our efforts were not assisted by the sight of the skipper, Chieftain and official photographer all reclining in comfort as they cheerfully consumed can after can of the chilled ale which had been so generously presented to the crew!

Non-stop rowing beneath that burning sun was certainly no joke and with the sweat pouring off our bodies and the blisters beginning to form on our hands, the mutinous murmurs of discontent became more vociferous. For the first hour of rowing we had shed the heavier sheepskins, but the entrance to the North Channel and the presence of so many spectators had dictated that we made our arrival in full Viking costume.

'It's alright for some!' commented Richard Young loudly. 'What about passing a can down, Eddie?'

'Can't possibly do that, it would interrupt the rhythm,' said the skipper.

'Now chaps, you're doing a grand job. Keep it up. Only three miles to go.' Refreshing words from Robin Bigland as he raised another can of beer in mock salutation.

'I'd love to join you,' said Arne Wisth. 'But there isn't a spare oar.'

'Have mine. Try this one,' chorused several voices.

With the ebb-tide reducing our actual speed to about 3 knots, Eddie Kaighin soon realised that our strength would be unlikely to last the required distance and he ordered the aft four oars to rest. Thankfully the rowers in those positions ceased their movements and leant wearily on their oars. Arne Wisth scampered forward and distributed cans of beer among them; but the skipper soon noticed that we were now only maintaining our position, gaining nothing, and ordered the resting oarsmen to finish their beer and continue rowing. The respite had been brief but essential, and for the next hour the process was repeated, the rest periods alternating between the aft and forward oarsmen. Thus by the time that Lerwick itself came into view an hour later, the beer had all been consumed and the crew were still forcing the longship into the strong tide, slowly but surely pulling her nearer to the quayside.

When we were still about half a mile from the place where we were obviously expected to land, judging by the dense throng of people waiting there, Eddie turned the *Raven* across the harbour in the opposite direction.

'We'll take her across to the other side, boys, then sail her down and give them a sight of her under full sail,' he said.

This change of course took us out of the mainstream of the tidal race and our speed visibly increased. At about the same time a sea-scout cutter came up astern and it was decided to give them a race.

'Ramming speed, Georgie!' cried someone to the stroke oar.

Immediately the tempo picked up and the *Raven* surged through the water with renewed vigour.

'Bloody Hell, the Chieftain obviously wants to water-ski!' came a gasping voice from the bow.

'Anyone thought how embarrassing it's going to be when we lose?' shouted another despairing voice, as the rhythm speeded up still further.

Regardless of how impressive a longship under full oar-speed looked from the shore (and we were to be told later that we had indeed looked a rare sight, skimming across the harbour), most of us were by this time beginning to feel the strain of driving six tons of ship against the tide for a couple of hours. Needless to say, our opponents in their lighter faster cutter succeeded in putting us to shame, and our excuses that we had been rowing for some time before their arrival on the scene and that we had spent the last six days in extremely uncomfortable and tiring conditions seemed inadequate even to ourselves.

At long last Eddie Kaighin gave the order to 'stow oars' and we thankfully pulled them inboard, our muscles aching with the strain, and hoisted the sail; the aft four oarsmen retained their oars in position for the final manoeuvring up to the quayside.

With the wind now abeam of her the longship heeled before it, and bore down under canvas in full splendour upon the ranks of spectators massed along the harbour frontage. Beautiful as the *Raven* looked under oars, we all knew that her graceful lines were accentuated when under sail and we could almost hear the cacophony of clicking as hundreds of cameras captured the sight as we swept around the end of the harbour and moved easily towards the steps below the reception committee.

That they were in fact the official welcoming party was made obvious by their striking apparel. Burnished breastplates glittered in the sunlight. Huge wings spurted from gleaming helmets and robes of brilliant colours flashed among the crowd. These were the Up-Helly-Aa Vikings, about whom we had already heard a great deal. Every January a world-famous celebration occurs in Lerwick when a mock longship is drawn through the streets of the town, the scene lit by thousands of flaming torches and in memory of the ancient past the ship is set alight – a dramatic reconstruction of a Viking funeral pyre.

These islanders were renowned for their intense sense of history and proud of their direct descent from those famous warriors of old. As such, we knew that our reception would be more a test of our drinking capacity than a congratulatory welcome on having successfully completed a difficult maritime crossing. As far as Shetland was concerned, anyone who claimed to follow in the wake of the true Vikings should consider the sea journey as nothing more than a period of relaxation before the real battles to be fought on land! For the first time in centuries a crew of so-called Vikings had voyaged from out of the east to their land, and there was no way that they were going to let such a challenge pass unheeded.

To a deafening cheer from the assembled crowd, *Odin's Raven* rubbed gently against the quayside and after four days at sea (six days after leaving Trondheim) the mooring ropes held her lively hull steady against the cold stone of the harbour wall. While the remainder of the crew furled the sail and stowed oars, Robin Bigland the Chieftain, Eddie Kaighin the Skipper and myself the Standard-bearer carefully climbed up the seaweed-covered steps. The solid quayside seemed to rock gently beneath our feet. Immediately we were swamped by well-wishers, cameramen, reporters and the Up-Helly-Aa Vikings themselves.

Thankful yet again for the steady support of our banner *Landwaster* I braced myself against a massive bear-hug from one of these eminent gentlemen.

'Congratulations, laddie,' he boomed, 'Nae doot ye'll be needing a wee dram o' this, tae set ye richt!' So saying, he produced a 40-ounce bottle of whisky and, having first taken a wee dram himself, he thrust the bottle into my hand. Then with a calculating look in his eye, he stepped back to study the form of the opposition.

Suddenly I was extremely aware of the responsibility that had been thrust upon me. I sensed that the eyes of the crew were upon me, waiting as they now were to climb the steps and join in the celebrations; and the expression on Robin Bigland's face suggested the dawning of a terrible fear that the months of hard training were about to disintegrate in the bars of Lerwick. With Bill Hook and his TV cameras very much in evidence, the honour of the crew was no longer a parochial matter but a national one, since it was certain that our arrival would be broadcast throughout the country. It was obviously not the time to decline the offer, or the challenge, of a drink. I only hope that my shipmates were not disgraced by my subsequent performance. After all those days at sea, by my soul that whisky tasted good.

It's not that we were all incipient alcoholics. The plain truth is that our weeks in Norway, during which we had consumed large quantities of refreshing but very weak beer, had obviously increased our appetite for alcohol far beyond our normal habits. Throughout the entire voyage, at virtually every port-of-call, we were challenged or felt duty-bound to display our prowess as trenchermen. The popular conception of the Vikings was of hard-headed men capable of drinking vast quantities of liquor; and we were expected to live up to this image. As a result, the crew of *Odin's Raven* felt they could allow no challenge to go unheeded, and (although sorely tried on occasions) they were never defeated. Neither did they disgrace themselves, nor come to blows. We were quite simply a hard-drinking, hard-working team.

On the other hand, neither the Shetlanders nor the crew of the longship were really prepared for the activities that unfolded during the two day's stay of *Odin's Raven*. This first landfall was an exceptionally emotional one. On our part we had just completed what we believed (mistakenly, as it later transpired) to be the toughest part of our voyage, and the feelings of achievement and relief were paramount in our enthusiastic participation in the celebrations. To the Shetlanders, we were in some form a reincarnation of their heroic ancestors, providing an extra dimension to their play-acting of ancient history. I mean this in no disrespect. Their will and determination to keep alive the traditions of their past was without parallel – an accomplishment to be envied rather than derided. Although the Vikings had colonised and greatly influenced all the Scottish Islands which we were later to visit, the waning of interest and knowledge in their illustrious forebears became more apparent the further westward we travelled, with only a few exceptions.

In the minds of us all, we received our only *true* Viking reception and send-off in those Isles of Shetland, until the day we reached our home port.

From the moment that we first stepped shakily on to that quayside in

Lerwick, the Up-Helly-Aa Committee took us to their hearts, each one of them 'accosting' his own particular Viking charge with the avowed intention of providing him with a memory of Shetland that would never be forgotten. If we had arrived with any thoughts of rest or sleep, such hopes were soon to be completely dashed.

The Galley-shed was the exclusive meeting place of the Up-Helly-Aa Committee and that is where we were rapidly transported as soon as protocol allowed. Steeped in tradition and nostalgia, the walls covered with murals depicting Viking scenes and portraits of past Jarls (Earls), the shed was dominated by a full-scale plywood replica of a longship. The effect was dramatic, almost calculated to encourage the festive spirit of reunion which had by now taken hold of us all. While the television cameras recorded the welcoming speeches a stunning array of bottles was ceremoniously unveiled – and battle commenced.

After two hours of what we were to realise was only to be a warm-up session, our hosts remarked that we had just completed a relatively tiring voyage and suggested a break in the proceedings for a period of a few hours. My own host, Charlie Simpson, a genial, bearded Islander, drove me unprotestingly to his house where I collapsed into the comfort of a 'real' bed, only to be awakened seemingly minutes later (in fact three hours had passed) at six o'clock in the evening. Some of my colleagues had not fared so well. The combination of lack of sleep and the sudden intake of strong spirits had served to open the flood gates to the exhaustion which we had fought back for the past few days. David Eames, a guest of one of the lifeboat crew, had been escorted to the kitchen of his host, presented with a full bottle of rum and exorted to 'Get some real drinking done.' Within a short time, Nature had come to Dave's rescue, and with a muffled apology to his surprised host, he gently rested his head on the table and fell into a blissful sleep. Richard Young had also been unable to fight off the tiredness during a protracted session, but in his case the need for slumber had overcome him while answering another type of Nature's call. It apparently took his host almost an hour to break into the bathroom in order to remove his guest to more comfortable accommodation. Georgie Kneale had arrived in his Valahalla. His quietness during the previous weeks had obviously been caused by total dedication to the mental preparation necessary to meet this ultimate challenge. Like the unveiling of a secret weapon he was suddenly and ruthlessly launched into battle. His Shetland opponent (and host) rose to the occasion magnificently, and whenever they appeared throughout the following two days it was as if two lost souls had been reunited by the bottle clasped so tenderly between them.

Afterwards, Robin Bigland noted the following in his log with reference to Jimmy, who had been Georgie's drinking companion '. . . He told me that he had been drunk for a week in anticipation of our arrival but the quantity that he had consumed in the last 48 hours had been the highlight of his life. Knowing the capacity of our own crew member who matched him, I could well understand the awe with which he spoke. I have seen some serious drinkers in my time, but this particular crew member (Georgie), although one of the smallest, really did possess the proverbial 'hollow legs' and when, as he put it, 'the taste was on him', the stuff disappeared as a river into the sea.'

The local dignitaries had arranged a banquet and ceilidh for that first evening and, although much enjoyed, it was only the prelude to the more intense celebrations which took place afterwards in the Galley Shed, continuing into the early hours of Sunday morning.

Brief snatches of the events which occurred that night drifted like spectral visions across my mind the following morning: the image of Odd Børstad, bottle in hand, earnestly speaking to one of our hosts whose closed eyes and semi-reclining position against the hull of the 'galley' seemed to suggest that he had already lost all interest in the general proceedings; Arne Wisth, whose inability to consume liquor in any great quantity was renowned, lying full-length beneath the grinning figurehead, his chest and stomach quickly utilised as a depository for empty bottles; the wild fiddle music and the rousing songs from our hosts charging the atmosphere with ghosts from ancient sagas, the scene made even more romantic by the presence of the huge paintings which lined the walls, depicting those legendary heroes of the Viking age.

How our shattered bodies stood up to the battering they received will forever remain a mystery. In retrospect our only consolation was that it obviously required a voyage of particular historical connotations to precipitate such celebrations. It was highly unlikely that any of us would have the opportunity to repeat an equally emotional journey.

At some time in the morning Charlie Simpson and I meandered slowly back to the comfort of his house. Our arrival interrupted yet another ceilidh, friends and neighbours having been invited in to meet 'one of the Vikings'. The particular Viking in question was, by this time, more than a little the worse for wear and it wasn't long before I made my excuses and disappeared into the peaceful solitude of the guest bedroom.

Our second day in Lerwick differed little from the previous one except that a few of the crew had, at least, managed to sleep for a few hours. In the morning we invited the Up-Helly-Aa Committee on board the longship, sailing her around the harbour for a couple of hours. Our genial hosts, having expressed a desire to handle her under oars, greatly amused us with their antics. They had to admit that the job was not as easy as it looked and began to appreciate how much training had been required to drive the *Raven* neatly and efficiently through the water.

The afternoon was spent in contrasting ways as far as most of the crew were concerned. A few continued to increase the profits of some well-known distillers, while others slept or relaxed on the *Raven*, Colin diving to check whether the 'straw keel' we had fitted in Trondheim was still in place. Alan Binns and I were driven around the Island by Charlie Simpson, who took us up to that massive blot in an otherwise beautiful landscape – the new oil terminal at Sullom Voe.

In the early evening we again met in the Galley Shed to continue the festivities which, judging by the appearance of one or two of the crew, had continued unabated throughout the day. This hospitality continued until the time for our departure at five o'clock the following evening. Somehow all the crew were reunited with their vessel without undue difficulty although Georgie Kneale, on being reminded that he was due on the boat in a quarter of an hour, was heard to mumble 'What boat?'

A moderate easterly wind had been forecast, and surrounded by scores of small boats and watched by hundreds of sightseers the longship reluctantly cast off her moorings and quickly picked up speed as she sailed down Bressay Channel – the 'Sooth-Mooth'. All of our new friends were aboard the escorting vessels; in fact, three of the Up-Helly-Aa Committee made the voyage to the Orkneys on board the longship – their dearest wishes coming true. As they turned back one by one the farewells were noisy and tinged with sadness. All of the crew felt that they were leaving some part of themselves behind on the island which had shown us such incredible hospitality. Modern-day Vikings from land and sea had met for a brief time and the resulting reunion had not only created strong friendships but also a kind of personal time-warp: a small nucleus of men had together created a tiny moment of history, the memories of which will not quickly be forgotten.

As we reached the mouth of the Channel the swell from the open sea caught the longship and in a few minutes her typical corkscrew motion reminded us that we were at sea again. In the gathering darkness, with her sail billowing out before a strong sailing wind, *Odin's Raven* plunged towards the Orkneys, the ancient capital of the Vikings of the Northern Isles, which lay a hundred miles to the south.

CHAPTER EIGHT

The Minch

Sailing a Viking ship in near perfect conditions is one of the greatest pleasures life has to offer. With the wind blowing strongly and steadily from the east, the *Raven* heeled over like a racing dinghy thrusting her way through the crests of the waves, as if rejoicing in her freedom once again. The spray hissed from the prow in great sheets, as the serpent's head dipped into the steep swell.

For those members of the crew who were not on watch, the first few hours since leaving Lerwick were a time for reminiscences or sleep – depending on how enthusiastically they had partaken of the final celebrations! The cool night air and frequent dousings with icy water from the bow quickly 'refreshed' those among us who were still suffering from the after-effects of the departure celebrations! As usual on a night-sail, the fore-part of the ship was soon a writhing mass of bodies. No cover could be rigged because of the conditions, and consequently it was simply a question of finding a vacant area of deck and lying down fully-clothed, with only the oil-skins for protection.

Wherever we landed, the *second* question we were invariably asked was 'Where do you all sleep?' The *first* enquiry was always, without fail, 'How do you carry out your ablutions at sea?' To the crew, now in our fourth week on board the *Odin's Raven*, sleeping on an open deck with no cover in all weather had become almost second nature to us. In retrospect it is understandable how such an uncomfortable mode of sleeping would attract comment from spectators, and many of the crew would probably have second thoughts now about repeating such a protracted voyage under the same conditions. Yet the fact that conditions on board were so crowded in some ways increased the comfort rather than added to the problems. Paradoxically enough, the compaction of a number of bodies not only provided some soft areas on which to lie, but also prevented one from being rolled across the deck with the motion of the ship.

The early evening was damp and cloudy; the rain which had let-up during the last three days had again discovered our whereabouts. Spirits were high, though, with memories of the Shetland Isles still fresh in our minds, and the mood on board was further enlivened by the announcement from Odd Børstad that the evening meal would consist of steak and wine! Unknown to most of us the Up-Helly-Aa Committee had insisted on providing us with the wherewithal to combat the discomfort of the leg to the Orkneys. The Bilge Rats immediately appropriated the wine, proclaiming themselves to be in charge of such contraband liquor, and with only one usable mug between the 3 Bilge Rats, the pouring of the wine followed the time-honoured pattern of:

'One for Eddie, one for us.'

'One for Robin, one for us,' etc.

Odd Børstad overcame the choppy conditions in masterly fashion, cooking two steaks at a time over the gaz and producing a mouth-watering meal. There were no garnishings and the meat was eaten straight off our knives.

'True Viking fare, this!' mumbled Shane Lucas, burying his face in an enormous slab of steak.

'It probably is,' Eddie Kaighin replied as he watched the sizzling frying pan in anticipation. 'Although they wouldn't have been able to cook it on board, it's highly likely that they wouldn't have had any qualms about slaughtering a local cow and cooking it over a campfire. They called it *strandhøgg* – a shore slaughtering.'

The picture remains vividly in my mind of the shapes huddled around the galley area, their faces lit by the eerie blue light from the gaz. Transpose that to a campfire on the shore (for the Vikings rarely sailed after dark unless it was essential) and the difference in time became immaterial.

'Have those Bilge Rats left any wine?' asked Robin Bigland, directing the question towards a tent-like structure which had been rigged amidships. This tiny shelter had been created by using Knut Skøgoy's army cape and had immediately been christened 'The Swamp' (addicts of M.A.S.H. on TV will realise the significance). Richard Young became known as Hawkeye, I became Trapper, and Rick Tomlinson was known for a short time as Radar. Of 'Hot-Lips' there was, alas, no sign.

That small square of tarpaulin was to be the only form of shelter when at sea and as such it was well frequented, although in really wet weather the originators usually insisted on their own rights to protection, evicting any 'squatters'.

During this meal, Nigel Wood was elected to the Honorary Order of Bilge Rats for the premeditated act of removing one of the few remaining 'Karrimats' and heaving it over the side in broad daylight in full view of the Chieftain. This naturally earned him a stiff reprimand, but as it created some extra deckspace the action was secretly approved by all. Although Alan Binns had left us in Lerwick (Hull University had only permitted him enough time off to complete the North Sea crossing), the presence of the three members of the Up-Helly-Aa Committee, who were accompanying us to Kirkwall, meant that the expected increase in the available deckspace could not yet be appreciated. The intentions of our guests were not only to enjoy the experience of sailing a longship but, more importantly, to learn as much about the techniques required as was possible in such a short space of time, since the Up-Helly-Aa Committee intended building a smaller, cheaper longship replica to sail to Newcastle in the summer of 1980.

Midnight came and went as we sailed past the shadowy outline of Fair Isle, the sea remaining choppy and the steady wind enabling our speed to remain constant around the 6-knot mark.

While most of the crew were asleep on the foredeck I prepared a net for a plankton haul. As a marine biologist researching for a Ph.D. concerning some aspects of crustacean life, in particular that of the lobster, one of the conditions of my being allowed the time off my research to undertake the voyage was that some form of relevant study was carried out whenever possible. The collection of data from samples of plankton taken across such a wide transect as the voyage would cover might enable me to determine if lobster larvae were present in any quantities. Such data would of necessity be extremely general and subject to a large number of variable factors, but the opportunity was too good to miss. I could at least be certain that the publication of the results obtained from a Viking longship would raise a few eyebrows in academic circles. Unfortunately a plankton net is a relatively delicate piece of apparatus, needing to be towed through the water at a very slow speed – something which the lithe *Raven* had difficulty in achieving. As a consequence I had already lost one net two days out of Trondheim, when a sudden gust of wind caused the ship to leap forward; the increase in strain parted the tow-line to the net. A telegram from Aalesund to the Isle of Man had advised the Marine Laboratories of my predicament and a replacement had been forwarded to Lerwick to await our arrival.

The actual process of making the plankton haul only took about twenty minutes but for that space of time the speed of the ship had to be reduced if at all possible. When under sail this involved the reduction of sail area, which required some extra hands on the mainsail downhaul – a job which was not normally appreciated at midnight!

'Bloody Jacques Cousteau's at work again!' grumbled Dave Eames. 'Plankton sandwiches for breakfast again.'

The results obtained from those hauls when analysed at a later date did, in fact, produce some interesting specimens, and although no lobster larvae were found the effort was not a total waste of time.

My scientific duties completed, I remained talking for an hour with Brian Cousins and his three colleagues whose turn it was for the 'graveyard watch'. With the Shetland Isles hidden in the darkness behind

us and Fair Isle fast disappearing in the murk, the conversation centred
on our time in Lerwick and how quickly we had re-adapted to the rhythm
and discomfort of our longship. Such shipboard-watches the first day out
of a harbour can have changed little in the years which separated us from
our ancestors. Armod's poem from the *Orkneyinga Saga*, translated by
A. B. Taylor, describes such a time, although in that particular instance
the longship was sailing in warmer, Mediterranean waters.

> *We watched o'er the sea-steed*
> *While o'er the stout gun-whale*
> *The billow breaks wildly.*
> *Thus duty is done,*
> *While the lazy land-lubber*
> *Sleeps by some maiden*
> *Soft-skinned and kind,*
> *Over my shoulder*
> *I gaze towards Crete.*

Substitute Lerwick for Crete and the mood remains the same,
regardless of the century.

The sixth of June dawned to find the longship rolling listlessly in the
long heaving swell, wrapped in a blanket of fine early morning mist. The
wind had dropped suddenly and our speed was now reduced to a meagre
$1\frac{1}{2}$ to 2 knots. Our anticipated arrival time at Kirkwall had been set at ten
in the morning, but with the first rocky outcrops of the scattered Orkney
Islands still vague shadows just visible through the grey drizzle, any
reception committee would have a long damp vigil.

The bleak and barren island of North Ronaldsay, which we passed
beneath a heavy curtain of rain, must have looked little different to the
thousands of Vikings who had made this passage before us. The Orkneys
were the centre of the Viking influence in the Scottish Isles for several
centuries when the Norse Earls of Orkney had ruled the waters which surrounded Scotland – including much of Ireland and the Isle of Man. One
of the most famous of the Earls was Sigurd Silk-Beard, who died in the
bloody battle of Clontarf, outside Dublin, in 1014 A.D.

It was of especial interest to me, as standard bearer of the replica, to
learn the legendary story of the original banner which I obtained from
George Mackay Brown's excellent history of the Orkneys, entitled *An
Orkney Tapestry*. Apparently the banner had one major drawback, which
was that whoever carried it would himself be cut down in battle. I was
given this book as a gift by my host in Kirkwall and when I read the
following description, my eagerness to continue as standard-bearer waned
rapidly:

'Earl Sigurd had a hard battle against Kerthialfad. Kerthialfad
advanced with such a rush that he scattered all the men in the front rank,

and smashed Earl Sigurd's army as far as the banner, and killed the man who carried it. Earl Sigurd got another man to carry the standard, and the hard battle went on. Kerthialfad immediately struck down this man and killed him and also the men round about him, one after the other. Then Earl Sigurd ordered Thorstein the son of Hall of the Side (an Icelander) to bear the banner. Thorstein was just about to lift it when Asmund the White said, "Don't carry the banner! Everyone who carries it gets killed."

"Hrafn the Red!" cried Earl Sigurd, "You carry the banner."

"Carry your own devil," said Hrafn.

The Earl said then, "Certainly the beggar should carry his own bag," and he tore the banner from pole and stuffed it under his cloak.

Soon afterwards, Asmund the White was killed, and then a spear transfixed the Earl . . .

Then the whole army broke.'

Although we did not expect any battles on our voyage, I handled the banner with some trepidation from that moment on.

We were all cold and tired by the time we rowed into Kirkwall harbour during the middle of the afternoon. The reception we received was quieter and more restrained than that in Lerwick, but nonetheless there were a few hundred people waiting to welcome us – a credit to their stoicism in the teeming rain.

While we were still some way off from the quayside we had noticed the unusual lines of a gaff-rig silhouetted against the skyline. This turned out to be a Grimsby sloop, vintage around 1850, which belonged to a group of Faroese businessmen. Robin Bigland and Eddie Kaighin later visited her, where they were offered a traditional Faroese welcome of whale blubber and dried fish. Eddie's description of this repast was blunt and to the point, whereas Robin described its taste as not unlike the rheested bacon that he remembered from his childhood in the Yorkshire Dales: although the flavour was not unpleasant, he wouldn't have relished making a meal out of it!

If we expected our 48-hour stay in Kirkwall to be restful, a preparation for the potentially hazardous crossing of the Pentland Firth and the infamous tides of the Minches, we were to be rapidly disillusioned. The *Raven* had no sooner rounded the harbour wall when a strident voice carried across to the longship.

'Anyone called Giffy on Board?'

This was a name by which Colin Bowen was also known and he shouted back in the affirmative.

'See you in the bar then!' came the shouted reply, more a statement than a question.

We asked Colin who his friend was.

'His name's Ronnie Spears,' said Colin, 'and he runs a pub which sells Manx ale.'

'What, not the real stuff?' said Richard Young, almost licking his lips in anticipation.

'Yes, all the way from the Isle of Man,' Colin replied.

The longship seemed to leap through the water towards the quayside as the thirsty Vikings took in the enormity of this sudden news and, in record time, she was neatly moored alongside. The expected celebrations were, however, to be delayed for some hours due to the protocol requirements which were part of every landfall.

After the initial welcome speeches and Robin Bigland's reply (which most of the crew could repeat word for word by now), we were introduced to our various hosts for the duration of our stay. The kindness and hospitality that was extended to us throughout the trip was overwhelming and to say that we were all extremely grateful would be an understatement. The major problem, and this was highlighted during our visit to the Orkneys, was the intense crew-spirit that had developed over the preceeding weeks. As any sailor will recognise, especially those who have travelled for long distances at sea, an integral part of a sea-going voyage is the time spent on land in the ports of call. The first few hours spent away from one's comrades act as a necessary winding-down and relaxation period but, all too soon, a yearning for the company of ship-mates comes to the fore again. The strength of this magnetic attraction is obviously determined by the relationship of the crew when confined together at sea; in our case the crew were living under such a set of unusual circumstances that the bond holding them together as a unit was singularly strong.

Within half an hour of landing at Kirkwall we were transported to various parts of the island by our respective hosts and were only to meet again, as a complete crew, at the two official functions which had been laid on for our benefit. Lunch-time next day was the first of these meetings, when the Town Council produced a magnificent banquet in our honour. It was here that we heard news of the monumental party the previous night in the pub which sold Manx ale, so we all agreed to meet at Ronnie's that evening. Having been royally entertained by Brigadier Robertson and his wife with whom I was staying, by ten o'clock in the evening I was reunited with most of the Vikings in Ronnie Spears' bar. The crew of the Faroese sloop were also there and a lively party ensued with much singing of sea-shanties, Manx folk songs and various other ribald verses.

In the early hours the party moved on to the Faroese boat; but, for some reason, as Nigel Wood and I walked past *Odin's Raven* we both sensed that it might be a good idea to keep an eye on her. In those northern parts we rarely found it necessary to keep a watch on board when in harbour, specially in the islands. Nevertheless we both felt this vague premonition that something might happen, so we declined the invitation by our Faroese friends and clambered down on to the *Raven*.

115

Two hours later, at four o'clock in the morning, it happened: a party of revellers called in to obtain some permanent reminders of the visit of the longship to the Islands, such as the oars and the weather vane. Between us, Nigel Wood and I managed to repel the boarders. It came as some surprise, therefore, later in the morning as we prepared the ship for sail when Bilge Rat No. 1 arrived carrying a 16-foot oar over his shoulder – having just retrieved it from Ronnie Spears' bar. To this day I don't know how it got there in the first place.

We were due to spend a further two days as guests of the people of Rousay, an island just off the north-western shoulder of the Mainland of Orkney, and it was thither that we headed during the morning of June 7. It wasn't until we had cleared the harbour entrance that Eddie Kaighin realised we were short of two men. Looking back towards the quayside we saw the frantically waving figures of Nigel Wood who had overslept, and Knut Skøgoy, who had been billeted in one of the outlying districts. With true Viking nonchalance they quickly commandeered a motor launch and rejoined us before the harbour disappeared from view.

This short trip was only expected to take two hours and so the 'Swamp' was soon erected, for a heavy drizzle had again set in, coinciding as usual with our departure and the time was spent recounting our various escapades. Much of the discussion on-board concerned the unwillingness of some members of the crew to be separated again on land but, as Robin Bigland pointed out, the accommodation arrangements were in the hands of our hosts; where Rousay was concerned Major Rio Ritchie had arranged our billeting among the residents of this small and thinly populated island.

Faced with the prospect of being 'marooned' in an outlying croft, six of the crew announced that they would prefer to take the ferry back to Kirkwall and stay there. Robin Bigland, sensing the mood accurately as always, agreed to this while not approving of it.

In the opinion of those of us who remained on Rousay, the 'breakaway' group made the wrong decision. Very definitely. Our arrival at the tiny jetty at the south-eastern corner of the island was witnessed by the smallest group of spectators we had yet encountered; but it transpired that it comprised virtually the whole population of the island (population 200)! Eddie Kaighin decided to display our skill as Viking mariners to the maximum and we sailed beneath the onlookers (it being low-tide and the top of the jetty fifteen feet clear of the water), the gunwale practically scraping the wooden supporting posts. We then carried out a wide sweeping turn, tacked and approached to tie up. As we came to a graceful halt and cast the mooring-lines up to the eager hands that awaited them, a Scotsman resplendent in kilt and sporran stepped to the edge of the jetty directly above our heads and enquired if Robin Bigland were on board.

'Yes, right here,' replied the Chieftain.

'Ah, Robin, you're looking well,' said the Scotsman.

'You're not looking so bad yourself – from where I'm standing!' said Robin.

After the welcome speech, everyone present repaired to the local pub, which turned out to be the only such establishment on the Island. Colin Bowen and I had already met the landlord in Kirkwall and had booked our accommodation in his hostelry on that occasion, along with Rick Tomlinson and Brian Cousins. Robin Bigland was to be the guest of the Major, intending to relax for a couple of days with some fishing and shooting.

Our stay on Rousay turned out to be the happiest two days that we were to experience throughout the voyage. Although we had not yet completed even half of the planned distance, the crew felt that the worst was over, and that only a pleasant cruise through the Western Isles lay before us. We were thus all lulled into a false sense of security. The celebrations in Lerwick and Kirkwall had been safety valves. Sadly, our pride in the appearance of the *Raven* had decreased rapidly since our arrival in Shetland; we were now neglecting our shipboard duties, and the longship was looking extremely unkempt by the time we reached Rousay. Some of the crew, like Brian Cousins, Nigel Wood, Rick Tomlinson and Rolf Hansen, for example, made every attempt to keep her relatively tidy, much to their credit , but the overall impression of the boat at this stage of the trip must have been a lack of pride on the part of the crew. Circumstances were soon to change things drastically, but those unforeseen events were still a few days ahead of us.

The people of Rousay took us to their hearts and the fact that it poured with rain for the whole of our stay detracted in no way from our enjoyment. On the first evening the local populace arrived at the pub from every corner of the Island to see the 'wild Vikings', and an impromptu ceilidh continued until well into the night. Nigel Wood and Shane Lucas played a guitar with their contrasting styles; Nigel with his quiet voice preferring to play a more restful folk-song type of music, while Shane attacked the instrument and sang with such intensity that the audience reeled visibly under the onslaught. Both types of music were much appreciated, however, and the inhabitants of that little island will no doubt remember for a long time Shane's rendering of 'The House of the Rising Sun' and Nigel's version of 'Streets of London'.

For those who were sleeping in the pub the evening's entertainment extended well into the early hours, but at least we did not have to get up until after lunch. Even then the dreary sound of the rain thrumming against the window suggested an even longer lie-in, but it was finally decided that a 'dive' would be the most suitable form of recreation on such a wet day.

For supper that evening therefore we had enjoyed fresh scallops washed down with wine supplied by our host, but the meal had been made even more enjoyable by the sudden appearance of our Chieftain with a request for a bag of chips! The tables had been well and truly turned for once. Apparently, after a hard day's fishing for trout, Robin Bigland's host had found the fresh air and the odd dram or two so stimulating that the thought of supper appeared to have slipped his mind! His offer of 'lobster beads' (whatever that meant) had been greeted with enthusiasm by our Chieftain; but the first bite nearly broke his teeth, because the repast had been served straight from the deep freeze! The sudden appearance, therefore, of our renowned gourmet with a humble request for chips, while the Bilge Rats tucked into a sumptuous meal, was greeted with ill-concealed hilarity. Robin Bigland took the banter in his stride, as usual, and promised to attend the ceilidh which our island friends had arranged for us later in the evening. He never did manage to keep the appointment, however, as he spent most of the night trying in vain to lose at snooker against an opponent who refused to admit defeat even though his ability had been somewhat reduced by his enthusiastic celebration of our arrival.

The ceilidh, which did not begin until midnight, was a resounding success and our departure at eleven o'clock the following morning was a relatively subdued affair – both on the part of the crew and the spectators. The noisy arrival of the rest of the crew as they returned from their sojourn in Kirkwall did nothing to improve our health. With Bilge Rat No. 1 in command it was to be expected that their form of transport would be unusual, but the thunderous clatter of a helicopter took us all by surprise.

The arrival of a large hamper addressed to Robin Bigland intrigued us all as well, but our curiosity was not to be satisfied until we had been at sea for an hour, the immediate problem of setting the sail and getting under way being more urgent.

Our next port-of-call was to be Stornoway in the Isle of Lewis in the Outer Hebrides. The direct route (in fact the only route) would take us due west before rounding Cape Wrath into the fierce tidal races of the North Minch. The Minches are reputed to be as hostile an area of water as the North Sea itself on occasions, and we hoped that our sea-luck would not desert us; but the first problem was to decide the best way in which to leave the inshore waters of Rousay. The most obvious route was to head directly west, between the island and Eynhallow, a small islet between Main Island and Rousay itself. The locals, however, had warned us of the extremely dangerous currents that ripped through the narrow channel, and since the longship was not the most manoeuvrable of vessels when sea-room was scarce, Eddie Kaighin decided to take her the long way round. This meant virtually circling the island anti-clockwise before being able to head out to sea, but the forecast was fine and a strong north-easterly wind augured well for a fast voyage. So after expressing our heartfelt thanks to our hosts of the previous two days, we hauled the yard aloft; released from her moorings, the *Raven* fairly leapt away from the jetty and the waving crowd.

The morning was sunny and pleasant, and the superb sailing wind added greatly to the enjoyment of being at sea once again. The pleasures of dry land were all very well, but the *Raven* was now 'home' to us all and, as such, we slipped back quickly and easily into the routine. Untidy as she was, the longship handled so well under these ideal conditions that the whole crew revelled in her speed and grace, the sail billowing taut above us and the fine spray blowing into our faces.

While the rest of the crew swopped stories and jocund banter, I watched the island of Egilsay slip past us to starboard as we tacked along the channel which separated it from Rousay. It was on Egilsay that Earl Magnus (later to be canonised as St. Magnus) met his death at the beginning of the twelfth century, murdered by his cousin Earl Hakon. He had crossed this very same sound to his doom. The picture of wild, untutored Vikings created by romantics of the Victorian age bears little relation to Magnus' decription as related in the 13th century Icelandic *Orkneyinga Saga*. According to that particular source, the man who died from an axe-blow across the top of his head had been tall and virile, with a vivacious expression, virtuous in his doings, lucky in war, wise, witty, quick with his tongue, noble-minded, generous, magnanimous, a sagacious councillor and extremely popular! One assumes this to be an exaggeration, but other records and legends do suggest that this Norse earl in particular was of an unusually noble character.

Similarly, the prevalent idea that the Vikings spent all their time bent on conquest and destruction is totally misleading. Certainly they would 'go a-viking', plundering during the summer months but in other respects their greatest achievements were as artists and craftsmen, as traders, not raiders.

Although our route lay westward, this sample of Skaldic verse as translated by G. Young, illustrates the choices open to a longship sailing from the Orkneys, as we were, at the height of summer:

Arni, Thorrald, Sven, Paul, Grettir, Harald,
The SEA WOLF is out of the shed, new tar on her hull.
The rollers are under the keel.
The women have put ale, salt meat, and bread on board.
As soon as the wave runs clean from Birsay
We will leave the Orkneys behind us,
The scarred hills and the creeled sounds,
And tonight we will lie at the mouth of a Scottish river.
Our voyage lies east this year.
We have heard of such towns – Aberdeen, Grimsby, London,
And the merchants who live in tall houses.
The churches have had enough of our swords,
And the girls who weave their words into curse or spell.
Our voyage does not lie west this summer

Among holiness and drifts of rain.
It is time merchants knew about us.
We will be back in time for the corn harvest.
You women, see that the scythes are sharp and the
*   barns swept,*
And the ale thick with honey.
We are tired of broken coast-lines.
This summer we deal in wool and useful currency.
They are not too beautiful, the girls in the east.

The women referred to in the poem may well have victualled the *SEA WOLF* with salt meat and bread but as the *Raven* rounded the north-eastern tip of Rousay, more exotic food suddenly appeared like manna from heaven for this modern Viking crew. With great ceremony, Robin Bigland carefully unpacked the large carton which had been delivered on board prior to our departure, to reveal the contents of a Fortnum & Mason food hamper! Apparently he had ordered it to celebrate our cross-ing of the North Sea, but the Post Office had obviously experienced some difficulty in tracking down the whereabouts of a Viking longship. Nevertheless, such a banquet could not have arrived at a better time, bearing in mind the Chieftain's unfortunate culinary experiences during our sojourn on Rousay. He certainly had the last laugh. Clearing the chart table of its impedimenta, he carefully unpacked the assorted feast and invited the crew to join him at luncheon. The sight of a 20th century longship bounding through the choppy waters, with the crew massed in the stern tentatively sampling such delicacies as pheasant in aspic and Beluga caviare, must have made the real Vikings turn in their graves! The chefs at Fortnum's would also have wrung their hands in horror had they been able to see the manner in which their meticulously-packed delicacies were attacked.

'You don't really enjoy this stuff, do you, Robin?' asked Dave Eames as he spread a layer of caviare on to a huge chunk of brown break. 'I mean, it's only for show, isn't it?'

'My dear boy, this 'stuff' is the staff of life,' Robin Bigland replied, with a pained look on his face as he watched Georgie Kneale thrusting an unsavoury sailing-knife deep into a jar of peaches in brandy.

'Must admit, the wine is quite good,' commented Brian Cousins, filling his enamel mug half-full with an excellent Madeira.

'One should really eat it with perhaps a little more finesse, Nigel,' suggested Robin plaintively, as he watched a leg of pheasant in aspic being ripped off.

The sharp report as the cork from a bottle of champagne sailed in a graceful arc towards the cliffs of Rousay, was the signal for a barrage of the usual disrespectful cries of 'Your bird, Robin!'

'Bloody good paste, this,' Eddie Kaighin mumbled through a mouthful of duck paté. 'But they don't give you much of it, do they?' (This having spread most of the contents of the delicate jar thickly on to a slice of bread).

It was a high-spirited and relaxed crew who watched the cliffs disappear over the horizon as evening descended. The wind had dropped and beneath a cloudless sky we sailed easily towards the small islet of Sule Skerry, – some 40 miles west of the Mainland of Orkney – our only navigational fix before sighting the Outer Hebrides. In such glorious weather, sleeping was only for landsmen, and the whole ship's complement was awake to experience one of the most dramatically beautiful sunsets of the entire voyage. With the north coast of Scotland a vague blur to the south, the blood-red sun sank gently towards the western horizon, the serpent figure-head silhouetted starkly against it. Conversation was reduced to quiet murmurs of awe as we revelled in Nature's beauty, made even more impressive by the appearance of a 'hunter's moon' shortly after the glow of the dying sun had faded from the horizon. This ghostly radiance reflected on the gentle swell lit the seascape of heaving water in a constrast of black and white which was quite breathtaking. 'As bright as day' describes the scene exactly, except for the lack of colour.

During the late evening, we sighted a Fishery Protection Vessel in the distance, which soon closed on us for a better look. As she circled, contact was made by radio and we were informed that they had been told of our presence in the area and had been on the look-out. This knowledge was comforting as were were approaching an area of water which has an extremely bad reputation among sailors, although the present conditions seemed to deny this. It was my turn at the steering-oar at the time and I asked Dave Eames why the Minches were so feared?

It was Eddie Kaighin, who was poring over the chart-table with Dave, who answered my question.

'First, thank your lucky stars, Mike, that we have got these calm conditions so far.' he said, 'I've been across here quite a few times and I've never seen it like this. It's always been extremely rough and wild because of the tides and currents. This area can be far worse than the North Sea, believe you me. I reckon Odin must be keeping a watchful eye on us. If we get all the way to Lewis with the sea like this,' he swung out an arm to encompass the gentle rolling swell which stretched to the horizon, 'then we'll have been luckier than most of us will realise.'

Odin, or whichever god looks after Viking longships, must indeed have been smiling on us, for the journey from the Orkneys to Lewis was completed in the most tranquil conditions – a welcome respite from the violent motion to which we had become so accustomed. What a pleasure it was to be able to sit safely on the gunwale, our bodies swaying with the gentle dip and roll, the sail billowing softly in the mild breeze. The voyage made by *Odin's Raven*, while obviously to be remembered for the adventure, the thrills, the narrow escapes, and so on, was made all the more memorable by the few idyllic days and nights that so rarely occurred. Such a time was that journey across the Minch.

At eleven o'clock that night we had sighted the pin-point of light which marked the lonely outcrop of Sule Skerry. Shane Lucas had relieved me on the helm and I was able to relax while watching the blackness of the moon-silhouetted rock grow nearer. The regular flash from the lighthouse attracted us like a moth to a candle, until I noticed with some concern that the prow of the longship had begun to drift away towards an even more inhospitable rocky islet which lay a few points to the south.

'Watch your helm, Shane,' said Dave Eames quietly.

'I am watching it,' Shane replied.

Slowly the *Raven* returned to her original course, once more heading towards the beckoning light; but a few moments later the same inexorable swing towards the other island was repeated.

'Shane, what the hell are you playing at?' Dave exclaimed, 'Watch the bloody helm!'

It was as if our training officer's passion for rock-climbing had hypnotised him. Mountains, rocks and cliffs, we knew, attracted Shane like a magnet, but the rest of us had no intention of being party to sailing a longship up such a deadly beach.

Midnight found the *Raven* hove-to a few yards off the jagged rock of Sule Skerry, where the steady flash of the lighthouse left one with the impression that the tenant had just slipped out for a while. We had been calling on the radio for permission to land for the previous half hour, but with no success. We were later to learn that the island was uninhabited; the light was an automatic beacon. The island may have been devoid of humans, but the shoreline was alive with the barking and shuffling of thousands of seals. We watched spellbound as the outline of the rocks shifted and altered, the bobbing heads silhouetted against the moonlight, creating a constant variation in the skyline. For half an hour, as the longship drifted quietly past the island, the crew gazed in fascination at the unusual sight, until the helmsman's cry of 'Get the sail up, boys,' broke the spell, and the gently-filling canvas drew us slowly away towards the west.

The following day dawned as dramatically as the sunset the previous evening, the colours differing only in intensity – pastel hues replacing the stronger, brighter colours of the dying sun. Few of the crew had slept through such an unusual night, but the warmth of the cloudless new day enabled us, for the first time on the voyage, to shed our heavy outer clothing and bask in the sun's rays. During the middle of the day the longship was visited by a huge school of dolphins, a chance ocean encounter which was one of the highlights of the voyage. For two hours these playful creatures amused us with their antics, passing so close to the sides of the ship that we could literally touch them. One of them, in sheer exuberance, performed a tail-dance for our benefit, skittering along the surface backwards as if practising for its next performance in one of those iniquitous prisons known as Dolphinariums. To see such beautiful creatures gambolling across the limitless expanse of sea brought home to me the inherant cruelty of keeping such mammals penned up in a tiny enlosure. The sheer pleasure they seemed to derive from their exhibitionist antics as they circled, dived and played around us, suggested the presence of emotions rarely accorded to species other than ourselves. One dolphin in particular, recognisable by a white scar slash behind its dorsal fin, would teasingly close right up to an outstretched hand and then, when almost within touching distance, turn slightly on its side, look up at the faces which peered over the gunwale, and suddenly turn away and rush in front of the bow, leaping forward with an amazing turn of speed. The natural grinning curve of the mouth enhanced the impression that this dolphin was enjoying itself immensely.

It was with real disappointment tinged with regret that we watched them turn, as if on a signal, and race away towards our destination, as if to warn those ahead of our imminent arrival. The sight of a whole school of dolphins leaping across the sea is one that few people are lucky enough to see in their lifetime, and we were all grateful for the opportunity to have witnessed such a rare phenomenon.

A few hours later a dark line on the horizon warned us that we were approaching our next destination, the Isle of Lewis. Thus the crossing of the Minches was completed under idyllic conditions, Nature having replaced the vagaries of the weather with the beauty of some of her other creations – a dispensation which, unfortunately, we were not to experience again.

In the Outer Hebrides, Sundays are strictly observed as a day of rest and consequently we planned to arrive in Stornoway the next morning. The early evening, therefore, was spent anchored in the sheltered beauty of Sheshader Bay on the Eye peninsula that juts out from Stornoway. Sabbath or not, within a few minutes of our arrival a small group of people had appeared on the beach. For those who wanted to stretch their legs ashore, B.C.'s inflatable dinghy was unearthed from a locker and with much wheezing and groaning was finally pumped full of air and moved alongside. This was the first time the 'tender' had been put to use. The remainder of the crew took the opportunity of starting the enormous task of cleaning up the longship. It was decided that the 'watch' left on board would clean up forward, while those who had gone ashore could tidy up aft of the mast on their return. It turned out to be a larger task than we had realised. The gentle sail from Rousay had provided opportunity for contemplation and discussion, and the ship had been allowed to fall into an unfortunate state of disarray. So now the deckboards were lifted and scrubbed, the lockers emptied and cleaned out, the stores neatly repacked and the deck area scrubbed and polished. The consequent difference in the ship and the morale of the crew was remarkable – no doubt assisted by the impression that the rest of the voyage would be as easy as the leg which had just been completed.

Robin Bigland was a little perturbed by the air of complacency which was now very apparent and he noted his concern in his diary: 'The particularly easy crossing of the Pentland Firth is in some ways unfortunate, because it has begun to give the crew a feeling that the voyage is an easy one. I know that this is not likely to prove the case and we have a long way to go yet.' Prophetic words, as we were all to realise before the week was out.

That evening in Sheshader Bay was, to me, the epitome of my dreams of how the voyage should have been for the whole journey. In the cool of the night, the bright moonlight again washing the sea with its soft radiance, we discussed the likelihood of the ancient Vikings also anchoring in this selfsame spot. The longship seemed to fit so comfortably into the surrounding scenery that it was impossible to imagine our forebears sailing past such an obvious anchorage. Seen from the shore the *Raven*, sail furled on the yard which rested on the supporting yokes, lay silhouetted against the silvery glitter as the small wavelets reflected the brilliant moonlight. Behind her the sea stretched away to the horizon, while all around the dark Hebridean cliffs rose steeply, overshadowing the tiny anchorage. With only a gentle breath of wind to ruffle the calm surface of the sea, the silence and feeling of ancient age that surrounded us was quite uncanny, an aura of timelessness that was felt by even the most unromantic among us.

It seemed a shame to break the tranquillity of the scene; but Robin Bigland and Dave Eames had taken the inflatable dinghy to try their luck at fishing and had drifted out of sight, and it took a lot of raucous bellowing before they came back into view. It should be noted (the division of labour being no different in modern times than it no doubt was a thousand years earlier) that the Chieftain was doing the fishing (without any success) and David Eames the rowing! On their return, I felt reluctant to ask Dave to row me around for another half-hour while I made a plankton haul, but in his usual cheerful fashion he readily agreed and the continuity of the 'Viking Plankton Samples' was thereby assured.

The return of those who had gone ashore for the evening heralded a general move towards our sleeping bags, and with only one 'watchman' awake to keep an eye open in case the *Raven* dragged her anchor, silence quickly settled over the idyllic little cove.

We awoke the following morning to yet another cloudless sky, the third in row, and the ship was readied for her entrance into Stornoway, the capital of Lewis. In such weather the opportunity for a swim was too good to miss and, donning my wetsuit, I dived down to check that the 'strawkeel' was still in position – which it was. By ten o'clock the *Raven* was ready for sea, and as quietly as she had entered it the longship slipped out the cove and headed southwestwards down the coast. The magnificent stark beauty of the cliff-lined coast rose up to starboard as we sailed close inshore. Some of those who had spent the previous evening ashore had met up with a local man who told them of the piles of rocks which had been built up above the only coastal watering place. Legend had it that if a longship were sighted in this very narrow inlet, the islanders would rush to the cliff-tops and hurl the boulders down on the unlucky trespassers. Passing the spot we saw how massive these rocks were (the few remaining cairns are now protected by law) and could easily visualise the damage they would have inflicted on a ship similar in design to our own.

We made our entrance under oars across a flat calm sea, with 'Action Man' (Knut Skøgoy) standing in the bow blowing his Viking horn with all his might.

'That bloody thing has got to go,' snarled Nigel Wood as yet another ear-shattering blast numbed our senses.

'The trouble is that he never lets it out of his sight,' said Richard Young, 'But as Chief Bilge Rat, I'll see what can be done.'

With a pride born of team-work we rowed in perfect unison across the harbour towards the large crowd who stood waiting on the quayside. When only a few yards off the steps, the Skipper's crisp orders rang out.

'Oars!' (the order to stop rowing after one more stroke).

'In oars!' Quickly the rowers pulled in their respective oars through the 'ports', laying them across the thwarts.

'Stow oars!' The final order. Starting with the bow-man, each oar was raised vertically before being carefully lowered into place and stacked along the inside of the gunwale.

'Make fast forrard – make fast aft!'

The final ropes were tied off, the kists replaced in position (having been moved into the rowing position) and the deck quickly tidied, all under the intent gaze of the scores of onlookers crammed along the length of the pier.

Stepping over the side on to the seaweed-covered steps, Robin Bigland was greeted by the local dignitaries, who invited the crew into the Customs building for a welcoming drink. Another town, another island; one step nearer the completion of the voyage that none of us really wanted to finish. Little did we know, on that gloriously sunny morning in Stornoway, how close we were to disaster and the possibility of a sudden and premature end to our epic journey.

CHAPTER NINE

Capsize

Our sojourn in Stornoway was brief but extremely cordial. It made a welcome change to discover that few compulsory functions had been arranged for us, thereby allowing time for shopping and sight-seeing. It was on Lewis that we first noticed both the difference in accent of the people, from the Norse–English so prevalent in Shetland (and, to a lesser extent, the Orkneys) to the softer vowels of the Scots Gaelic, and also the decrease in emphasis on the Viking heritage – the Lewismen preferring to remember their Scots ancestry. This was not surprising when one recollects that the Western Isles suffered more pillaging than 'settling' at the hands of the Norse invaders.

After thirty-six hours of restful interlude the crew reboarded the long-ship at 11 p.m. on the Tuesday night and prepared for a night sail down the coast to the Isle of Skye. It was unfortunate that because of the possibility of inclement conditions it was necessary to make this leg of the journey during the hours of darkness, since it meant that some of the most beautiful scenery of the Scottish Isles would pass by unseen; but with a three-day stop-over planned in Portree, on Skye, we could hope to have a chance later on to view the splendours of these rugged mountain vistas.

For the three hours before the departure time the crew had been entertained to an excellent farewell dinner, made even more enjoyable by a liberal supply of wine. It was therefore a merry bunch of Vikings who eventually settled themselves into positions for rowing, the wind having dropped away to nothing. The large crowd overlooking the ship from their vantage point on the jetty heard Eddie Kaighin give the orders which would send the *Raven* out into the darkness across the placid waters of Stornoway harbour.

'Stand by oars!' The full complement of rowers grappled with their cumbersome burdens, raising the heavy oars into a vertical position.

'Cast off forrard – cast off aft!' With a loud splash the mooring ropes hit the water, to be quickly hauled in and neatly coiled. The longship rocked gently as Rolf Hansen and Robin Bigland moved across the deck with the heavy ropes.

'Starboard side, push us off with your oars!' With one accord, seven men thrust against the slimy stone of the pier, forcing the ship away from the wall until enough space had been created to enable the oars to be used.

'Standby.' The order for the rowers to hold their oars in readiness, parallel to the water, the blades poised to make the first stroke.

'Taking your time from Georgie – give way, together!' came the command.

Normally, on the final word, fourteen oars would crash simultaneously into the water, the first short, sharp stroke sending the boat surging through the water. Unfortunately on this occasion, the farewell dinner on land had taken its toll of the co-ordination between mind and body where some of us were concerned. As a crew we had always taken pride in our efficiency at both rowing and sailing at all times, but never more so than when we were the cynosure of hundreds of pairs of critical eyes. In Stornoway harbour, alas the departure of *Odin's Raven* must have looked like the ungainly antics of an inebriated spider, the oars rising and falling with little semblance of rhythm.

As we rounded the beacon which marked the harbour entrance, a position from which we could no longer be seen from the shore, Robin Bigland could contain himself no longer. His face suffused with anger and humilation, he rushed to the mast, jumped on to a kist and exploded.

'That was the most deplorable exhibition that I've ever seen!' he shouted. 'I've a good mind to stop the trip right now, and I mean that. I'll put you all on a plane and send you straight home.' He continued in the same vein for a couple of minutes until he had vented his anger and run out of expletives. Although it was unfortunate that such a rebuke had been necessary, it was not before time. Not only did it serve to remind everyone that Robin Bigland was in overall charge, and perfectly capable as we well knew of cancelling the voyage on the spot, but it also cleared the air dramatically. Since the passages across the two most hostile stretches of sea had been successfully completed, the feeling that the journey was now a cruise had been growing by the hour. Behaviour and discipline on board had become too relaxed, with a consequent loss in concentration and alertness. Robin's free-and-easy attitude with the crew, which had paid enormous dividends initially in breaking down any barriers which might have existed, had been taken advantage of by some of the members. Under the mistaken assumption that the Chieftain was prepared to sit back and allow events to take their own course, liberties had been taken which tended to precipitate the rapid disintegration of the hitherto excellent teamwork.

The disappearance of a third of the ship's complement back to Kirkwall from Rousay had been one example. In Stornoway, one or two men had absented themselves for virtually the total duration of our stay, and on one semi-official occasion the lack of enthusiasm for the function had resulted in the gradual disappearance of almost the whole crew. When during the course of the evening our hosts had requested some involvement from their guests, Robin found, much to his embarrassment, that none of the Raven's 'minstrels' or entertainers in other fields was present.

In retrospect therefore, his forceful reprimand was timely; individualistic tendencies being all very well on land but, where such a complicated sailing vessel as the longship was concerned, teamwork was the most vital ingredient – and instant obedience to orders.

Robin's own version of the admonishment, recorded in his diary soon after the event, was incorrect in one respect. He wrote '. . . so on leaving Lewis I was sharply reminded of the fact that the crew had begun to feel that the voyage would now be easy, by their general attitude, many of them having drunk too much prior to our departure. I'm afraid it was necessary to give them a stern reminder that this was not a pleasure cruise and that we had a very serious undertaking ahead of us. I think my sharp words sobered them up, for the rest of the evening was spent in a much more subdued fashion.'

This last comment was not entirely accurate because that journey down to Skye, at least for the first four or five hours, was one of the more memorable evenings of the voyage. Almost as if to prove to the Chieftain that the crew were still united and aware of their responsibilities, the worst affected of the oarsmen were voluntarily replaced and, to the rhythm of a seemingly endless cycle of songs, the longship glided across the starlit sea, a ghostly silhouette from another age. The gaunt cliffs of Lewis and, later, Skye echoed to the sound of men's voices raised in song. It was a mood which recreated the past without anybody being consciously aware of it. The entertainment thus created not only sobered up those for whom it was necessary, it also re-united the whole crew as one – including Robin Bigland. The singing gradually died down in the early hours and when our watch stood down at 4 a.m. the only sound was the gentle creak of the oars against the oarports and the splash as the blades hit the water – this time in perfect unison.

I awoke at eight o'clock to find the longship riding lazily on the mirror-calm water, at anchor in another of those beautiful highland coves. The majority of the rest of my shipmates were still asleep; Eddie Kaighin and Robin Bigland were in their hammocks, slung between the yokes and the mast. I was told by Rick Tomlinson who was brewing up some coffee, that due to the ideal conditions and the exertions of the rowers during the night, we had covered this short leg unexpectedly quickly – so much so that we were now moored only twenty miles or so north of Portree, our next port of call.

'Why aren't we going straight in?' I asked.

'Apparently, Robin contacted them from Lewis,' replied Rick, 'and they requested that, if we were able to manage it, could we arrive after six o'clock, so the town pipe-band could be on hand to welcome us!'

'Great!' was my comment, as I accepted a mug of scalding coffee. 'I wonder if the original Vikings so courteously advised them of the time of their arrival?'

Since the final legs of the voyage were relatively short hops between islands, and we were able to give reasonably accurate indications of our movements our arrivals could be advertised over the local radio, thus giving as many people as possible an opportunity to view the longship at her best – when at sea. However unusual and interesting she may have been to view when moored to the quayside, she was obviously a more dramatic picture when under sail.

With the whole day in front of us, a number of the crew opted to go ashore and stretch out on the grass in an effort to catch up on lost sleep. The bay was surrounded by wild, towering hills, the grassy tussocks almost kissing the sea as they swept down the hillside. The sheep grazed on the precipitous pastures with the ease and aplomb of mountain goats, although it is almost certain that any sheep that lost its footing would find a watery grave. While Rick Tomlinson, Dave Eames and Colin Bowen stretched out on a grassy knoll to sleep, Robin Bigland, David Scott (the BBC reporter) and myself collected driftwood and built a small fire. There was no real need for extra heat, for the sun appeared at regular intervals through the sparsely scattered summer clouds, but it seemed 'the thing to do'. A few hundred yards away, her image reflected in the mirror-stillness of the water, *Odin's Raven* lay dwarfed by the backdrop of massive cliffs. That inexorable feeling crept up on us again that we were following in the exact wake of our ancient predecessors. There was no way that one or more longships had not anchored in this same cove, wild crews taking the opportunity to land and cook their meal over a camp-fire, similar to the one around which we sat.

The utter peacefulness of the scene remained unbroken until midday when the arrival of Bill Hook and the BBC camera crew announced that our idyllic sojourn was over. The wind had gradually increased during the morning and the BBC, woefully short of film of the longship at sea, were taking every opportunity to make up this lack. The afternoon was therefore spent sailing up and down the coast while David Eames rowed a non-too-enthusiastic cameraman around in the now quite choppy sea, both getting soaked through in B.C.'s extremely small and remark-ably unstable inflatable dinghy! With the filming completed, the *Raven* returned to the scene of our morning sojourn to land Bill Hook and his party, whose intention was to go ahead to Portree in order to film our arrival.

By four o'clock the weather had deteriorated considerably, the rain slanting across the water directly into our faces as we tacked the *Raven* southwards towards our goal. As the wind increased it also shifted direction and the conditions quickly became uncomfortable. With the longship sailing extremely close to the uninviting lee-shore, her 15 degrees of leeway accentuating the danger, it was decided to use the engine. The difference in the motion of the boat was immediately apparent. Instead of riding over the steep waves and sliding down into the troughs, the *Raven* under power crashed into the water with a force that sent quivers along her entire length, the broken wave-crests smothering the decks with spray. The extra dampness thus created had little effect on the crew as the driving rain had already penetrated all but the stoutest protection, and most of us were soaked to the skin. After the previous week of fine weather, this sudden and unexpected change in the conditions made that short haul to Portree the most uncomfortable couple of hours of the whole voyage.

Portree lies at the head of a natural V-shape bay and as we rounded the headland and turned towards the harbour, the wind came on to our quarter enabling us to sail up the bay in magnificent style. Undeterred by the drenching rain and strong winds a number of small boats had come out to meet us, bobbing around the longship in the short, vicious sea. David Scott and Jan Riddell of the BBC documentary team had cadged a lift in a high-speed dory powered by a 125 h.p. Chrysler outboard and they literally leapt across the water, bounding across the waves in bone-jarring fashion. Viewed from the longship the spectacle was quite dramatic, the effect emphasised by the look of alarm on their faces! We were to come to know the owner and helmsman of the dory, Tex Urqhart, very well during the days to follow, unfortunately under less welcome circumstances.

The presence of a piper in one of the boats added a touch of Highland authenticity to the occasion, although the strangled squeak which occasionally emanated from his instrument, due no doubt to an excess of water in the works, rather detracted from the overall impression. Similarly the vociferous orders from Bill Hook (aboard yet another boat) in his attempts to clear some of the flotilla out of the way while he tried to film us with the piper in the background, tended to mar the freedom of expression one felt that such an occasion required.

Much to our surprise we noticed that the quayside was packed with people to whom the attraction of seeing a Viking vessel under full sail was obviously great enough for them to brave the appalling conditions. With the gusting wind in our favour we were able to sail right up to the quay, and our arrival was greeted not only with loud and prolonged applause but also with the grand sound of the pipe-band arrayed in all their finery, their furry bearskins drooping a little in the damp. It was one of the more exceptional welcomes that we were to receive, and the interest and enthusiasm for us and the longship set the scene for the next few days.

It had been planned that we would stay in Portree for 3 days, the whole crew being billeted in a cosy guest-house only a few yards from the harbour. One of the greatest delights as far as we were concerned was that no official functions had been arranged for us, except for our expected attendance at the nightly dances in the 'Gathering Hall' – a chore we were only to willing to undertake. Without further ado, once the longship had been moored safely and the decks cleared of ropes and sheets, the crew collected their personal items together and squelched up the road to the guest-house. Within an hour of our arrival, every airing-cupboard and radiator was festooned with dripping clothing as, for the first time since leaving Norway, time was available to empty the kists completely and sort out the conglomeration of articles which had accumulated. The warmth of the hospitality and cosy surroundings soon had its effect and, for perhaps the first time on dry land, most of the crew were in bed at a reasonable hour.

The following morning found the crew much refreshed and eager to explore the surrounding countryside. The weather had improved a little, the driving rain giving way to a persistent drizzle, but the wind remained gusty, the spume flying across the waters of the bay. With no particular wish to clamber up the hillsides in such conditions, a number of us wandered down to the longship, only to find it swarming with schoolchildren. Alarmed at first at the thought of the chaos such a boarding party could so quickly create, we were relieved to observe the harassed figures of Robin Bigland and Shane Lucas (the latter having acquiesced to insistent demands that he dress up in his Viking costume), both of whom were engulfed in the melee of excited children. We decided that discretion was the better part of valour in the face of such overwhelming odds and quickly retreated to the safety of the bar in the Rosedale Hotel which overlooked the quayside, impervious to Robin's plaintive cry of 'Come on chaps, you can't leave me on my own with this lot!' Couldn't we just!

It was no surprise to find the BBC crew already ensconced in their customary positions at the cocktail bar, and in no time at all our infallible technique (uncharitably referred to by the cameraman as 'begging') had obtained the round of drinks necessary to celebrate our narrow escape.

David Scott and Jan Riddell were still shaky from their toboggan ride in Tex Urqhart's dory the previous day, while Bill Hook was earnestly trying to convince Eddie Kaighin that the conditions were ideal for filming the *Raven* at her most dramatic.

'Hell, Bill, do you realise it's gusting up to Force 8 out there?' I noted a sense of desperation in Eddie's voice; the prospect of spending the afternoon in the warm comfort of the bar was fading rapidly as the conversation continued.

'I know, Eddie,' wheedled Bill, 'but it's reasonably sheltered and we'd get some fantastic shots of her at full speed.'

Eddie was still not convinced that it was a particularly good idea, but now Bill played his trump card; 'I know you're probably right, Eddie,' he said. 'It *is* a little dangerous. I just thought that it would be fun to see how fast she really can go.''

It was like a red rag to a bull. I'm quite sure that if Bill ever decided to change jobs, psychology would be the obvious choice. At lunch-time Robin Bigland was acquainted with the proposal, and his ready agreement no doubt stemmed from his own desire to test the longship under conditions which guaranteed an exhilarating sail. In what later proved to be a stroke of good fortune, the only available members of the crew at the time were the most experienced in sailing, with the exception of Nigel Wood and Ganger-Rolf Hansen who were sightseeing somewhere. Fate plays idle tricks and I opted to travel with the film crew on the converted trawler, the *Ferrara*, which they had chartered; my intention was to take this golden opportunity of photographing the longship under sail – something which, as a crew member, I had not been able to do yet.

At one o'clock on June 14, *Odin's Raven* slipped her moorings and sailed briskly out into the bay, her bow slicing into the steep, choppy waves, the froth bubbling behind her as she rapidly picked up speed. Before leaving the quayside Robin Bigland had to disappoint a number of local dignitaries who had requested permission to accompany him, pointing out that it was a sail purely for filming purposes and any unusual faces would upset the continuity of the documentary. He had never previously refused to take any one and, in retrospect, it again seemed that some unconscious premonition must have directed such a decision. Similarly, Eddie's decision to transfer some of the kists on to the quayside to allow more room on deck was something that had never previously even been considered.

Consequently, when the *Raven* sailed out of Portree that day, she did so with a crew of highly experienced sailors, none of whom was likely to panic in the event of a disaster. It is unlikely that the same could have been said if the whole complement or extra passengers had been on board. With Eddie Kaighin on the steering oar, Robin Bigland and Brian Cousins controlling the sheets and Dave Eames, Rick Tomlinson and Colin Bowen to cope with the sail, she could be handled as efficiently as if the whole crew were aboard.

From the comfort of the day-cabin on the *Ferrara*, with Rick Tomlinson's camera slung around my neck as I had left mine in my kist on board, I watched her graceful hull bound through the water. For an hour she sailed up and down the Sound which separates Skye from the mainland: one minute storming past us at a speed far too fast for the camera-boat to match, the next virtually becalmed as the fickle wind dropped away completely. Bill Hook was having a field-day, his every wish coming true as he directed the cameraman to capture the most spectacular shots. With her sail reefed, the longship scudded through the spray-tossed water like a playful puppy, her course criss-crossing ours as she alternately shaved across the bows or cheekily raced up astern, as if nudging the *Ferrara* along.

Having used up one film from a position out on the deck, I went below to replace it with a new one.

'Tough work being a Viking, Mike, isn't it?' said a grinning Dave Scott.

'It's hell out here,' I replied, proffering my empty glass for a refill.

At that moment a sudden squall caught our boat broadside and we heeled over before its potent force. Bill Hook was on the bridge, talking to Eddie Kaighin over a portable two-way radio, the link used to direct filming sequences from a distance, and I heard him exclaim jokingly, 'What are you doing sitting there, Eddie? We've got a gale over here!'

Glancing out of the window I saw the *Raven* virtually becalmed about half a mile away. Suddenly, the white square of canvas altered in profile and seemed to become narrower.

'Jesus Christ, she's going over!' yelled Bill Hook.

In a stunned silence we watched her slowly tilt over and then, quite suddenly, the sail disappeared, leaving the hull rising clear of the water.

'Oh my God,' I said, as I leapt up on to the deck.

'Keep filming, keep filming,' bellowed Hook to the cameraman, who quietly nodded his assent; the capsizing of a Viking longship was all in a day's work!

'Never mind the bloody film!' I shouted. 'Let's get over there fast!'

My anxiety was understandable. One doesn't live cheek by jowl with others for six weeks without feeling dread when they suddenly disappear into a most unfriendly sea.

The skipper of the *Ferrara*, more used to cruising around the placid waters of the Mediterranean, rose to the occasion magnificiently and had already turned the boat towards the stricken longship, but that journey across the half-mile or so that separated us seemed to take an endless time. The camera was still churning away beside me as we neared the capsized boat and, in retrospect, one realised that priorities differ at such times, depending on the circumstances. The disaster 'made' the documentary as far as Bill Hook was concerned, and certainly it did add the touch of drama essential to good television. But my only thought, once I had counted six figures safely on the hull, was that my ship lay there wallowing at the mercy of the waves which were becoming more alarming as the weather worsened. The whole crew, without exception, not only had pride in their vessel but also a strong feeling of emotional attachment. The dull, sick feeling in my stomach grew in intensity as the full import of what had happened began to sink in.

'What the hell happened?' asked David Scott as he stood beside me in the bow while we were still some minutes away from the wreckage of what had been, only a few minutes earlier, a graceful longship flying through the surf.

'I've no idea,' I replied. 'But that gust must have caught her unprepared.'

What had actually happened during those few hectic seconds was not pieced together until some hours after the event, and that evening, Robin Bigland attempted to relive the event in his diary.

'As we sailed out into the open water,' he wrote, 'all of us felt the elation of a good breeze and the fine vessel moving so gracefully, as always, through the water. The BBC were telling us that they were getting good quality shots and we all felt that the possibilities of an excellent afternoon's sailing were there for the taking. It's funny, in retrospect, small things pile up to produce an overall picture that shows what might have gone wrong, in a small way initially, gradually building up to the culmination. The wind was obviously playing strange tricks. It backed and veered and, on one occasion as we were tacking, we found ourselves passing through almost 260 degrees on the same tack! Nevertheless, it was an exhilarating experience and we were enjoying it to the full.

'The events of the next few minutes kaleidoscope in one's mind because of the awful inevitability of what took place. We were just recovering from the tack already described and the boat had picked up way again. We were close-hauled. I was seated aft and had just passed over the port sheet to Brian Cousins. I remember that he made a remark to the effect that this was testing sailing. Quite suddenly she started to heel and I remember seeing the first flecks, little spurts of water through the oar ports, and then, all at once as 'green' water began to pour over the gunwale, she heeled and began to go. I had that moment of extreme clarity looking at Brian's face, his gaze met mine and there was a mutual look of astonishment between the two of us. Next thing, I plunged into the water, realising that it was important to clear the rigging of the vessel. I was under for several moments and had to duck beneath one of the shrouds to clear myself before coming to the surface. As I surfaced, I was conscious that the water wasn't that cold but that in ducking under the shroud my woollen hat had caught and come off and I was immediately thoughtful of the loss of the hat which I treasured. All sorts of jumbled emotions came to mind. I thought of the small Christmas tree in the stern of the vessel (a present from Norway) and what a pity it was that we would probably never be able to bring it back to the Island.' (In fact, it did turn up a few days later, somewhat the worse for wear after its immersion in salt water.) 'Miraculously, both the stones that we were carrying, stowed in the bilges, one a rock from the beach for the Rotary Club and the other a portion of stone from Trondheim Cathedral, somehow were preserved.

'I saw that the boys, Eddie Kaighin, Brian Cousins, Rick Tomlinson, Colin Bowen and David Eames were all in the process of scrambling on to the starboard side of the vessel. Utter confusion in the water, where everything capable of floating was jumbled about. I swam to the side of the vessel and also clambered aboard. I found myself clutching a bottle which turned out to be a sample of North Sea Oil we had been given in the Ninian Field. To my regret, I found that I couldn't quite gain a firm hold on the hull, so I had to let the bottle go. It floated away and was never recovered.'

Colin Bowen could not recall the actual events leading up to the capsize in any great detail. In his position in the bow, he felt the longship begin to heel, looked up and saw Eddie at the helm 'six feet up in the air'. Realising she was going over and, mindful of the coils of mooring ropes and the anchor on which he was standing, which could so easily ensnare him underwater, he jumped over the side. Even so, he was caught under the sail for a short time, but his training as a diver came to his rescue and there was never any question of panic. Brian Cousins and Dave Eames also remembered little about those frenzied moments except hearing Eddie's shouts of 'Let go the sheets!' and 'Look out, lads, she's going over!' Brian also recollects saying to Robin Bigland, 'It looks like a gust coming up,' just before the squall hit.

Rick Tomlinson, utilieing his experience of dinghy-racing in which a capsize is not an uncommon occurrence, simply walked up the side of the boat and clambered on to the starboard side, high and dry! Eddie Kaighin retained his grip on the gunwale as the *Raven* went over, climbed back on to the hull and set about the process of retaining some sort of order in the chaos.

By the time that we on the *Ferrara* arrived on the scene, the mainsail had been cut loose, the life-raft inflated and the precious cargo of mail-bags safely recaptured; in fact, the first words I heard as we closed on the stricken vessel were those from Robin Bigland exhorting the others to rescue the £15,000 worth of first-day covers (luckily sealed in waterproof floating containers) which we were transporting from Norway to the Isle of Man. For some obscure reason, known only to fanatics of philately, the value of those covers increased dramatically as a direct result of the catastrophe!

The water surrounding the half-submerged longship was literally covered with floating debris. Most of the loose equipment was made of wood and the sea was littered with kists, deck boards, oars, plastic bags and all the other impedimenta that had accumulated during the previous five weeks. Even as we watched, the disaster area visibly increased, the tide and wind beginning to disperse everything in different directions.

From the bow of the *Ferrara* I heaved a line across to Eddie Kaighin who attached it in the first instance to one of the pine yokes. There was no way that this could stand the strain and as soon as the tow-line drew taut the yoke was wrenched from its seating and flew through the air towards us. On the second attempt the line was fixed to the mast and, as the strain was taken up, slowly but surely the ship righted herself. Unfortunately, with no scuppers in the original design, there was no available exit for the tons of water held in the hull, and although the mast could be raised to the vertical there was no stability, and the ship quickly settled back on to her side. After half an hour the skipper of the rescue boat decided that the best thing was to tow her to the beach, about two miles away; and even though we realised that such a course of action could spell disaster for the longship, as she would break up very quickly in the steadily worsening conditions specially if grounded on a hard rocky beach, there did not appear to be any alternative.

The real problem, which had become apparent soon after our arrival on the scene, was that there were too many 'chiefs'. While Robin Bigland bellowed at me to ask the skipper of the *Ferrara* to radio for the life-boat, Eddie Kaighin was adamant that she could be righted and was shouting orders about the positioning of the tow-rope, and Bill Hook was also trying to assist in all this decision-making. I was surprised that the skipper of the *Ferrara* remained calm for as long as he did, but finally he ordered the crew of the longship to come alongside in the life-raft and stated that the only solution was to run the *Raven* ashore. The repeated radio-calls for assistance had met with no response, probably due to the close proximity of the mountains affecting the transmission range. In any case there was little cause to summon help as none of the crew was injured and a perfectly adequate rescue-boat was on hand. Eddie Kaighin and Robin Bigland both realised that the skipper of the *Ferrara* was now in total command, and was perfectly entitled, if he so desired, to drop the tow once the crew were safely on board.

With the life-raft moored alongside the *Ferrara* and the sodden, shipwrecked mariners aboard, the tow-line tautened and the longship swung into the wake of the rescue-boat as the slow haul towards the beach began. As soon as he arrived on board Eddie Kaighin discussed the possibilities with his rescuer, and finally it was agreed to try to tow the longship back to Portree harbour, about five miles away.

For the next two hours we crawled across the choppy sea, the tow-line disappearing into the water as the longship became totally submerged, the force of the tow, even at slow speed, driving her beneath the surface. Dave Eames and Rick Tomlinson, having borrowed the Zodiac inflatable carried by the *Ferrara*, spent most of the time bouncing across the waves collecting as much of the debris that was manageable, breaking open the floating kists and removing the contents. A passing fishing boat also joined in the search successfully retrieving most of the larger equipment such as the oars and deckboards.

Eddie Kaighin, still obviously shocked by the suddenness of the calamity, was trying to explain to Bill Hook the cause of the capsize. Such discussions were to continue among all of us over the next few days, but the basic facts could not be argued. The combination of such a massive area of sail and a sudden gale-force gust of wind, estimated as at least Force 8, had been the causal factor; coupled with the problem of releasing at least six sheets in a few seconds and the lack of scuppers, so that once 'green' water started coming over the side then nothing could stop the inevitable happening. In retrospect, the only way in which the capsize could possibly have been averted was to have dropped the sail to the deck immediately the oncoming gust was suspected. One learns by mistakes and our failure to recognise the importance of just such an action was a consequence of trying to learn the technique of sailing an ancient untried vessel in such a short space of time. We were not infallible! The lesson had been learned the hard way, and from that time on, even in the calmest weather, the main halyard was manned constantly; in fact, just such a precautionary action *did* have to be taken during the very last minutes of the whole voyage!

A capsize was the one thing we had all feared and it was pure luck that it had occurred under such convenient circumstances, with a rescue-boat on hand, only a few miles from shore and with a reduced crew on board. If the longship had gone over in the middle of the North Sea, or on any one of the legs from Lerwick onwards, when we were never accompanied by other boats for any length of time, it required little imagination to picture the situation. With a full complement aboard, some of whom might be sleeping, the confusion of bodies, ropes, kists and assorted paraphernalia would almost certainly have resulted in injury or, as most of us were only too aware, death. Even had we survived the capsize itself, having seen how little woodwork actually remained above the surface and bearing in mind the areas of sea we had crossed which were totally devoid of shipping, the danger of prolonged exposure with no means of sending a Mayday signal would have been just as serious.

Thoughts such as these must have passed through all our minds as, in the early hours of the evening, the sad little procession finally came to a halt alongside the quayside in Portree; the Vikings not involved in the events of the afternoon had heard the news and were waiting anxiously as we arrived. Within minutes of tying up, Colin Bowen swam out to the masthead, lashed on a rope and, with the help of a number of willing bystanders, the *Raven* was once again raised into a vertical position, although the hull was still totally submerged. After ascertaining that low-tide was not due until 4 a.m., when the local fire-brigade, who had immediately offered their services, would attempt to pump out and refloat her, everyone repaired to the Guest-house for a hot bath, a change of clothes and a meal.

Most of us were obviously depressed by the turn of events, for we assumed that the voyage was probably now over, or at least severely curtailed. Robin Bigland, however, never one to concede defeat easily, had already set the necessary wheels in motion, to enable the longship to become ship-shape again at the earliest opportunity. When the arrangements with the fire brigade had been completed he rang his wife to acquaint her with the facts, especially as regards the safety of the crew, because the media have a habit of distorting or exaggerating such occasions, often with unnecessarily injurious effects on the families of those concerned. Within a couple of hours our wives and relatives had received the bad news about the *Raven* but were assured that no crew member had been hurt in any way. Our Norwegian friends were not so lucky, however, as one of their national papers actually announced that some of the crew had been lost!

The engine of the *Raven* had been immersed for several hours and it was obvious that it was going to require a major overhaul, but the local garage, Machrea's, agreed to prepare themselves for a rush job. Robin Bigland's next most important priority was to bolster the morale of his crew, and with this in mind he returned to the boat to find a disconsolate Eddie Kaighin. He recorded in his log: 'I found him in bad shape since he was taking the capsize very personally. I'm afraid I was a bit tough with him. We still have a long way to go and there's no room for self-pity in a skipper's job. If the boys see him go under, they'll soon lose heart and then where shall we be?' Whatever Eddie's personal feelings, he kept them well hidden from us, and whether as a result of Robin's talk or by dint of his own resources his overt reaction to the disaster was a determination to see the longship once again gracefully riding the waves.

If Robin Bigland had any fears about the morale of his crew disintegrating, they were soon allayed. The dance that evening, during which we were invited to choose a local 'Viking Princess', soon took our minds off our own problems. Such entertainment provided the ideal outlet for any worries or fears concerning the future. During the course of the night, however, the crew's irritation with the BBC film crew finally came to a head and it was a miracle that no blows were struck. Throughout the course of the voyage, although we had been warned to expect the presence of the media for most of the time, the domineering methods used by Bill Hook to obtain the film he desired had begun to wear down our patience, even though we accepted that his job was to produce the best possible documentary record of our voyage. On this particular occasion, though, the mood of the crew was such that all we really desired was to be left alone with our own problems – namely, the refloating of our vessel and the safe continuation of the voyage.

Although low-tide was not due until 4 in the morning, at one o'clock Bill decided that he wanted to film the pumping out and he started chivvying us all to leave the dance and get down to the harbour. Tempers began to run high, and by the time we had all assembled on the quayside there was not one of us who would have grudged him an accidental push over the edge into the sea. The fire brigade had also been unceremoniously hustled down to where the longship lay, still almost totally immersed; but beneath the harsh lights of the BBC cameras, the pumping out commenced.

For me it was an intensely emotional moment as the great spume of water from the hose belched over the top of the ship and she slowly rose up from her watery resting place. It was like raising one of the ancient Viking boats; first the gunwale becoming visible, then what remained of the deckboards, until finally she was floating on an even keel, the glaring lights accentuating her damaged woodwork. The deck, devoid of all the kists, oars etc., was a skeleton of ribs and trapped debris, the gaping holes left by the missing deckboards exposing her barren insides to the world. She looked a gutted wreck of her former beauty and it seemed an impossibility that she would ever be sailed again. But within minutes of the hoses being removed, the essential work of re-fitting the engine began. Those of us who were not immediately involved returned to the Guesthouse to grab what sleep we could before the hard work really started.

The following four days were a combination of hard work during daylight hours and hilarious relaxation in the evenings.

The morning after the capsize an inventory of missing items was made and initially it appeared that a great deal of equipment had been lost. However, with the help of the local population, passing fishermen and enthusiastic tourists, much of the floating debris was recovered from the sea and surrounding beaches. Tex Urqhart and his powerful dory came in extremely useful now. Even on the day of our departure a kist and a sleeping bag were returned to the boat by some tourists who had found them some miles along the coast. Consequently, although everything was soaked through, very little of the most essential equipment remained unrecovered. Perhaps the biggest blow to the ship was the loss of the log book along with the spare sail, our only form of covering when conditions allowed. Similarly all the food had provided an unexpected meal for the local marine fauna, and the heavier equipment such as the radio, echosounder and ship's bell had obviously plummeted straight to the bottom of the channel. Most of our Viking gear had also gone missing, due no doubt to the heavy woollen garments quickly becoming waterlogged, but the loss of our banner, *Landwaster*, was, to me, a very personal disappointment.

By eleven o'clock on that first morning the engine was again in working order, much to the disappointment of the sailors among the crew. Essential as it had proved to be on certain occasions, many of us had hoped that its sudden enforced silence was to be permanent!

The capsize had occurred on a Thursday, and by Sunday evening the sail was again sheeted up and hanging limply from the yard. Most of the deck-boards which had been found were re-fitted, and only three new ones had to be made by local carpenters; these excellent people, who had rallied round enthusiastically in our time of trouble, had also carved two new yokes to hold the yard when not in use and a number of the smaller wooden accoutrements which had not been found at sea.

During those hectic days, other events had occurred which were unrelated to the problems associated with the longship.

Apart from the nightly dances in the 'Gathering Hall', some of which had been organised entirely for our benefit, our entertainment centred on the bar of the Rosedale Hotel and the crew of the Naval Auxiliary Vessel *Goosander*, which was moored close to the longship. On one memorable afternoon, work on the longship was interrupted for a time as selected members of the two crews met in a jousting match on the calm waters of the harbour. Having 'appropriated' a couple of local dinghies, 3 men from each crew rowed out to do battle for the honour of their respective vessels. It was a slightly one-sided affair when one considers that one of the dinghies was so small it tended to sink under the weight of the combatants long before they were within reach of their opponents, but by exchanging boats after each joust any disadvantage was thus nullified, supposedly. After five such matches the result was declared an honourable draw at 3 wins each! As all of the participants had ended up in the water in any event, honour was served all round.

The concordance with our fellow mariners continued every evening in the quayside tavern. This hostelry was dominated by a well-built buxom barmaid, Helen, whose habit of leaping across the bar in her pursuit of her arch-heckler Jimmy, from the *Goosander*, was quite an awe-inspiring sight. Jimmy, a true Glaswegian with the sense of humour for which that city is justly famous, often had the room rocking with laughter – for example, with his description of his wife, who was 'so ugly that I rent her out to the local farmer as a scarecrow and the birds bring back the things they nicked two years ago!' Apparently she had the further misfortune to suffer from 'straight hair and curly teeth', and used to be a mental nurse who used her husband for homework!

The memories of those relaxed evenings in that hospitable town included the evening when Eddie was promoted to Chief Bilge Rat; it had been decided that the feat of actually capsizing a longship rated a life membership of the society. The customary pint of beer was poured over his head as B.C. read him the riot act, usurping for a time Robin Bigland's position as Chieftain.

Now that we knew that the *Raven* would be continuing the voyage, although the unforeseen delay had caused the cancellation of the projected 'leg' to Dublin, the morale of the crew was again at its zenith and we were all anxious to be on our way.

All the oars had by now been recovered, as had all but one of the kists. With the inflation of the main life-raft after the capsize we were to make the rest of the trip with only the smaller 8-man raft available for use in emergencies, but few of us showed any concern about that; presumably each of the sixteen crew-members assumed that he would be one of the lucky eight!

Tobermory, on the Isle of Mull, was to be our next port of call, and so, on Tuesday, June 19, the *Raven* once again prepared for sea. This time Eddie Kaighin was taking no chances, and before setting sail we loaded about half a ton of shingle into bags and positioned them in the bilges in an attempt to increase ballast.

Robin Bigland had given Odd Børstad the wherewithal to purchase a suitable meal to celebrate our recovery from the potential disaster of the capsize, and he and Nigel Wood came aboard just prior to our departure time with their arms loaded with huge steaks and bottles of wine. Our send-off was as noisy and cheerful as our arrival had been six days earlier, and, with Tex Urqhart circling around in his dory at something over thirty knots, the great sail was hoisted once again and the longship drifted gently away from the crowded quayside. Saddened as we were by our departure from such a friendly and hospitable community, without whose assistance the continuance of the voyage would have been in jeopardy, we were nonetheless thankful to be on our way again, although the memories of the generosity of the people of Portree remain with us all to this day.

On a glorious summer morning, *Odin's Raven* sliced through the sparkling water, a warm gentle breeze driving her away from the scene of her misfortune along the Sound of Raasay towards the Kyle of Lochalsh, the narrow channel which separates the Isle of Skye from the mainland.

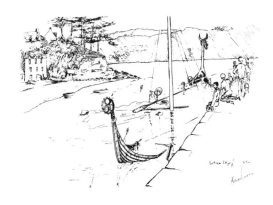

CHAPTER TEN

Corryvreckan Whirlpool

The route from Skye to Mull passes through some of the most breathtak-ingly beautiful scenery in the whole of Britain, and as if in reward for our endeavours over the previous few days we were granted perfect summer weather for the voyages. Beneath a cloudless azure sky the longship glided across the rippling surface of the sea, her crew revelling in the hot condi-tions. For the first time since the departure from Trondheim we were able to strip off our shirts and sunbathe, half-clad bodies littering the deck. The loss of equipment as a result of the capsize had created extra stowage space below the deck, with the result that a great deal more room was made available in 'the living quarters'. The sudden demise of the bulky liferaft allowed a more comfortable steering position to be adopted and, as we approached the Kyle of Lochalsh, Dave Eames had fashioned the remaining raft in such a way that he was steering from virtually a reclin-ing position!

The only obvious signs on board that we had recently been involved in a disaster were that the main down-haul halyard was manned constantly, and there seemed a decided reluctance to take up position on the leeward side of the ship! I have to admit that for the first couple of hours sail I made certain that I was sitting high on the windward gunwale within easy reach of one of the stays! It was to take a few days before our confidence returned completely and a number of the crew deemed it safer to remain awake during the hours we were at sea!

The actual motion of the boat seemed little different even though we had taken on the extra shingle ballast in Portree, the longship creaming over the top of the waves in her usual lively fashion. The sheer thrill of being at sea once more, combined with the glorious weather, served to keep everybody in high spirits, even when a unanimous groan heralded the arrival of yet another TV team.

We had just passed through the Kyle of Lochalsh and were heading south-west down the Sound of Sleat, rowing easily beneath the hot sun (our sailing wind only lasted from Portree to the Kyle), when our visitors drew alongside. Now that the *Raven* was virtually on the home run, our proximity to land enabled the media to contact us with much greater ease – the speed of modern travel reflected in their ability to ricochet about the islands while we sailed lazily along, revelling in such a slow but vastly more satisfying mode of transport. In fact, this particular camera crew were the BBC *Look North* team whom we had last seen on a freezing February dawn during the months of training. On that occasion they had been involved in filming one of our overnight hikes over Snaefell, the highest mountain in the Isle of Man, and the alacrity with which they had purchased our refreshments at the hostelries along the route had endeared them to us forever! Consequently we greeted them as long-lost friends, co-operating with their every desire in a manner that would have made Bill Hook green with envy.

Overlooked on either side by the stark beauty of the Scottish highlands, the longship made her way steadily in the warmth of the afternoon sunshine towards the open sea at the mouth of the Sound while the film crew meandered precariously among the oarsmen, conducting random interviews and taking close-up shots of hirsute bodies as they sweated at their task. Our visitors soon departed, well satisfied with their afternoon's work, and soon after their boat had disappeared from view we came out from the lee of Skye, where the sudden re-appearance of a pleasant breeze enabled the oars to be stowed and the sail set once again.

Apart from the vague presence of distant fishing boats we were alone on the sunlit waters, a situation we all preferred and one which seemed to fit more aptly our status as Viking voyagers. That particular evening, as we sailed across the gently heaving swell, past the gradually darkening mountains of Eigg and Muck, we became spectators to one of the most dramatically beautiful sunsets that many of us had ever been lucky enough to experience. It was at times like these, when we were completely alone with Nature, the surroundings undefiled by anything that could be classed as 'modern', that the historical implications of our voyage were emphasised most strongly; even the sudden incursion of a passing coaster whose course carried it photogenically across the fiery path of the dying sun detracted little from the feeling of antiquity which enveloped us. Although each member of the crew must have his own particular and different memories of the voyage, I know that the evening sail off the Ardnamurchan peninsula is remembered by all, if only for the unparalleled beauty of the scene. The evening meal of steak and wine, to celebrate our 'rebirth', no doubt added to the general atmosphere of contentment. A glass of wine in one hand, an enormous steak speared on a knife in the other, while watching the molten glow of the sun spreading across the horizon, viewed from the gently rocking gunwale of a Viking longship, is one memory which all of us will carry to the grave.

It was an evening for reminiscences, for the discussion of future plans, for talk concerning the safety of the *Raven*, since the shock of the capsize was still very much on our minds — and for those so inclined, the perfect environment in which to exercise the vocal chords as the sound of men's voices raised in song echoed across the empty sea.

The onset of darkness acted as the signal for sleep, and the murmurs of conversation gradually died down. Soon the only sounds to be heard were the slap of water against the hull and the whistle of the wind in the rigging. Our turn for the graveyard watch had again come round, and I noted with amusement that few of my sleeping comrades were prepared to risk being encapsulated in a sleeping-bag cover, with memories of the capsize so fresh in our minds!

With the disappearance of the last rose-coloured streaks of the sunset, the wind had risen and the longship heeled to the increased pressure, the white foam which marked our passage through the water contrasting with the darkness surrounding us. In the early hours of the morning the deeper blackness of the hills of the Island of Mull loomed in front of us and the problem of locating a safe anchorage presented itself. The sky had clouded over with the rising wind, and the starless night made the darkness virtually impenetrable; after one attempt at anchoring in which we fouled a rope from a fishing net, Eddie Kaighin decided that our only alternative was to cruise between the mainland and the island until the onset of dawn enabled us to navigate less hazardously. With the wind gusting unpredictably and some hours of travelling on a reciprocal course ahead of us, the engine was utilised, allowing most of the crew to sleep in relative peace — or as much as the short, steep sea would allow them.

At first light a small jetty was sighted, seemingly unrelated to any signs of habitation, and thankfully we moored alongside. Night watches were quite monotonous in any event, but the utter boredom of having to negotiate an identical stretch of water for hours on end, twenty minutes towards one light visible on shore then twenty minutes in the opposite direction, was enough to drive a helmsman to distraction. How the original Vikings coped with the situation when unable to see a safe anchorage, in a confined channel, the sea too rough for oars and the wind so fluky that it necessitated an exorbitant number of 'tacks', had to be left to the imagination. It was, however, the one occasion when the majority of the crew was grateful for the presence of the engine, regardless of how much they abhorred the fact that we had to have one.

The grey light of dawn spreading across a murky cloud covered sky out of which a steady persistent rain had begun to fall illuminated the sleeping figures of the entire complement of *Odin's Raven*. Moored in such an obviously uninhabited spot it had seemed unnecessary to retain a watchman, and everybody took the opportunity to obtain some rest; the previous long hot day and the tension of being at sea again had taken its toll of our energy. As far as I can recall it was the only occasion when the longship was 'en route' between ports of call that all sixteen of the crew had attempted to sleep at the same time. I soon found my cramped position totally untenable, and after wriggling out from the press of bodies around me I climbed on to the dripping planks of the jetty and surveyed the mass of bodies.

Tied up to the satisfying stability of terra firma, everyone felt that the chances of a capsize were reduced to a minimum! Consequently the deck was a tangled conglomeration of blue and yellow Gortex, most of the crew having opted for the warmer, but not necessarily drier, conditions created by the sleeping-bag covers. It was as if a swarm of giant caterpillers had decided to nest among the oars and kists; the occasional mass of thick, untidy hair or a sudden movement as one of the bodies squirmed from one uncomfortable position to another only served to heighten this overall impression.

Few men showed any displeasure at being woken from such a disturbed slumber when the smell of hot coffee permeated through to their nostrils and breakfast was soon completed. Morning ablutions did not occupy a great length of time as usual, mainly because we all slept in our oil-skins in any event, and Tobermory would presumably provide better facilities.

During the process of cleaning the frying pan by tapping it on the gunwale, the handle broke and the remnants disappeared into the sea. Nobody took a great deal of notice until it was observed that Shane Lucas had changed into his swimming trunks. We watched in amazement as our hardy Viking clambered over the side into the icy water and proceeded to grope around for the missing article. In the opinion of all on board, seven o'clock on a cold drizzly morning was not the ideal time to stand up to one's chest in very chilly seawater for half an hour. To give Shane his due, he pursued his task with enthusiasm but with a resounding lack of success. Eddie Kaighin's cry of 'Stand by to get the sail up, boys!' brought a halt to the rescue attempt and soon the longship was sailing slowly away from her night's abode, a gentle intermittent breeze causing the sail to crack loudly as the fickle wind repeatedly died away to nothing.

When still a couple of miles from our destination the yard was lowered and the oars unshipped, and with the drizzle alternating with heavier showers of rain we rowed the longship into the calm waters of Tobermory harbour. This was perhaps the quietest reception to date, the inclement conditions obviously affecting the enthusiasm of the local people. However we were grateful to find that accommodation had been arranged in the rather plush Western Isles Hotel which overlooked the harbour. Having spent such an uncomfortable night the luxury of a hot bath followed by the tempting proximity of a soft mattress soon took its hold, and by the middle of the afternoon hardly a Viking could be seen.

Next morning, Brian Cousins, Dave Eames, Rick Tomlinson and myself decided to tidy ourselves as best we could under the circumstances, and we invaded the local launderette accompanied by a number of large

145

plastic bags containing approximately three weeks of washing. For two hours we plied the washing machines with such a variety of clothing that two of them gave up the struggle, emitting a succession of groaning and wheezing sounds which we found quite alarming. By midday the four of us were virtually reduced to T-shirts and underpants, taking complete advantage of the opportunity even to the extent of washing the clothes we were wearing at the time. The reason for this unusual event was that we had been invited to attend a lunchtime banquet, reputed to be of such a quality that one felt the occasion demanded some improvement in our normal unhygenic appearance.

Our stay in Tobermory revolved around this magnificent luncheon which took place on the second day of our visit in honour of the Governor of the Isle of Man who was due to join us for the occasion. The banquet had been organised by one of the sponsors of the voyage, Geoff Atherton, but because of the extremely heavy low clouds and torrential rain which persisted throughout the day, their plane was unable to land on the island. Thus the consumption of the splendid feast was left to the crew, and the gluttony that prevailed was filmed by an envious documentary team, Bill Hook having rejoined us in Tobermory.

This superb meal, which consisted of lobster, salmon, cold ham and roast beef salad and all the trimmings, all washed down with champagne and other wines, was certainly well received by the crew, our only regret being the absence of our generous sponsor. The climax came when Arne Wisth attempted a solo rendering of some Norwegian tune, tapping on a large number of glasses of his favourite tipple, vodka and orange, with a couple of knives. For some obscure reason none of the glasses produced exactly the desired vibrations, thus necessitating constant refills and subsequent large sips, the whole performance accompanied by Odd Børstad on 'spoons' and Knut Skøgoy on 'tables' (apparently the percussion department)!

After such a gargantuan feast it was not surprising that the soporific effects soon made themselves felt and the remainder of the day passed by unnoticed by the sated gourmets.

In the evening the BBC requested our attendance at a local discotheque so that they could film the leisure activities of modern-day Vikings. It was a purely artificial occasion, the glare of the television lights serving to make most of the revellers feel self-conscious, with the exception of the cook of *Odin's Raven*. The enormous figure of Odd Børstad rampaging across the dance floor with the sure-footedness of an inebriated elephant was a sight which will long be remembered by those who were present. The heat from the lights was so intense that he had found it necessary to remove his T-shirt, thus displaying his ample stomach, a sight which produced gasps of sheer amazement from the assembled onlookers. His exertions were such that when his successive partners returned to their tables, the damp patches on their dresses advertised the intensity of Odd's

Norwegian bear-hugs! In high spirits the party was transferred to the hotel bar where it continued until the early hours.

Due to the delay caused by the capsize, the intended extension of the voyage incorporating a visit to Dublin had been cancelled. This also reduced the pressure on the schedule, which was planned to culminate with our arrival in Peel on the Isle of Man at a set time on July 4. Now, with a day or two in hand, we were invited by the Argyll and Bute District Council to stop over in Oban on our way south to Islay, our last port of call in the original plan. Friday morning therefore found a rather fragile crew preparing the longship for the short journey down the Sound of Mull. The forecast for the day was not one to instil confidence, giving winds of Force 5 to Gale Force accompanied by heavy rain. The festivities of the previous 24 hours had in no way obliterated our very real fears as to the safety of the *Raven* in such conditions, and the driving rain which had continued unabated since our arrival on Mull did nothing to improve our spirits.

Our presence in Tobermory had obviously made itself felt and a very large crowd braved the inhospitable conditions to cheer us on our way; the departure was also enlivened by the late appearance of some crew-members who had, in a spirit of goodwill, tidied up the hotel bar after the devastation caused by the merry-making of the previous evening. That they had been well rewarded for their endeavours was obvious by the ungainly and hazardous manner in which they boarded the vessel. It was lucky for the rest of the crew that the gentlemen in question were not due on watch until after our estimated arrival time in Oban.

The vigorously waving crowd quickly disappeared behind a curtain of rain as the longship surged out of the harbour into the uninviting rough seas that awaited her in the Sound. But for our nervousness concerning the stability of the vessel, the first two hours' sailing could have been very enjoyable. The initially strong wind had quickly dropped down to a steady Force 4 and on a broad reach we plunged towards the mouth of the Sound at an average speed of 6 knots. It was still noticeable, however, that most of the crew preferred the relative security of the windward gunwale, regardless of the drenching rain and spray, to the greater shelter available on the lee side of the ship. With the *Raven* heeling over exuberantly before the wind it would have been an unimaginative person who settled himself so close to the water as it hissed past the hull only a few inches below the lower gunwale!

Bill Hook had arranged a meeting between ourselves and the *Highland Seabird*, a fast twin-hulled pleasure cruiser/ferry, somewhere off Oban, and radio contact with this ship verified the fact that the wind was still dropping – if a gale had been in the offing we would have almost certainly returned to Tobermory. The constant television filming to which we were now subjected was a direct result of the proximity of our present route to the mainland and the short distances between landfalls. From Norway until we had reached Portree we had been for most of the time the sole occupants of the seas surrounding us. However, between Portree and Oban our presence could be easily detected and our position quickly ascertained. For this period we felt that we had become no more than extras (unpaid, I might add) on the documentary film, and the whole purpose and historical significance of our voyage appeared to have slipped into the background. Our hosts in Skye, Mull and Oban made only passing references to the men in whose wake we were following, and one got the distinct impression that the importance of the Viking heritage of the area had been usurped by the more intense interest in later Scots history, the clan rebellions, for example, and the era of Bonnie Prince Charlie. We became for that short period of time simply a tourist attraction, which was not surprising as it was the height of summer; few people seemed to recognise the significance of the voyage or even that it could be classed as a dangerous undertaking. Thankfully, we were to find that from Oban onwards we escaped from such a constricting 'goldfish bowl', the media only interrupting our solitude once more before our eventual arrival on the Isle of Man.

Although it might appear from previous comments that the presence of the camera crew working with Bill Hook always caused irritation or friction, I must emphasise that most of our meetings were extremely amicable. It was a kind of love-hate relationship, the crew accepting that Bill had a difficult job and, more often than not, we acquiesced to his wishes; at the same time the aura which seemed to surround the longship and those aboard was something which we guarded most jealously, and the frequent incursions into our very close and private 'family' could not help but create a certain resentment. Our relationship with Bill Hook, David Scott, Jan Riddell and the camera team was always friendly, however, if a little sardonic at times, and apart from the incident on the night of the capsize, they were always made welcome whenever our paths coincided.

Their arrival in yet another chartered yacht ('No wonder the TV licence has gone up again!' remarked one of the crew) at our rendezvous point with the *Highland Seabird* was the signal for yet more filming of the longship at speed, this time contrasted with the dramatic sight of the *Seabird* roaring past her at 25 or 30 knots. The arrival of the Oban lifeboat on the scene led to a number of comments concerning our reputation for stability since the incident off Portree.

'Hey Bill, are you expecting another capsize?' Eddie Kaighin called on the radio to the TV boat.

'You can never be too careful!' was Bill Hook's reply.

In fact the lifeboat crew, having heard of our imminent arrival, had decided voluntarily to escort us into Oban harbour. For all the jocular comments that were being bandied about, their presence was very reassuring, especially as there were still quite a number of us whose confidence in the safety of the *Raven* had not quite been completely restored.

The rain continued unceasingly throughout the afternoon, and in our exposed position we were all thoroughly soaked but not necessarily miserable. When the lifeboat drew alongside and asked if any of us would like to come aboard for a cup of warming tea (the manoeuvres required for the filming had not allowed our galley to be utilised), the stampede for the side nearly caused a second capsize!

With the *Highland Seabird* preceding us at high speed towards Oban, those who had been lucky enough to gain access to the lifeboat revelled in the luxury of a roof over their heads and the scalding hot tea burning their throats. The sight of our shipmates hunched in the stern of the longship, their backs to the driving rain, made us realise how very exposed and unprotected our vessel really was; and it was with a tinge of regret that we left our benefactors after such a welcome respite.

As we entered the harbour at Oban we were again surprised and grateful to see how many spectators had braved the conditions in order to welcome us. The quayside was packed with people and it was apparent that the local tourist office had handled some very short-notice advertising with conspicuous success.

When we finally moored to the appointed jetty at eight o'clock in the evening it was an extremely wet and chilled crew who climbed ashore, leaving two of our number on watch for the evening; it was not a pleasant chore under the circumstances, and they made short work of unfurling the sail and stretching it across the foredeck as a shelter. For the rest of us the accommodation was in complete contrast to the luxuries experienced in Tobermory – it was the basement of a Youth Club. It was a jolting reminder that we were meant to be tough and hardy Vikings and that the comforts of the Western Isles Hotel must be considered as a very untypical form of accommodation.

Although our stopover in Oban was unscheduled the presence of the longship had obviously been well advertised, and when I went on watch at eight o'clock the following morning a large crowd of onlookers had already gathered on the quayside. As usual it was raining and the morning was spent tidying up the ship beneath the protection of the sail/tent, which also served to hide us from the scores of onlookers. This was our first experience of a mainland port in the tourist season since leaving Trondheim, and the constant procession of spectators to and from the ship was certainly very different from the quieter harbours of the islands. Few of us were enamoured by the continual requests to put on our Viking clothes (mainly from American tourists), and few such articles of apparel had survived the capsize. Nevertheless, Shane Lucas finally consented to satisfy their evident curiosity. In our opinion, this was a singularly foolish thing to do; as we suspected, with such a continuous turn-over of excited visitors, he was not allowed to change back into something more suited to the inclement conditions for the rest of the day.

Our final day in Oban dawned 'fine and sunny' (the shipboard expression normally used by anyone who climbed to the top of the mast to check the weather up there)! We were particularly grateful for this change for the better as we were expecting the imminent arrival of our benefactor of the sumptuous banquet we had been given in Tobermory, Geoff Atherton. At midday, beneath a cloudless summer sky we welcomed him and his passengers on board the ship which his efforts, along with many others, had enabled us to put to sea. We were particularly pleased to see Kathy Lewis again, along with Mick Kneale and his wife Cath. Mick had been one of the obvious candidates for the crew until his unfortunate accident a few weeks prior to our departure for Norway. As Geoff had missed the previous luncheon he had arranged on our behalf, he decided to repeat the festivities while in Oban. Yet again we were presented with a magnificent repast, to which we did more than justice.

If one gains the impression that our voyage had degenerated into a succession of magnificent feast, this is entirely understandable, but not necessarily true. On these two occasions we were certainly feted and the champagne flowed like the proverbial water, but when one realises that we were now relatively close to home, this was just a foretaste of the celebrations that were to follow when we reached our destination. Behind us lay over a thousand miles of unpredicatable sea, the memories of the cold, dampness, the wind and storm, and of course the capsize, still fresh in our minds. Ahead, only two hundred miles separated us from our families and the tumultuous reception we had been warned to expect on our arrival. We knew that our progress had been well reported in the Isle of Man and the constant stream of telegrams we had received since our departure from Norway continually reminded us of the importance of our voyage to the people of the Island. Small wonder, therefore, that we were beginning to feel that now the worst must be behind us. Complacency, I may add, certainly had not re-appeared among the crew, our experience off Portree having put paid to that. We were to remain in a state of perpetual alertness when at sea (a condition which could be construed as one of 'healthy fear') until the moment when we actually jumped over the side on to the beach at Peel. However, as each landfall brought us one step nearer to our destination so the tension on board was relieved more quickly and our enjoyment of the situation increased with the knowledge that, all too soon, our unique experience would be a thing of the past. The whole atmosphere that surrounded the crew, whether they were on board the longship or at some function ashore, was one of 'enjoy it to the utmost while you can!' We all realised that the voyage was quite literally 'the trip of a lifetime', and the odds on any of us ever being able to repeat such an experience were very remote. Consequently, as we drew inexorably nearer to home, our determination to savour every passing moment increased in proportion. Although the letters which accompanied Kathy Lewis, the first mail that most of us had received since leaving Norway, reminded us that our waiting families were now only a couple of hundred miles south

of us, such poignant anticipation seemed only to increase our determination to savour to the full our last few days at sea.

That final evening in Oban turned into a kaleidoscope of events which
summarised this overall feeling. For example, Robin Bigland's speech at
the dinner given in our honour by our hosts, the local council, for the first
time strayed from the usual serious expression of gratitude for the
hospitality afforded to us, to what can only be referred to as a risqué reply
full of double entendres, most of which were easy to interpret!

The party, which continued on board the longship until dawn, turned
out to be the last of such affairs that was to be held. The word 'party'
unfortunately conjures up a picture of noisy crowds and blaring music
which, for obvious reasons, was never the case as far as we were concerned. What usually happened, as it did on this occasion, was that a number
of the crew would return to the longship with a few drinks, content to sit
and talk together throughout the night. Often, though, late-night revellers
would be invited on board as is the custom among the yachting fraternity
the world over. On the evening in question, the low state of the tide had
left the *Raven* fifteen to twenty feet below the level of the jetty, the only
method of access or egress being by way of a rope. The scene can well be
imagined when a group of Scotsmen who had obviously partaken of a few
drams requested permission to come aboard. Their descent via the rope
was certainly novel, although all but one negotiated it successfully. The
last of their party seemed to experience great difficulty in actually finding
the rope in the first place and, fearful for his safety, we advised him not to
attempt the descent.

'Och, I'll be alright,' he slurred, his hands finally making contact.

So saying, he slid towards us with undoubted gracefulness but, with his
face a picture of bewildered consternation, continued his journey below
the level of the gunwale, and ended standing up chest-deep in the water.
He was no 'wee Scot', and it took four of us to haul him inboard.

In retrospect I found this frequent revelry when on land, which was
uncharacteristic of most of the crew under normal circumstances, an
interesting phenomenon. Most observers or critics would probably assume
that a more sensible occupation the night before sailing would be to rest as
much as possible in readiness for the energetic activities involved in
working such a complicated ship – bearing in mind that she had a proven
ability to carry out sudden and disconcerting manoeuvres! My only con-
clusion was that it was the knowledge of the potential dangers inherent in
a voyage such as ours, in virtually any type of weather, that created such
occasions. The methods of relaxation pursued on land were therefore
encouraged not only by the imminence of the next departure, but also by
the relief at having successfully over come the dangers that lay behind us.

Such a theory quickly became more plausible when, as we sailed out of
Oban the following afternoon in the usual damp and gusty conditions, I
studied the faces of my companions, which no doubt mirrored my own

expression. The strong wind and choppy seas were not new to us and it could be assumed that, after nearly five weeks under similar conditions, we would all have been relatively relaxed and confident. Although outwardly the jocund remarks relieved the monotony of the long hours, there was a powerful undercurrent of tension. The sudden whitening of knuckles when a stronger gust heeled the ship further over and hands gripped more tightly on to the gunwale or a nearby sheet; the crew-member sitting with the main halyard in hand ready to drop the sail the instant the order was given, or even before such a command, if he thought the situation warranted it; the fewer people asleep on the foredeck, with the exception of Arne Wisth who again stared unblinkingly at us from the bows; and a number of other almost indefinable differences all showed the increased tension on board. Apart from the obvious thoughts about one's own safety there was the added fear that the voyage could still, so easily, be brought to a premature end when we were practically in sight of our goal. The discussion about what lay ahead of us as we approached the Isle of Jura did nothing to slacken the tension.

'What do you mean "We're going through a whirlpool"?' I questioned Eddie Kaighin, butting in to his conversation with Robin Bigland.

'That's where we're going, boys,' he replied, to the crew in general. 'The Corryvreckan Whirlpool lies just behind that island.' He pointed to the small island of Scarba which lay off our starboard bow. 'If you hit that on a high spring tide with an onshore wind, then things can get exciting.'

'Is it by any chance, I mean just for the record, you know, to satisfy my curiosity – is it a spring tide today?' came a quietly plaintaive query from Richard Young.

'No, it's alright, Richard,' laughed Eddie. 'And anyway we're only going to pass through the outskirts of it. The centre of the whirlpool lies between Jura and Scarba, but our course lies across the edge of it. Anyway, the tidal race is probably more dangerous!'

Odd Børstad, who had been gradually assimilating all that was said, turned to me and said, in rather an anxious voice, 'Eddie is going to take us through a whirlpool now, is he?' I patted him on the shoulder in what I considered to be a comforting manner, before replying:

'Don't worry, Odd, Eddie's as experienced at taking a longship through a whirlpool as he is at taking one beneath the flame of an oil rig!'

Odd's sudden look of relief quickly changed to an expression of horror as the import of what I had just said sank in.

Thus it was with the crew in a state of nervous anticipation that the longship approached the dark area of ruffled water which marked the outer extremities of this famous whirlpool. The wind which had held us steadily on course for the previous three hours suddenly eased, which did nothing to reduce the feelings of anxiety in the heavily charged atmosphere. To sailors who know these shores, the Corryvreckan certainly has no reputation for the production of unpredictable and often violent seas, and if treated sensibly and with respect for its power, passage through the straits can be made with relative ease in modern boats. Although we had no plans to go near the centre of the vortex, for those of us on board without such intimate knowledge of this well-known feature of the area, our imagination ran riot. Pictures of sailing ships whizzing round in ever decreasing circles until they disappeared into a bottomless hole flashed through our minds as we felt the first effects of the unusual currents, a gentle but insistent tugging at the wooden strakes beneath our feet.

The sky had clouded over completely and the rocky shores of Jura, Scarba and the Mainland loomed close on either side as we entered the narrow mouth of the Sound. The atmosphere was electric with tension, the like of which we had never experienced. In the cold grey evening light, the longship sailed through that dark mysterious stretch of water, a seething mass of eddies and tiny whirlpools. Black ripples would suddenly erupt into waves large enough to cause the crew to grip their handholds tightly, yet the next minute we would glide serenely across a calm sea as black as pitch, the swirls and cavorting of the currents churning around the periphery until once more we felt the greedy waves pluck hungrily at our vessel. The whole area reeked of an awesome, frightening power which waited only for the word before unleashing its ferocity upon our frail cockleshell of a boat. It was as if the *Raven* were picking her way carefully across the surface of a bubbling, simmering, giant's cauldron which at any moment could suddenly erupt into a boiling turmoil of frenzied sea. That such a force lay waiting beneath us was illustrated graphically by the distant waves which crashed violently against the rocky cliffs of Jura, the spray rising 40 to 50 feet into the air before thundering down into the maelstrom beneath. The tremendous vibration one felt on the steering oar as the current plucked viciously at it, wrenching it in random grabs, and the incredible acceleration when a tidal rip held us inexorably in its grip, carrying the longship along at seven or eight knots, produced an impression of such careless might that the experience was totally unnerving – but unforgettably exhilarating. Corryvreckan has a justifiable notoriety. What that witches' brew could produce when Nature provided all the necessary ingredients was best left to the imagination, and I sincerely hope that no ancient longship ever ventured unwittingly into such waters unless the conditions were ideal.

It was interesting to hear, at a later date, of a theory produced by a Dutch historian who had sailed through the centre of this turmoil during a local sightseeing cruise. Apparently he claimed that the description in ancient Greek mythology of Jason passing through the whirlpool exactly fitted the brooding landscape which surrounded Corryvreckan. Not only that, but the recorded duration of his journey and the rough direction could have brought him to the exact spot! Such deductions are best left to experts in that particular field, but it is certain that the overpoweringly depressing aura that enveloped the place could lead romantic minds back into the shadowy mists of time. The picture can be imagined as an ancient Greek galley or, in our particular case, a Viking longship traversed the whirlpool, men straining desperately at the oars and the helmsman fearfully gripping the quivering tiller while the vicious tides hurled the ship to and fro, the jagged rocks and black staring cliffs waiting in anticipation on either side – and over all, the thunderous clouds rolling across the storm-laden sky. Dramatic stuff, but then the seething turmoil which so often lies hidden beneath the mists that roll down from the mountains of Jura encourages the mind into the realms of drama.

When finally the motion of the longship became more consistent it was clear that we had reached the outer limits of the troubled area, a final burst of short steep waves petulantly spitting us out into the 'normal' sea, and the *Raven* became a hubbub of noise as our experience was discussed by an awed crew.

With the low cloud cover and the gusty conditions, darkness came early that night and with it a cold north wind which chilled us to the bone. The contrasts in weather that we experienced on the voyage only lacked a blizzard or hurricane for completion, but we little expected such a low temperature so far south at the end of June. In the intense blackness of midnight the *Raven* crept slowly and cautiously into the shelter of a small bay nestling at the southern end of Jura, our only guide a single speck of light on the shore which we presumed emanated from a croft or farmhouse. With a shattering noise the anchor was dropped over the side and we came to a gentle halt, the sudden silence only broken by the occasional bark of a lonely seal somewhere out in the darkness.

For the few hours that remained until the dawn light once again gave us an opportunity to see our course, few if any of the crew managed to sleep. The cold wind and icy drizzle cut through our protective clothes and, unable to move around to any great extent, we huddled together for warmth on the open deck. The gallons of coffee produced by Odd Børstad during those long hours of the graveyard watch were gratefully received, but only succeeded in making the cold more intense once the sudden warmth had dissipated. Eddie Kaighin's cry of 'Get the sail up boys!' as the cold light of dawn crept tentatively over the horizon was met with a cheer of relief, and rarely had the vessel been made ready for sea in such haste – so much so that Odd Børstad, who had been cooking breakfast when the order was given, was left holding his enormous frying pan complete with 16 sizzling eggs. In a kind of stupified horror we watched him as he shrugged his shoulders angrily and tossed the entire contents over the side. As if in slow motion our breakfast sailed serenely through the air and landed in the cold, grey sea – tiny splashes that extinguished any hopes of hot food for the next few hours. This was not the first occasion that our otherwise thoughtful skipper had caused such hardship. More often than not he would give an order which sent us scurrying to our positions, coffee mugs and sandwiches flying in all directions, without realising at first the chaos he thus caused. The problem was that he would be poring over the chart-table calculating the necessary course and, without looking up, would suddenly issue an order. Unfortunately this had occurred quite frequently during meal-times, but Odd Børstad had always taken such interruptions in good spirit. This particular morning, however, the cold sleepless night had left its mark on all of us, and the cook, the most equable of men normally, was no exception.

Once under way there was no further chance of hot sustenance and we resigned ourselves to a long, hungry day. Our route lay due south towards the harbour of Port Ellen on the southern coast of Islay, the last of the Scottish Isles at which we were to call. The weather for a change was ideal for fast sailing, the sky overcast but with only the occasional fine shower of drizzle to cause us any discomfort. 'Reaching' before a strong north westerly wind we surfed our way down the Sound of Jura at a steady 8 knots, the *Raven* swooping over the waves with her unique and delicately graceful action. It was the perfect sea for her, the knife-like prow splitting the crests of the waves at just the right angle to send the spray cascading on either side, very little actually falling inboard. It was exhilarating sailing and the unusual sight of two killer-whales as they moved majestically past us heading northwards, their sleek black backs dipping rhythmically into the rolling waves, was an experience not easily to be forgotten. With such careless power seemingly at their disposal, it was unlikely that even the turbulent waters of Corryvreckan would cause them much discomfort.

By mid-morning, Odd Børstad's natural good humour had returned and the warmth of his coffee soon dispelled the last of our memories of the cold sleepless night and the loss of our breakfast. It was at about this time that somebody noticed three small specks approaching us from Jura. As they came swiftly towards us we discerned that they were canoes, or 'kayaks', each powered by a single paddler. We were amazed at the speed with which they closed on us, for although the wind had abated slightly we were still forging ahead at an estimated four or five knots. When our visitors finally caught up with us and came alongside we tied their flimsy looking craft to our cleats and invited them aboard for coffee, having ascertained that their next port of call was also Port Ellen, still some twenty five miles distant.

During the following few hours the *Raven*, with her convoy of kayaks nestling astern like ducklings behind their mother, sped southward, and we listened in fascination to the stories our guests recounted of their various exploits. We had come to consider our own voyage as a fairly hazardous and adventurous undertaking, but to listen to this completely self-effacing trio, two ladies and a gentleman, none of whom with all due respect could have been under fifty years old, made our trip appear very

155

mediocre in comparison. Having circumnavigated Ireland the previous year (a casual off-the-cuff remark) they were at present engaged in an extended voyage around the islands of the Outer Hebrides. In fact they had come through the Straits of Corryvreckan only 24 hours before our own lively passage across the outer extremities of that turbulent area! We considered the longship to be somewhat of a cockleshell but the sight of those tiny craft bouncing like corks in our wake made our own efforts seem very small in comparison.

The presence of our surprise companions, or rather their kayaks, necessitated constant adjustments to our speed, to avoid swamping the frail structures. We had learnt by now that the alteration of the sail area by relatively minor adjustments in the height of the yard caused an immediate reaction in the forward speed of the longship. With the wind blowing constantly from one direction, but varying in intensity, this meant a busy few hours for Richard Young and myself on the main halyard as we tried to keep a steady speed. Hauling the heavy yard up and down at any time was tiring work, but having to carry out minor adjustments all the time was particularly strenuous and in some ways we were extremely grateful when our guests took their leave some five miles out of Port Ellen. Although we had enjoyed their company, the need to reduce our speed meant that we had missed the opportunity of really testing the longship on a long run in near-perfect sailing conditions. Perhaps the experience of meeting such resourceful people made up for the loss, although the sailors among us were not necessarily of the same opinion.

In the early evening, an extremely tired Viking crew sailed into the midst of perhaps the most evocative reception we were to encounter on the whole voyage. The now familiar wail of the bagpipes lured us towards the crowded jetty. As we sailed across the last few yards of water which separated us from those that awaited our arrival, the beautifully clear and melodic sound of children's voices singing a Gaelic song of welcome echoed across the harbour, drifting towards the distant rolling hills which lay capped by misty clouds. Eddie Kaighin was obviously so overcome that, for the first and only time on landing, he misjudged the distance from the jetty and our arrival on Islay was accompanied by a resounding crash as the great serpent-head on our prow devoured, rather than hissed at, part of the landing stage!

We were to stay on Islay for three days, as the guests of Rod and Sue Walker in their hotel, the Machrie. It was to this hotel that the crew repaired, where the comfort and good food once again provided the sharpest of contrasts to our lives as boat people. It was this constant fascinating metamorphosis that etched experiences so deeply into our memories.

The day following our arrival the crew were conducted around the Bowmore Distillery, Islay being famous for its production of malt whisky. Such an event guaranteed a 100% attendance and the learned arguments on the quality of the product required the tasting of a large number of samples. We felt, quite naturally, that as we had been warned that our presence would be required in a number of similar establishments on the island, our prognostications on the subtle differences between individual malts called for extensive research at each distillery. The evening seemed to arrive more quickly than normal and, with it, the crew of our sister ship, H.M. Submarine *Odin*. In view of the island ceilidh which followed such a meeting, the residents of the hotel must have been extremely glad that most of us were billeted in the beautifully equipped little cottages adjoining the hotel.

It had been arranged by Bill Hook (who else!) that the submarine and the longship would be filmed together at sea, a meeting of ships that spanned a thousand years. Robin Bigland, Richard Young, Arne Wisth and myself had accosted the captain at a convenient time during the ceilidh with the request to accompany him on the submarine during the filming. To this he had immediately assented, and on yet another cold and showery morning we were duly ferried out to the waiting vessel. I don't think that man has devised more deadly-looking ships than these hunters of the depths, the overwhelming sense of evil exemplified by their morbid black colour, the darkness totally unrelieved by any recognition number or letter.

Her Majesty's submariners are, by the nature of their calling, hardy men and we had nothing but admiration for the self-control that each man must exert to live harmoniously, as they undoubtedly do, in the desperately constricting confines of the dripping cigar tube that is the interior of a submarine. God knows we were short enough of space on *Odin's Raven*, but the interior of *Odin* left us stunned by the sheer non-existence of any spare 'Lebensraum' whatever. A fascinating experience was to peer at the *Raven* through the attack periscope as we submerged and then surfaced alongside her. The sea was extremely choppy, a Force 8 gale in the offing, and to my certain knowledge there were some very sore heads (on both vessels) moving uneasily on the waters that day, but every man in both crews performed with discipline.

Robin Bigland recorded in his diary, following this meeting between the two *Odins*:

'In the case of *Odin* (the submarine), those who wear the porpoise badge do not earn it lightly, but our own boys really do look like a crew. I think I can allow myself a moment of justifiable pride in their achievement. Eddie is a damned good sailing master and I made a good choice in his selection. For the rest, they have all fulfilled and exceeded my hopes and expectations. It is a pity Alan Binns isn't with us now, I think it would have done his old heart good to see the mature crew in action.'

Our stay on board the submarine was extended due to the difficulty experienced by the BBC helicopter in locating us, a thick sea mist having virtually obliterated this epic meeting. Nevertheless, far too soon for us, a remorseless clatter announced their arrival and we transferred back to the fresh air (and dampness) of our own *Odin*, while the submariners who had been afforded the reciprocal honour on board the longship returned to the confines of their submarine. A generous gift of champagne from the Royal Navy toasted this unique mid-ocean event, and with the wind increasing by the minute the two examples of such differing eras of maritime power went their separate ways: the *Odin* to the silence and coldness of the deep ocean, her thin, deadly shape sliding quickly and purposefully below the mounting waves; while the *Raven*, bucking and gyrating in the short steep seas, sped back into the safety of Port Ellen harbour, her crew soaked through but well pleased with the morning's work.

That afternoon Robin Bigland received our replacement Viking costumes which had been generously loaned to us by the Up-Helly-Aa Committee in Shetland who had learnt of our misfortunes. With all due respect to our good friends in Lerwick, after our own homespun clothing the new gear looked better suited for a quick performance of *The Prince and The Pauper* on stage, with its velvet and garish colours. Although we realised the importance of landing in Peel properly attired for the occasion, our hearts quailed at the thought of wading ashore clothed in purple tunics, golden breastplates and sheepskin-covered wellington boots! The mutinous mutterings which rapidly grew in volume, interspersed with hysterical laughter as various crew-members tried on different combinations, were quickly quelled by Robin Bigland's unequivocal decision that either we wore the garments or made our own. There followed a concerted rush for the least colourful of the clothes, followed by a dedicated search through the out-houses adjacent to the hotel for old 'Viking' sacks or anything which could be converted to tunics. In the event such combinations proved perfectly adequate, but we all deeply regretted the unfortunate loss of the original gear to which we had grown very attached or, to be more truthful, which had become very attached to our bodies!

After a very rare early night, there followed a day during which we allowed ourselves to be transported from one function to another. This included a luncheon, a trip to the local lifeboat, visits to the Laphroig distillery, a dairy (a strange combination which amused us greatly), the local hospital and, of course, the inevitable museum. Our last night on Islay was spent in predictable fashion, the hotel bar and local discotheque receiving the dubious benefits of our presence. Perhaps such activities were not the most sensible in view of the forecast for the next day which gave strong winds and rough seas. Breakfast the following morning was a quiet affair, the crew half-listening to the moaning north-westerly wind as it drove the cold sleeting rain across the fields outside the hotel. Our schedule was now necessarily tight; it was essential that we arrive on the Isle of Man in four days' time, the day before Her Majesty the Queen was due to open Tynwald, the Manx Parliament, whose celebration of the Millennium was the initial motivation for our voyage, and we knew that only a full-blown gale would keep the longship moored to the jetty, so we prepared ourselves for an uncomfortable night's voyage to Portpatrick, our final port-of-call before Man itself.

Before saying our farewells, we were driven to the grave reputed to be that of Godred Crovan, known to all Manxmen, quite mistakenly, as 'King Orry'. History relates how he became the first documented Viking ruler of the kingdom of Man, and possibly the Western Isles, the ancient domain through which we had voyaged during the previous four weeks. It was a poignant moment as we stood in the drenching rain beside that ancient grave among the wild heather and rock-strewn landscape. It was virtually certain that we had followed the route taken by this Icelandic-born Viking of old as he travelled throughout his domains nearly a thousand years before us, and on that bleak Islay hillside our paths had crossed yet again. As a token of our respect we left some wild flowers on the massive headstone marking the site but, in retrospect, if Godred Crovan had been half the warrior history claims him to be, then perhaps those fierce blue eyes would be crinkling in laughter as he looked down from Valhall and saw our little offering!

In the early hours of the afternoon we set sail beneath a leaden overcast sky, the promised north-westerly driving us quickly away from the little jetty and the good friends we had made during our brief stay on that beautiful island. The pouring rain had continued unabated throughout the day, and with the wind almost directly astern we were in for a very wet but fast sail, down past the Mull of Kintyre to the small port of Port-patrick on the Mull of Galloway.

Unknown to us, as we rounded the buoy which marked the outer limits of the harbour, the sea was to have one final attempt at bringing our voyage to a premature end in its reluctance to allow such a ghostly messenger from the past the pleasure of a final easy passage to her ultimate destination.

CHAPTER ELEVEN

In the wake of Godred Crovan

Tradition states that when Godred Crovan came to the Isle of Man in 1079 he landed on a bright starry night. Those who waited on the shore asked from where he had come and, in answer, he pointed up to the Milky Way. 'Yonder is the road whence I came,' he replied, 'and along that star-spangled dome is the way that leads to my country.' Since that time, the Manx translation of the Milky Way has been Raad Mooar Ree Gorry, or 'The Great Way of King Orry'. (The name Godred in Manx was Gorree, since anglicised to Orry.) It is thought that Godred's home was on Islay and it was on that island that he died, in 1095, although Manx tradition has it that he died on Man, his remains lying buried at Maughold on the North East coast.

In the gathering gloom of the evening following our departure from Port Ellen the heavy rain clouds moved menacingly over the longship, thus putting paid to any possibility of the *Raven* following 'the Great Way of King Orry'. The strong north-westerly wind, estimated at Force 5 or 6, blew from almost directly astern, driving the *Raven* before it. The rain, our constant companion for the majority of the voyage to date, never let up for an instant, forcing those of the crew who were not on watch to find what shelter they could below the gunwale.

The route from Islay to the southern-most promontory of the Mull of Kintyre lies open to the Atlantic, the ocean swell forced to become shorter and steeper as it squeezes its way down the narrow North Channel which divides Ireland from Scotland. For the first few hours of the sail the tide and wind were certainly not in empathy with each other; the resulting waves crashed against our hull and showered us with yet more water. The violent pitching and rolling of the ship kept any movement on deck down to a minimum, and the crew were glad that no sudden coarse-changes were in the offing which might have necessitated altering the set of the sail. Conversation on board was sporadic, most of us wedged tightly

Sleeping positions when safely anchored. Two's company, three's a crowd, sixteen is ridiculous!

Brian Cousins fixing the sail to the yard arm. A dangerous job in rough weather.

The 'swamp' open for business!

Approaching Stornoway, Isle of Lewis.

The Chieftain and Helmsman relax at anchor.

Under full sail, a few seconds before disaster struck.

The old and the new. *Odin's Raven* sails past H.M.S. *Mohawk*, off Peel.

The final landfall at Peel, July 4th 1979.

between the kists, curled up in almost foetal positions as we tried to protect ourselves from the constant drenching from both the spray and the rain. Most of us were either trying to sleep or were lost in our own thoughts. We were now very close to home, the voyage nearly completed, and our brief period as Vikings almost over. As our vessel reared and plunged her way towards the Isle of Man, my mind flicked back over the last seven weeks and, like turning the pages of a photograph album, the memories came flooding back. I was lost in a reverie of our stay in Norway when Nigel Woods' voice brought me back to the present.

'What on earth's that over there?' he exclaimed, pointing out across the port bow.

The huddled figures crouched between the kists slowly unfurled, and keeping our anorak hoods tied tightly around our faces as protection we peered over the gunwale across the turbulent sea. In the distance a small black object some two miles ahead slowly emerged from the foaming wave-crests, solidifying into the familiar shape of the conning-tower of a submarine.

'It's not the *Odin*, is it?' somebody asked, as our visitor from the depths drew nearer.

'No, it's too big,' said Robin Bigland, who was peering at it through his binoculars.

'Looks like a nuclear sub, judging from her size,' Eddie Kaighin commented. 'And she's really moving, too.'

It was indeed an impressive sight: with the rain-blurred shadow of the mountainous Mull of Kintyre looming behind it, the menacing black conning-tower, rising vertically from the sea, forged past a few hundred yards off our port side — the massive bow-wave and rapidly-widening wake churning the sea into a creamy froth. As we watched, two figures appeared on top of the conning tower, each with an arm raised in greeting. We acknowledged the unusual meeting in a similar fashion and I wondered what kind of picture we, in our turn, presented to them. With the open Atlantic behind us and the *Raven* surging spray-covered into the steep white-capped seas with her sail full-spread before her, we must have looked a dramatically spectacular sight.

As quickly as she had surfaced she disappeared, slipping quickly and silently beneath the surface into the quieter and presumably much calmer depths of the ocean.

'Was she one of ours?' Georgie Kneale enquired of no one in particular.

'No way you can tell,' replied Richard Young as he resettled himself below the gunwale. 'They don't carry any identification marks and, if you remember the lads on the *Odin*, even their hats just say H.M. Submarine, with no name printed on them.'

'Must have seen us on their periscope and popped up for a quick look,' Eddie remarked as he snuggled himself down by the chart-table, returning to his task of navigating us safely down the North Channel.

The brief flurry of excitement proved too little to keep the conversation going and soon everyone was again concerned with their own thoughts, and the more urgent problems of trying to stem increasingly frequent trickles of water which percolated through our oil-skins.

The low clouds presaged an early onset of darkness as the *Raven* closed on the Mull itself and the expected Atlantic rollers began to make themselves felt. The tide had turned, and running with the wind as we were, the motion of the longship altered accordingly. Instead of crashing into the short seas, these larger waves tended to lift the ship up as they rolled beneath and carry her on their crests for a short time and then as they swept on their way we seemed to slide backwards, the figurehead lifting into the sky as the stern dropped down into the deep troughs.

When my turn arrived to take over the helm, sometime early in the morning, we were passing through the narrowest part of the North Channel. In such a comparatively constricted area, the waves shortened and increased in height, the crests breaking into sheets of foam as they lifted us on their backs. It was a totally new experience as far as I was concerned and I have to admit to being a little nervous until I had grown used to the quite exhilerating motion. Standing at the steering-oar, a safety rope tied around my waist, I was looking along the length of the ship. The effect of such a movement therefore was far more exaggerated than it had appeared from my previous position, amidships. With the approach of each wave, the stern would be lifted up at an acute angle to such an extent that I had to brace myself against the tiller to avoid falling forwards. The bow of the ship would drop away until it was pointing down into the blackness of the trough between two waves, before slowly rising as the apex of the wave rolled beneath us. The virtually flat bottom of the long-ship emphasised this movement as we really were 'floating' on the water, following the contours of each wave like a piece of driftwood as it rides the combers up to the beach. As the crest of each wave creamed along the keel-plank, the *Raven* would be carried forward with careless abandon, literally surfing with almost a third of the hull out of the water, the foaming crest stretching out on either side as it surged along the length of the ship. When the crest passed beneath, so the stern would suddenly drop down into the following trough, the sail cracking viciously as the wind spilled out, and the serpent head at the prow soaring upwards to leave me, on the helm, some ten feet below it. The whole dramatic sequence was immeasurably heightened by the surrounding darkness, against which the whiteness of the breaking wave tops formed a striking and eerie contrast.

'Try and hold her steadier, Mike,' shouted Eddie Kaighin against the howl of the wind as the bow swung out fifteen degrees from our course, the surging waves taking command of the steering-oar.

'I can't do anything about it, Eddie,' I yelled back to him in the comparative lull between waves. 'She just swings away of her own accord.'

All my energies were now concentrated on trying to hold the tiller against the powerful force of the waves, there being little point in trying to follow the compass course. The state of wind and sea was such that any direction other than that in which the waves themselves were moving would have placed us in immediate danger of broaching, and we had first-hand knowledge of what would happen if the sail was allowed to turn broadside to a wind of such strength.

The conditions were now such that none of the crew were content to site comfortably beside their kists. Most of them were standing near a rope or sheet, with two on the main halyard and Rick Tomlinson on the Rakke downhaul, in case the sea took command and swung us around sideways.

Eddie Kaighin, working on the old adage that 'you never learn any-thing unless you experience it', was close at hand in case I required his help, but was content to allow me to remain on the helm if I so desired – which I certainly did. It was one of the most exciting experiences of my life, not doubt heightened by the very real danger that was present, but this was the kind of sailing for which most of us had originally volunteered. At that moment in time we felt closer to the original Vikings than on any previous occasion, especially as the particular area of sea was renowned for such conditions, thereby implying that our predecessors had quite certainly experienced journeys of a similar nature.

Nevertheless, after half an hour of the strenuous effort required to hold the vibrating steering-oar as steady as possible, I was beginning to feel extremely tired and was just about to request a relief when I noticed that most of the crew had turned and were staring behind me, their faces registering a certain amount of consternation.

'What are you all staring at?' I shouted, more than a trace of nervousness creeping into my voice.

'Don't worry, Mike,' Robin Bigland said, managing to raise a grin even though he was extremely worried about our safety. 'But I advise you not to look behind you.'

Nothing could be more guaranteed to rouse my inquisitive nature at the best of times, but under the prevailing conditions turning my head to look behind was a rapid reflex action!

The size of the approaching wave, the object of everyone's alarmed looks, seemed to me to be higher than any comparable object I could bring to mind. It was afterwards estimated at no more than 20 or 25 feet high, but as the stern started to lift and the bow to drop with a sickening plunge I was convinced that it was on a par with the North face of the Eiger.

'Just hold on and try and keep her steady, Mike!' yelled Eddie Kaighin.

I didn't bother to attempt an answer; the force of the water as it sucked at the steering-oar required all my attention. The phrase 'going up like an express train' sprung into my mind as the massive wave picked us up like a piece of flotsam, driving us through the darkness amid a maelstrom of foaming surf. There was no way that I could hold her, and inexorably the bow began to swing across the line of seething water. Five degrees, ten, fifteen, twenty; how far she went I've no idea, but the sudden heel as the sail caught the full force of the wind and the massive inrush of 'green' water which poured over the gunwale, drenching Arne Wisth who had taken refuge right up in the prow, brought a leap of fear into our eyes. 'My God, she's going to go', I thought, as Eddie Kaighin grabbed the opposite side of the tiller and together we heaved against the inexorable strength of the sea. Slowly, very slowly, the *Raven* swung back on to her course and everybody heaved a sigh of relief, especially those who were on the main halyards. They had been poised to drop the yard to the deck, an emergency measure which nobody fancied having to carry out even as a last resort. A controlled lowering, yes; but to let go of the main sheet and allow that solid tree-trunk of pine to crash to the deck complete with 60 square metres of billowing sail was a desperate measure in the extreme. Yet if the *Raven* had continued swinging broadside-on, there would have been no alternative.

The wave which had been the cause of the excitement disappeared into the darkness ahead and, as if sulking at its lack of success, the sea began to ease a little almost immediately, although the waves still loomed menacingly large as they rolled relentlessly beneath our stern.

'Okay Mike, I'll take over now,' said Eddie Kaighin once the danger had passed. I nodded thankfully and transferred the safety rope to his waist.

'You Bilge Rats have all the fun,' was his parting comment as I staggered forward along the pitching deck, my aching arms grabbing for handholds on any available object, animate or otherwise. His comment was obviously a reference to Richard Young's predicament earlier in the voyage when, on the way from the oil-rigs to Lerwick, he had suddenly found himself holding the full weight of the steering oar, the leather strap attaching it to the fulcrum having suddenly split apart.

It was not until five o'clock in the morning that we neared the entrance to the harbour at Portpatrick and, with the heavy swell allowing no margin for error, a drenched and exhausted crew raised no objections when the engine was started up. As the *Raven* glided through the incredibly narrow entrance the soaring swooping rhythm ceased, and we suddenly found ourselves moving sedately across the stillness of calm waters towards a vacant mooring. Shivering in the cold of the dawn hour, sixteen bleary-eyed men peered around at the other boats in the harbour. We had heard that some Manx boats had planned to come up to Portpatrick to meet us and to act as an escort on the final leg of the journey down to Peel. Sure enough, on three other yachts the 'Three Legs of Man' flag rustled gently in the breeze, the high walls of the quayside sheltering the harbour from the main force of the wind, which had in any case fallen quite rapidly during the previous hour.

With our vessel safely moored to the satisfying stability of the stone quay, most of the crew settled down to sleep; but Colin Bowen, Robin

Bigland and David Eames climbed the steps to the road flanking the harbour where they were accosted by some late-night revellers who insisted they join them for some coffee and a celebratory glass or two. Some others in the crew, with that gleeful sense of mischief that invariably accompanies the rude awakening one is about to deliver to a friend enjoying a well-earned rest, raided one of the Manx yachts in the sure knowledge that after a few understandable grumbles they would be afforded a most cordial reception.

For my own part the strenuous activity and lack of sleep since leaving Islay had left me totally exhausted and, with utter disregard for the persistent drizzle, I lay down full length on the deck of the longship and collapsed into a dreamless sleep.

After what seemed like minutes, but in fact was four hours, I was nudged into awareness by the sound of piercing children's voices, somewhere above me:

'I tell you, they ARE alive, I just saw one move!'

'Doesn't look very comfortable, does it?'

'Real Vikings didn't wear oil-skins anyway!'

I peered up at the quayside from underneath my arm, to be confronted by a crowd of onlookers staring down at the ship.

'Hey, look, that one's waking up'. The surruptitious movement of my head had been noticed and, since the noisy presence of spectators rendered further sleep impossible, I eased my stiff body into a sitting position. The voices had woken the rest of the crew who had remained aboard so, with an alacrity born from experience we climbed to the top of the quayside, fended off the usual questions such as 'When does the raping begin?' and 'Have you got a loo on board?' with Viking-like grunts and made our way to the Mount Stewart Hotel where Mike, the proprietor, made us all most welcome.

A relaxing session in the bar at lunchtime was rudely cut short when Colin Bowen arrived to inform us that our presence was once more required on the ship: apparently we were to put to sea again and effect a second arrival, in order that we could be properly and officially welcomed! Later reference to Robin Bigland's log acquainted me with the events which led up to this highly unusual and ill-received (by the crew) decision.

'At about 7.30,' he wrote, 'I went to the Port Patrick Hotel for breakfast accompanied by Colin and David. An excessively garrulous waiter badgered us throughout the meal with what he obviously thought were hilarious references to our likely prowess as Vikings with the local girls. We were heartily glad when he was called away to the telephone! I succeeded in persuading the receptionist that a room with a shower was the least form of hospitality fitting to be offered to a Viking Chieftain with some of his crew. We were provided with what had to be the noisiest bedroom in the entire hotel, being at the foot of the main staircase, it being also the habit of the numerous children who infested the place to jump the last 3 or 4 steps to the floor. However, we were dog-tired and arranged ourselves rapidly for sleep. To my fury, after what seemed like a few minutes there was a heavy knock on the door. A chambermaid was eventually admitted, who looked with some wonderment at three strangely arrayed, hirsute men sharing the same small bedroom, but told me a local Councillor was seeking a meeting with me in Reception. Cursing the unfortunate man for a thoughtless churl under my breath, we met, and he launched into a lengthy diatribe about how we were expected at 3 o'clock in the afternoon, a big reception had been laid on and other considerations, indicating that it was damned thoughtless of us to upset his plans! Frankly, I could cheerfully have committed violence upon him but, summoning some shreds of self control, I patiently explained that we had travelled through the night in a tricky sea in a small boat and that whilst whenever possible we fitted in with local requirements, there was no anchorage of any description available to us in the sea conditions which prevailed at the time and we had therefore been forced to arrive in Portpatrick as best we might. I did not spare him details of the perils of the deep and it was a rather chastened local Councillor who thanked me most effusively when I offered to take out *Odin's Raven* to the open sea again that afternoon and be escorted in by the local lifeboat to music by the local pipe-band.'

We always found it amazing that on nearly every one of our landfalls our arrival coincided so closely with the estimated hour. In Lewis and Skye, for example, the longship had travelled with such alacrity that we were only too grateful for the extra hours thus gained, to relax and recover from the previous 'leg'. In Portpatrick the opposite had occurred, and this lack of awareness of the difficulties inherent in piloting a vessel such as ours, let alone the ability to effect an entrance at the precise time requested by the local council, was met with some irritation by the crew. Nevertheless, to please our hosts, the crew, still very tired and grumbling vociferously about the ridiculousness of the situation (the longship having lain in full view of everyone for the last nine hours), rowed out of the harbour into the choppy water. The presence of the lifeboat did nothing to lessen our antipathy towards the perpetrators of this outing, some of the crew taking it as a personal affront to the seaworthiness of their craft! In point of fact the boat in question was so laden with local dignitaries and photographers that in the event of a catastrophe it was far more likely that we would become the rescuers!

The prevailing conditions of a lively sea and pleasant breeze created an enjoyable sail as we journeyed up and down the coast for an hour or so, at one stage providing the passengers on a passing Manx ferry, the *Ben-My-Chree*, with an unscheduled preview of the longship.

At the appointed hour we entered the harbour for the second time that day, but this time under sail. As the wind was in the right quarter, Eddie Kaighan produced a superb example of seamanship and brought in the *Raven* in a wide sweeping curve, helming her neatly alongside the appropriate steps. It must be admitted that for all our complaints at having to make the extra trip out to sea, the reception afforded us more than compensated for the rest we had been denied. The whole area of the harbour was a mass of clapping, waving people, many of whom, we were later to discover, had travelled quite long distances in order to welcome us to Portpatrick. A large pipe-band serenaded our transition from ship to land, their stirring music leading the melee that followed, supposedly a parade along the main road of the town.

Our second day in Portpatrick developed into one of complete contrasts. The morning was occupied with a number of interviews for television, Bill Hook having crept quietly back on to the scene, arriving by way of the common motor-car for a change.

In the afternoon, Robin ordained that a full dress-rehearsal of our final landfall was a necessity, to prevent any last-minute unforeseen problems arising that could embarass us in front of the expected multitude at Peel. We had been reliably informed, from telephone conversations with our families, that a reception committee of an estimated 15,000 to 20,000 people would be on hand to welcome us home.

Accordingly the longship was again manned, this time under oars, and for two hours we practised running her ashore on to the small sandy beach inside the harbour. It was, in fact, very important that such a manoeuvre was given maximum attention, as at no time during the voyage had a suitable opportunity presented itself, all our landfalls having been carried out alongside convenient jetties. Certain discomforts inherent in such an operation became quickly apparent, not the least being the tendency for our boots to fill rapidly with water when we jumped into the shallow surf. This was not only uncomfortable but when, as the plan required, we tried to reboard the longship, the excess weight demanded an almost superhuman effort and a most ungainly scrabbling at the gunwale!

It was intended that we walk up the beach, across the area of sand which would be kept clear of sightseers, and present the varius gifts we had recieved to the Governor of the Isle of Man and the Bishop. For example, we planned to hand over the symbolic stone, hewn from the 12th-century structure of Trondheim Cathedral, presented by the Bishop of Trondheim and transported with us on the voyage. Robin Bigland was to give this to the Reverend Vernon Nicholl, Bishop of Sodor and Man, it being intended that the stone should be incorporated into the fabric of St. German's Church in Peel, which was to be made the new Manx Cathedral.

Three of our friends who had sailed from Man to meet us, John Martin, Stuart Collister and Jan Maugham, stood in for the Bishop, the Governor and Lady Paul respectively. Having perfected our landing technique, which necessitated wading ashore, two men having previously taken out 'springs' which were to be attached to two strategically placed posts, the crew then formed a semi-circle while the ceremonies proceeded.

John Martin as the Bishop took his part very seriously and managed to keep a deadpan face against some of the more irreverent comments to which he was subject, but Jan (as Lady Paul) found the event a trifle more disconcerting as she attempted to fend off the amorous advances made towards her, such behaviour no doubt encouraged by the words 'I want to marry a millionaire' which were emblazoned across her T-shirt! If the crew intended to react in a similar fashion with the real Lady Paul, she was in for a big surprise!

The Governor's wife, 'Godmother' to the *Raven* and her crew, was as we well knew blessed with a cheerful sense of humour, but Robin Bigland requested that none of us should make any comment to her about the cake which she had so generously presented to the crew, via Kathy Lewis, at Oban. With all due respect, her Ladyship's culinary prowess had defied even our wide-ranging palates, as well as dulling our seaman's knives! The only crew-member who had consumed some slices with alacrity had been Dave Eames but, unfortunately, as we had learnt from long experience, such a test in no way guaranteed the edibility of any food.

The successful completion of the practice session was over-shadowed by the certain knowledge that on the day, in spite of Robin Bigland's absolute belief in both his and Kathy Lewis's powers of organisation, the 'clear area of beach' available to us would in fact be a seething mass of people – thereby nullifying all of our careful plans. Within 48 hours we were to be proved utterly correct, with a vengeance!

That evening, the night before our departure on the final leg, Robin gave a private dinner party for the crew alone in the Portpatrick Hotel. It was to be his own personal 'thank you' to the crew for assisting him in the realisation of a dream which had occupied most of his waking moments for the previous eighteen months. As such he spared no expense, and provided a most sumptuous meal. Realising that the proceedings were likely to become fairly rowdy, Robin had cautioned the manager that we needed somewhere a bit off the beaten track. This he certainly provided, and we might just as well have eaten in the cellars! However, such a lowly setting in no way detracted from the excellence of the cuisine. Knowing the capacity of his shipmates, following the pre-prandial champagne and canapes, Robin provided a bottle of Chablis for each member of the crew to accompany the fish and a bottle of Chateau Meyney to accompany the entree. The party was a great success, to put it mildly!

Everybody became tremendously sentimental, and as often happens when emotion begins to overtake the Islander, we fell to abusing each other roundly at the same time telling each other what tremendous fellows we really were. Several crew members made speeches and, as Robin recorded in his log, '. . . There was a moment or two when I might easily have "piped my eye," so freely had we drunk and so warm was our comradeship.'

Perhaps the best speech made by any of the 'other ranks' was that by Arne Wisth, who was more than a little the worse for wear. He was utterly unable to complete a single sentence, collapsing with laughter every few words until, finally, he just slid quietly under the table to ringing applause from us all.

Robin's own speech so moved his crew that most, if not all, were hard pressed to fight off the emotions that welled up within us. Our vessel had carried us across 1,800 miles of some of the most dangerous waters in the world and had been our home for the previous two months. His eloquent words so mirrored our own feelings, although in prose that few of us could match, that I requested a copy of the speech, which I now reproduce in its entirety.

The Chieftain's Speech given at the Farewell Dinner in Portpatrick – Monday July 2, 1979

'Our Somerleid is about to pass into memory. The last Vikings will soon have swallowed the scraps of the Magic Mushroom that rolled back the centuries to the days when our soul brothers rode their own long serpents west over the sea. So the dream of yesterday wakens into today's reality. Let us take a moment or two for reflection before the dream fades for ever and gather round us for a moment the shades of Godred Crovan, our own King Orry, and Sigurd, Earl of Orkney and Somerleid, Lord of the Isles. Men who carved themselves names etched deep in the steely history of these Western Isles, bid them welcome to the table and toast their immortal memory. Soon, some of us for the last time, we shall step aboard our old friend and secret mistress, *Odin's Raven*. We all know there were two ravens of Odin, Hugin and Munin, Thought and Memory, but she is well named for she is both, never far from our thoughts and for ever in our memories. Shall any of us ever forget her undulating grace as the sail fills and she glides across the ocean, proud, gracious, a thoroughbred, a true mistress, Sea-Wife and Sea-Mother, bearing us and protecting us from the sea, the old grey widow-maker with whom she alone holds communion. Down the years we shall look on her perhaps in company with a crowd of idle-tongued, unknowing sightseers and the memories will come flooding back and we shall blink and swallow as though the cooking smoke from Odd's galley was once more in our eyes. So my brothers I ask you now to raise your glasses and drink with me to our ship, the thought of her and her immortal memory.

   To our ship, *Odin's Raven*.'

The toast completed, there were only two options open to the crew. Either we collapsed into a scene of emotional reminiscences, or we channeled such overwhelming feelings along a more physical avenue, and it was this latter direction that was taken. With one accord the entire crew

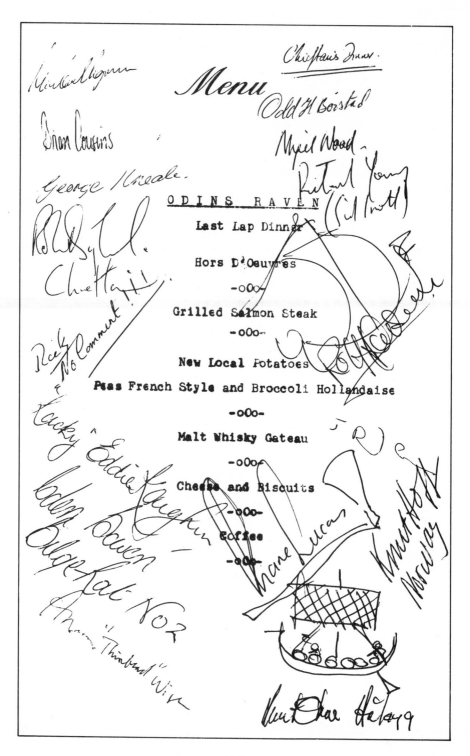

raised the Chieftain aloft, still seated in his chair, conveyed him in state through the conveniently-placed French window and deposited him, in situ as it were, in the hotel swimming-pool. The scene that followed reminded one of an early nineteen-thirties Keystone Cops comedy. One after another the rest of the crew found themselves immersed in the warm waters of the heated pool, either having entered of their own volition or with some genteel assistance from exuberant shipmates. Some, with a view to continuing the celebrations elsewhere in relative comfort, removed most of their clothes before taking the plunge, a precaution which was rendered completely ineffectual by the giggling, gnome-like figure of Arne Wisth who circumnavigated the disaster area, throwing in all such discarded apparel to their respective owners.

The hotel manager sallied forth from the relative safety of the building, only to retreat a short time later minus the sleeves of his dinner jacket. In a similar vein, several of the guests who ventured too close to the furore left the scene in haste when a number of sodden Vikings in various states of undress began to move purposefully towards them, their eyes agleam with demonic intent.

The manager had an understanding nature, or possibly he reckoned that the odds were not entirely in his favour, and he took the demise of his jacket in good part, eventually joining some extremely damp and bedraggled Vikings in the bar for a drink – diplomatically refraining from commenting on the virtual nudity of his drinking companions. As regards the attitude of the residents who through their own lack of forward planning happened to pass us in the confines of the hotel, it can only be described as one of awestruck fear, a little like the completely sober new arrival at a party who finds himself in the middle of a bacchanilian orgy and smiles and winks in encouragement to all he meets for fear of being pulled down and pillaged, or worse, on the spot!

The remainder of the night was, inevitably, spent on the town, a hostelry called the Downshire receiving the dubious honour of our company. The vision of Brian Cousins engrossed in a deep and earnest conversation with a large rather perplexed ginger cat on the steps of the hotel at approximately three o'clock in the morning adequately summarises the success of the evening in my opinion!

Tuesday, July 3, was sunny, and for most of the day lethargic Vikings were to be found in various states of repose all over the town. The quietness of solitude that most of us sought was not entirely due to the excesses of the previous night. It was a time for preparing one's mind to accept the reality of the situation. The adventure was almost over. The next day would see the culmination of the voyage, our successful return to the Island where it all began, and then back to the routine of modern life. The obviously pleasurable anticipation of being reunited with one's family was tempered with the knowledge that the unique experience of living closely confined with fifteen other men for so long would become just a memory – the in-jokes and the repartee quickly disappearing into the mists of time.

The somerleid was over, and suddenly the make-believe was fading, reality walking briskly forward to meet us. Home-coming, families, wives, girlfriends, responsibilities, all crowded in like familiar relatives with concern written on their faces.

What sort of reception would we get from our own people?

How had our families really fared with the stresses and strains brought about by our absence and endured, even as did those Viking wives of old, when their menfolk went year by year across the expanse of grey, unforgiving sea? Many a modern Viking looked reflectively into his drink that night, seeing in it shadows of the readjustment to the real world he knew would be his lot from the moment his feet touched the sands of Peel Bay.

For Robin Bigland, it was with a growing sense of relief that he welcomed the final twenty-four hours of the voyage. The culmination of a dream, perhaps, but he had lived for many weeks with the constant concern that something unpredictable and radical would go wrong and that the whole voyage, so precariously balanced as it was, would be thrown into chaos. He knew, as did we all, that we had our detractors and cynics on the Island who had predicted many times failure for the voyage, and we were aware that their gloomy forecasts could so easily have been proved true. The return to reality therefore, from Robin's point of view, was merely a relief that the planning and massive support of so many friends and helpers was at last to be vindicated.

By mid-afternoon on that penultimate day of our historic voyage the crew began to coalesce into small, quietly-spoken groups, none of us really sure how to accept the inevitable. Brian Cousins, Nigel Wood, Colin Bowen and myself found solace in a half-hearted game of pitch and putt, an activity to which was gave so little concentration that we succeeded in losing six golf-balls – apparently a record for the course. Others were drowning their sorrows in the Downshire or relaxing beneath the hot sun amid the grassy tussocks which fringed the shoreline.

Evening found us enjoying a final meal at the Mount Stuart Hotel before we sauntered down to the longship in groups of twos and threes to prepare her for our final departure. We were in no mood for a noisy or rapturous send-off and consequently the departure time had been set for 4 a.m., it being estimated that to leave at such an unearthly hour would ensure our arrival off Peel in time for the festivities, regardless of the weather. In fact the night was incredibly still, scarcely a ripple disturbing the mirror-calm water of the harbour. Our desire to leave Portpatrick in silence, to slip away in the quietness of the dawn, was shattered by the noisy arrival of the revellers from the Downshire Pub who, no doubt in good faith and with the best of intentions, celebrated our departure by showering us with what seemed like a never-ending hail of rice! Having scoured the longship from stem to stern in readiness for the morrow we were singularly unamused, and after a hasty conference with Robin Bigland, Eddie Kaighin gave the order to cast off the moorings.

Thus our intended silent departure became an ear-splitting crescendo of shouted farewells, off-key choruses from our well-wishers and a cacophony of blaring car-horns that could probably be heard on the Isle of Man. The number of lighted windows that suddenly appeared around the harbour as we rowed towards the entrance was ample evidence of the noise-level attained, but we were touched to notice the coloured lights in front of the Portpatrick Hotel flicking on and off in an obvious gesture of farewell.

For the journey to Peel we were accompanied by two of the Manx yachts, whose modern abluting devices were in constant use by the *Raven's* crew, a seemingly continuous stream of anxious Vikings passed from one boat to the other. The reason for such decorum, having utilised the 'gunwale system' until that time, was not only the close proximity of female company on board our satellites, but more in anticipation of the presence of hundreds of prying eyes when we arrived off our destination.

Her graceful lines highlighted by the pastel shades of the most breathtaking dawn that we had experienced, the longship glided across the gently undulating swell towards the low grey shadow on the horizon that was her final destination – home.

At eleven o'clock, beneath the glare of a cloudless summer sky, *Odin's Raven* hove-to some five miles off the port of Peel, our swift passage from Portpatrick uninterrupted by any last-minute intervention from the sea, whose mood had decided our every movement. For once, Father Neptune had resisted the opportunity to play with our fragile cockleshell and, as if applauding our insolent passage across his domain, presented us with conditions that could not have been more perfect.

There is a tradition on the Isle of Man that the God Mananan, who lurks in the mountains, shields the Island from any attack from the sea by shrouding his domain in an impenetrable mist, thus hiding it from any would-be invaders. The perfect weather we experienced that day seemed to place a seal of approval on our voyage; truly we were coming home.

Only one uncertainty marred those hours before the final run in to the shore, and that was our lack of knowledge concerning the whereabouts of the femboring, *Munin*. Remembering the threat her skipper had pronounced, of racing us to the Island, we had no idea whether he had either already reached Peel, or was lurking close at hand to steal our glory. Repeated questioning of the Harbour Board over the radio only served to increase our fears, as it appeared that the *Munin* was expected in, or at least was thought to be in the vicinity. We had requested that a Norwegian flag be brought out to us in order that our Norwegian shipmates could sail in under their own National emblem, placed on the same staff but below the 'Three Legs of Man', and it was during the radio discourse that followed this request that we learned of the possible presence of our rivals.

'Don't worry, lads,' Eddie Kaighin said, as we all began to discuss ways in which we could frustrate any such plans, 'If they try and cut in before us, the Harbour Board launch will sort them out!'

In the event our fears were groundless, for the *Munin* had turned back after reaching Shetland; but at the time we had no way of knowing this.

A light south-westerly breeze enabled us to spend the afternoon sailing backwards and forwards across Peel Bay, giving the rapidly increasing crowds on shore an opportunity to view the longship under sail. We were due to make our actual landing at 6 p.m. exactly so that the full panoply of the planned pomp and ceremony could be brought into effect. It was a joke among the crew that the Governor was required to attend another function at seven o'clock and thus the conquering Vikings had been requested to begin pillaging on the dot of six, and would they mind ceasing their activities at a quarter to seven, precisely?

The direction of the prevailing wind put paid to any thoughts of sailing into the beach and so we prepared ourselves for a long and of necessity immaculate spell at the oars. Peel is the centre of the Viking tradition on the Isle of Man and the local 'Vikings' would be quick to scoff at any performance that did not rise to their own and everybody else's expectations.

The hours ticked by with increasing sluggishness, the crew growing more irritable as they sweltered beneath the hot sun, for the presence of the media had required the donning of our heavy Viking costumes. A constant procession of TV camera crews circled the longship among the growing armada of small boats whose numbers increased as the minutes ticked by. The dramatic arrival of the frigate *Mohawk* served to increase the excitement of the occasion and then, with only an hour to go before the designated time for our landfall, the bane of our lives appeared again in the shape of a large and very noisy Norwegian helicopter.

'Oh, God, here we go again!' exclaimed Nigel Wood, as the creqrushed to their positions in readiness for some rapid activity on the sail.

'They can't be so stupid as to risk causing a capsize now, can they.' This from Richard Young as he positioned himself beside me on the main halyard.

'Ever heard of a T.N.C.U. (Typical Norwegian Cock-Up)?' I replied dryly.

'Stand by, everybody!' shouted Eddie Kaighin above the deafening clatter of the engine as the helicopter crept towards us. 'Don't wait for an order from me; if he gets too close, drop that sail fast!'

As if mesmorised we watched in horrified fascination the approach of the huge circle of flattened water that signalled the onrush of wind which could so easily capsize us, even at the final hour of the voyage. David Eames, standing on one of the kists, was shouting profanities at the perpetrator of our discomfort, his violent hand gestures needing little international translation and being recorded with obvious glee by a nearby Independent Television cameraman; the resultant film, shown on the News that evening, captured perfectly David's obvious annoyance.

The helicopter, with various cameramen dangling out of every available orifice, continued its inexorable passage towards us and suddenly we realised that it wasn't going to pull away. With an unexpected rush of air that nearly resulted in disaster, the downdraught caught the sail and the *Raven* heeled over sharply, the serpent-head leaning over sideways at an acute angle, a fierce red eye glaring up at the cause of its humiliation.

Even as Brian Cousins yelled 'Drop it!' Richard Yound and I let go the main halyard, controlling the rope as it whistled through our hands as best we could. With a loud crack the yard hit the gunwale, the foredeck party frantically grabbing at the canvas as it flapped viciously across the deck. Reluctantly the longship righted herself on to an even keel as the helicopter, seemingly well pleased with the chaos it had caused, finally consented to pull away, and circle off towards the open sea.

'Get the sail up again, boys,' said Eddie Kaighan, 'Quick as you can!'

Robin Bigland, seeing visions of his pride and joy being towed into her home port before the cynical eyes of the thousands of waiting spectators said 'If that idiot tries it again, don't leave it so long; get the sail down as fast as you can!'

Richard Young and I exchanged grimaces as we blew on our rope-burned hands.

'I don't believe it!' Brian Cousins muttered beside me 'He's coming in again!' Our heads jerked round in astonishment. It was unbelievable, but true. The helicopter was clattering towards us only a few feet above sea level, the dreaded circle of wind-battered water creeping across the sea with the churning waves that surrounded it leaping hungrily towards us.

While David Eames repeated his gesticulations and the rest of us shouted various imprecations at Norwegians in general (much to the embarrassment of our foreign shipmates, who also appeared baffled by what seemed a determined attempt to capsize us), the helicopter headed directly towards us and yet again we brought the sail crashing to the deck.

'What the hell is he playing at?' enquired Rick Tomlinson of the world in general. 'That pilot must be mental!'

Obviously deciding that enough havoc had been created for one day, the helicopter finally headed towards the land and disappeared into the distance.

'If I ever meet up with that fellow, I'll personally throttle him!' fumed Nigel Wood.

We were amused to hear the I.T.N. commentator on the News that evening state that the helicopter had 'blown down our sail!' Obviously he was not a nautical man.

The only advantage gained by the sudden excitement was that the time had passed very quickly, and, Eddie Kaighin gave the order for a final run past the *Mowhawk* under sail taking up our rowing positions.

As we came under the lee of the frigate, its large bulk effectively blocked the wind and we quickly lost our forward impetus. To our great delight Eddie Kaighin, ever the man for the occasion, had no hesitation in cupping his hands to his mouth and yelling, 'Would you mind moving your ship please, you're taking our wind!'

We watched in amazement as the frigate duly moved slowly astern, her unexpected activity resulting in a sudden ducking for a solitary wind-surfer who had been cavorting around near her stern, blissfully unaware of his impending doom until it was too late. Happily he was unhurt, but we observed that he elected to remain aboard the rescue craft which had gone to his aid.

With the harbour now close on our starboard side the sail was lowered for the last time, neatly furled and lashed on to the yokes. There was no time for emotion but I, among others, gave a small sentimental tap to the rolled-up canvas as the last lashings were tied off. The kists were quickly positioned for rowing, the oars lowered and pushed out through the oar-ports and with a final 'Give way together lads!' from Eddie Kaighin we started across the half mile of water that separated us from our final landfall.

There was little need for Robin Bigland's exhortation to 'Give it all you've got, boys, bags of pride!' We had no intention of repeating the fiasco of Stornoway again. The single splash and 'clunk' as the oar blades hit the water in perfect unison and the wooden shafts banged against the oar-port told us that our strokes were all in time. There was none of the usual banter and backchat, everybody intent on concentrating on the man in front, anxious not to be the one to catch a crab or cause a sudden loss of rhythm, and regardless of the boats that fussed around, the passengers shouting their welcomes across the water towards us.

Two parallel lines of converted lifeboats which were used as longships by the local Vikings during their annual races and reincarnation of the historic landing that we ourselves were now celebrating, lined our route to the beach and, as we passed them, their crews cheered and clapped us on our way.

Robin Bigland, from his position aft, gave a running description of the scene that lay before us but which none of us dared turn our heads to view. We already realised that the original estimate of 15,000 people had almost certainly been attained but the surging multitude of people that met our eyes when, at last, the longship slid gently on to the sloping sands of Peel was unbelievable.

The whole beach was a riot of colour and the mass of cheering spectators stretched back on to the promenade completely encircling the bay. As we leapt over the gunwale with the precision gained from our practices in Portpatrick and waded ashore, our previous doubts were quickly realised. The loosely roped-off area of beach, supposedly kept free for the ceremonies relating to our arrival, rapidly disappeared beneath the hordes of people pressing forward towards the longship. The V-formation we had intended to adopt for our walk towards the Governor and the assembled reception committee disintegrated into a free-for-all battle against the swarms of children who descended like locusts upon us.

I never managed to reach the appointed position, being brought to an abrupt halt while still some yards distance by an enthusiastic well-wisher of the pre-pubital variety, who grabbed hold of my sword in an attempt to wrest it from my possession.

'Come on, Mister, let's see if it's real!' came an insistent piping voice.

'Garn, betcher he's not a real one, anyway,' presumably from a comrade in arms.

Robin Bigland was apparently under similar duress as he vainly attempted to address the Bishop in the sombre tones suitable to the occasion, at the same time trying desperately to fend off another detachment of inquisitive youths who had set themselves the task of obtaining some Viking apparel as a memento of the occasion.

It was with a feeling of great relief that we heard Robin Bigland give the order to return to the *Raven* in order to row the final two hundred yards into the harbour itself and land in the comparative safety of the more securely-held area in which our wives and families were waiting patiently. It was however necessary first of all to remove a number of limpet-like small bodies who had clambered aboard during our brief absence and, as we pushed off from the beach, the last survivors of this incursion were prised off the gunwale and nonchalantly dropped into the shallows.

Practically deafened by an endless stream of congratulations from the packed crowd that lined both sides of the narrow harbour, we rowed up to our moorings where, for the last time, the order to 'stow oars' was given.

All too quickly we were ferried ashore, the longship having very sensibly been moored in the middle of the harbour; the time for any private farewells to our vessel was relegated to some later hour. There, on that heaving quayside, among the vibrant and noisy revellers, we were reunited with the families whom we hadn't seen for two months. The relative peace and quiet inside the Viking longhouse to which we rapidly repaired enabled us to greet our loved-ones in slightly less public surroundings, although the presence of an assortment of press photographers reminded us only too vividly that for the next few hours at least we were still the Vikings of *Odin's Raven*.

It was also a time for reunions with others equally involved in our adventure, such as Kathy Lewis and all the rest of them who had done so much to make the voyage the success it had obviously become: Alan Binns, whom we had last seen waving a sad farewell in Lerwick, and innumerable other faces we remembered from somewhere but couldn't put a name to.

And, of course, our families. It wasn't the time or place to allow full rein to our emotions but, to me, the sight of my two young children, their first hesitant steps towards a bearded fur-covered figure as my wife gently pushed them in my direction suddenly turning into a joyful cavalry charge as recognition dawned on their faces, more than made up for the weeks we had been apart. Lifting them up into my arms I looked over their heads at my wife, our eyes met, and we both knew that no words could remotely describe our emotions at that moment in time.

Later that evening, the festivities over, the crew slipped quietly away, few farewells needing to be said. While my family waited in the car, David Eames rowed me over to the longship to collect my belongings and, as he ferried the first load ashore, for a few short minutes I was alone.

The silent and empty deck rocked gently beneath my feet as I slowly walked across those well-remembered planks. The sounds of gaiety and laughter echoed in my ears and the memories came flooding back. One thousand eight hundred miles lay behind me but I could remember every moment with crystal clarity. The empty silence of the Norwegian Fjords, the noisy crowds of Oslo, the spray crashing inboard as we fought the sea off Startpoint; the eerie sound of the seals on Sule Skerry and the playful antics of our dolphin friends off Lewis. The sick feeling in the pit of my stomach as I watched the greedy waves ride over the naked hull when she capsized off Portree. The idyllic splendour of the painted sunset as we sailed past the Isle of Eigg. The heart-stopping fear that clutched at my body as the sea fought to wrest the helm from my grasp off the Mull of Kintyre; and now this elegant lady of the seas, this ancient reincarnation of the graceful beauty of a past age, lay resting at her moorings, quietly satisfied with the completion of her arduous task. I looked up at the mast as it swung slowly across the star-studded heavens and listened for the last time to the gentle lap of the ripples against the hull.

With an overwhelming feeling of emotion I touched the smooth roundness of the mast, then turned and climbed into the waiting dinghy.

'She's a beautiful ship isn't she, Mike?' Dave Eames said quietly as he rested on his oars, both of us looking back at the shadowy silhouette of the longship.

'Wherever she goes from now on,' I replied, 'she'll carry the hearts of sixteen men with her.'

We looked at each other and Dave nodded. Nothing else needed to be said. There are some thoughts that can never be put into words.

While life rushes by in panic against time
Young men sit out youth and grow old in their prime
Then I find tranquility in a far distant place
Away from the noise and the terrifying pace.
On quiet sunlit seas or by soft chuckling streams
I sit all alone, in peace, with my dreams.

Michael Ingram. *Odin's Raven*
July 2, 1979

APPENDIX

Odin's Raven

Eddie Kaighin, the helmsman of *Odin's Raven*, a seaman of experience, had gained much of his knowledge 'under sail' on board the *Naiad*, an old gaff-rigged cutter built in 1884. Although fascinated by the intricacies of old-fashioned sailing, he had never imagined that he would be in command of a vessel whose rig dated back a thousand years.

Odin's Raven was modelled on the celebrated Gokstad ship, which was excavated from a Viking burial mound near Sandefjord in Southern Norway, in 1880. Most of the vessel – the hull, two parts of the mast, some oars, a gang plank and numerous other articles had been meticulously preserved by the blue clay that had been heaped over the mound; but the rigging had completely rotted away.

The measurements of the Gokstad were as follows: She was 76'6" long, 17'6" wide, and 6'4" from the bottom of the keel to the gunwale amidships. In contrast, because of the cost of building a vessel of similar size and the length of time it would require, *Odin's Raven* was designed as a two-thirds scale replica, 50' long with an 11'9" beam and 4'6" in height. With a freeboard of about 18" she had a draft of 3' on the keel and 4'6" to the bottom of the steering-oar. Oak was the chosen material for the hull and the construction methods were copied with particular care to detail, even down to the grooves which decorated the strakes. She was fastened in clinker fashion with galvanised iron nails while the frames were fixed to the completed hull (unlike modern methods of ship-building where the reverse is common practice), by lashing them with nylon. The original Vikings used spruce roots as 'ties'. Such a method of construction allowed the vessel to flex, resulting in a cork-screwing motion in heavy seas. The lack of 'thwarts' produced a tendency for her to 'pant' which was particularly noticeable when beating into a head sea.

The steering oar (see Fig. 1) was fastened on the starboard side, secured by passing a rope through the boss on which it pivoted, as well as by

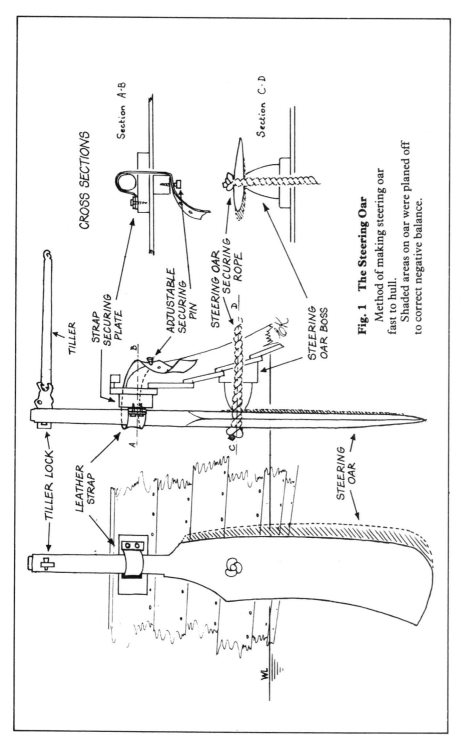

Fig. 1 The Steering Oar

Method of making steering oar
fast to hull.

Shaded areas on oar were planed off
to correct negative balance.

181

virtue of a leather strap attached to the gunwale. In the early days of the sea trials in Oslofjord, the negative balance of the helm made itself obvious, tending to pull into the 'hard over' position, a movement which required some strenuous muscle power to return it 'midships'. However, by trimming a few inches off the leading edge of the oar this effect was relatively easy to correct. Similarly, the overall thickness of the steering oar (two inches at it's midships cross-section) created a substantial amount of 'drag', a problem remedied by planing down the inside surface, thus creating an aerodynamic design more in tune with the original on the Gokstad. The final result produced a tolerable negative balance and virtually no drag at all. As the oar extended below the depth of the keel, the strap was designed to be adjustable to allow the oar to tilt when the vessel was beached.

The oars, mast (30' high), gangway and deck-boards were fashioned from pine, while the sea-chests (or kists), which doubled as rowing benches, were made out of marine plywood.

The whole boat, from the top of the mast to the keel, inboard and outboard, was treated with several coats of an oil called Trekfast. This concoction, the smell of which was very akin to 'Stockholm tar', provided protection from the nalt water and atmospheric effects, preventing any drying out and a consequent splitting of the wood.

When fully-manned, *Odin's Raven* was propelled by fourteen oarsmen and, including the 'Chieftain' and helmsman, she carried a crew of sixteen (see Fig. 2). If scaled down proportionately, the oar-ports would have ended up practically on the waterline and unless the vessel was to be powered by a crew of dwarfs (two-thirds scale humans), the 'ports' had to be fitted in the sheerstrake (top) instead of the third strake down.

For the same reason the T-shaped Yokes, designed to support the yard and sail when not in use, had to be built to the original Gokstad size of six foot six inches.

During the critical sea-trials, which were carried out during the days immediately following the launching, a number of teething troubles soon made themselves felt.

Fitted as she was with a 20 h.p. engine, she proved extremely difficult to manoeuvre under power, but the Helmsman discovered at an early stage, much to his amazement, that she would answer the helm equally as well regardless of whether she was going ahead or astern!

The first major problem, however, was that caused by the surface area of the hull available to the wind. The high sweep of the bow acted as an immovable 'jib' causing the head to 'pay off' all the time, but short of drastically re-designing the classic lines of the longship, there was no obvious remedy and the problem remained with us, although when fully-loaded and ballasted this tendency was reduced to some extent.

The first full day of sailing occurred five days after the launching, the intervening period having been spent whipping and splicing all the

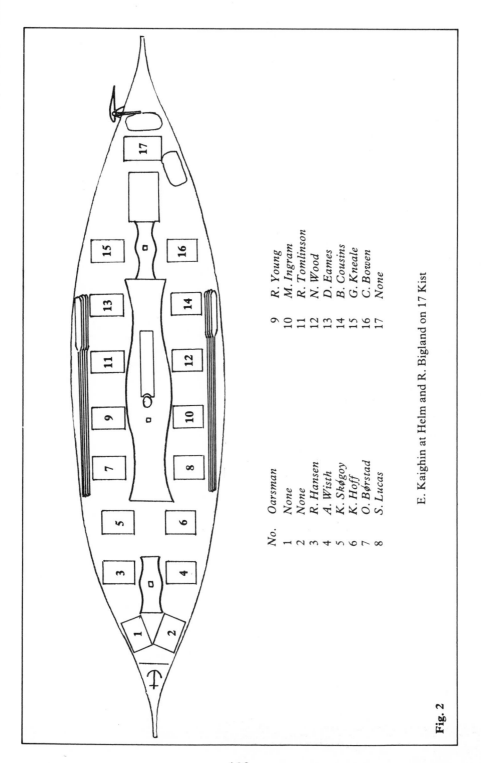

No.	Oarsman
1	None
2	None
3	R. Hansen
4	A. Wisth
5	K. Skøgoy
6	K. Hoff
7	O. Børstad
8	S. Lucas
9	R. Young
10	M. Ingram
11	R. Tomlinson
12	N. Wood
13	D. Eames
14	B. Cousins
15	G. Kneale
16	C. Bowen
17	None

E. Kaighin at Helm and R. Bigland on 17 Kist

Fig. 2

various sheets and ropes and bending them on their respective positions. At such a time the advice offered by Eric Rudstrom, an experienced builder and sailor of squaresail rigged Fembørings, was of incalculable value. As a result of this initial sail, two problems became apparent. In the first place the *rakke*, a banana shaped timber device used to hold the yard against the mast (see Fig. 3), continually twisted around, snagging with the downhaul halyards. Secondly, the method of securing the 'tack' to the samson post proved unsuitable for setting the sail to the best advantage. Each time she was paid off on to a different course a new position for the 'tack' was needed, a little further aft. Rolf Hansen, an experienced squaresail enthusiast, solved both problems with comparative ease. As regards the *rakke*, he redesigned it into a semi-circular shape which slid more easily up the mast, and from then on it gave no further trouble. His suggestion of a *seglestikke*, ('sail piece') which was an iron bar inserted through a hole drilled in the sheerstrake, solved the difficulty with the 'tack'. The 'sheet' was looped over this bar, outside the hull (see Fig. 3), the slack being taken in through the aft oar-port. By drilling three such holes a variety of adjustments could be made to the set of the sail, when close-hauled. To release the 'tack' the bar was simply withdrawn.

Another device, new to the modern-day sailors on board, was the *priare*, two of which were utilised to hold down the foot of the sail (Fig. 3). Each comprised a system of 3 tails of rope fastened to the sail, joined at a block from which a single rope's end led to a shackle fitted to the deck. These ingenious devices dated back as far as the Viking period, and proved to be so efficient that they were still in use up until the 19th century when the fembørings were constructed.

Eric Rudstrom had advised the helmsman that the fore and aft trim was likely to be of critical importance where the performance of the long-ship was concerned. By moving a single man from the bow to the stern the trim could be altered by 4 or 5 inches. Experiment soon showed that by shifting the off-watch crew forward a better performance was achieved when close-hauled; when running, the reverse procedure was required, the vessel becoming easier to control with the majority of the weight aft. Consequently, throughout the voyage, many a sleeping Viking was to be rudely awakened by the cry of 'Everyone aft of the mast', or vice versa, depending on the required trim.

Inclining the mast, fore or aft, was a standard procedure among fembøring sailors, but such a manoeuvre had not been anticipated by the designers of the longship. By altering the standing rigging the mast could be moved a few degrees, so after some experimentation, it was inclined permanently five degrees aft, a position in which it was decided that the vessel produced her best all-round performance.

Perhaps the most valuable piece of practical advice to be gleaned from Eric was the effect created by lowering the yard a little, without altering the running rigging. This produced the equivalent of an instant 'reef',

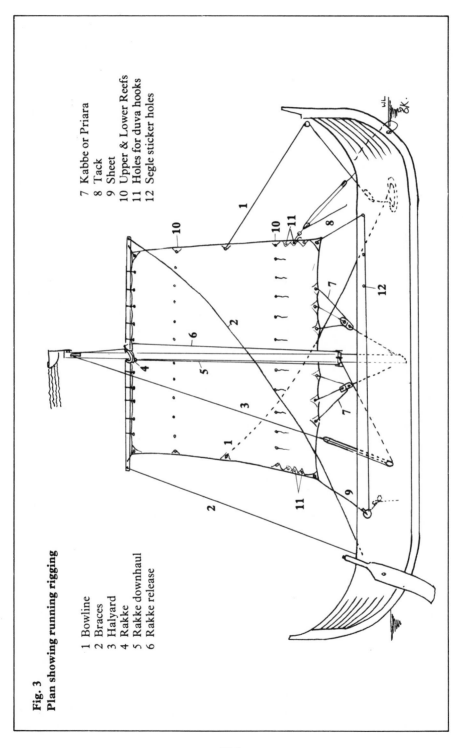

Fig. 3
Plan showing running rigging

1 Bowline
2 Braces
3 Halyard
4 Rakke
5 Rakke downhaul
6 Rakke release

7 Kabbe or Priara
8 Tack
9 Sheet
10 Upper & Lower Reefs
11 Holes for duva hooks
12 Segle sticker holes

thus an extremely useful method for reducing sail-area during squally conditions.

Beating to windward was a completely unknown quantity with the longship and few people would hazard a guess as to how close she would sail or how much leeway she would make. It was therefore a pleasant surprise to discover that with the wind strength at about Force 4 (which produced her best performance), she could sail, without pinching, with the wind 55° to 60° on her bow. With the leeway estimated to be approximately 10° to 15°, this meant that the longship could sail about 70° off the wind, when beating. The performance deteriorated with either an increase or decrease in wind speed, but the fact that the vessel could sail to windward at all was greeted with much relief.

When sailed close-hauled a potentially dangerous situation could very quickly appear if the 'head' was allowed to come too high into the wind. In such a situation, the sail was likely to back on to the mast, possibly with disastrous results to the vessel. When in doubt (or trouble) a square-rigger has to be paid-off and headed down wind, unlike modern fore and aft rigs.

The actual process of tacking was one which required some entirely new innovations, especially with regard to the use of the oars (Fig. 4), and was the most complicated manoeuvre that had to be performed under sail. It could only be attempted when the wind strength was less than a Force 5, otherwise her head would fall off before the wind was directly on the bow (in-irons). The successful completion of a tack required the participation of most of the crew, each of whom had a specific function. The sequence of events which followed the order 'Stand by to tack!' was as follows: In the first instance the helm would be put hard-over to bring the vessel's head into the wind, and the order 'Give way together!' produced the necessary extra turning power from the two bow oarsmen. The use of the oars was essential to keep the head coming round to windward, but as a result the forward movement of the ship was dramatically decreased. Eventually she would stop and, with the wind directly on to the bow, she would begin to move astern. At this juncture the helm was put hard over in the opposite direction, which is where the operating efficiency of the steering-oar when going astern came in most useful. The sail would then help to box her round and when she had gathered way the oars were taken in. With the wind at about 45° on the new bow the order would be given 'Round with her!' and the subsequent actions would be carried out simultaneously. The yard would be braced around, the bowline let go, the tack released and the *seglestikke* inserted in the opposite hole; the sheet would be let go, pulled forward and looped over the newly positioned *seglestikke* to become the new tack, and the old tack pulled in to become the new sheet. The oarsmen would then rig the tackle to harden the luff and the continuous bowline would be hauled tight and made fast. As she began to make her way forward on the new course the various lines, such

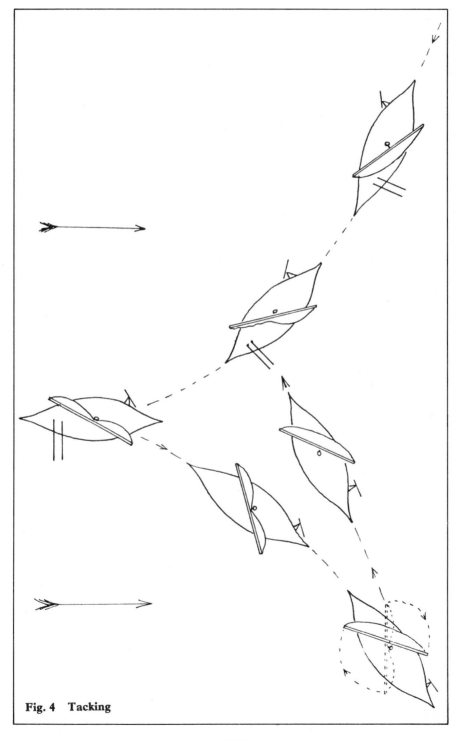

Fig. 4   Tacking

as the *priares*, would be adjusted to set the sail correctly. One can readily understand the dread with which the initial order to prepare to tack was received by the crew, especially during periods of rough weather!

It was, of course, possible to wear ship to alter course, but with the presence of such a long keel the longship required a large area of sea in which to turn, the end result being the loss of hard-earned distance to windward gained during the previous reach. Indeed on one occasion early on in the sea trials when wearing ship on a lee shore, the skipper had to order the sail to be dropped and the engine started to avoid running upon some particularly evil-looking rocks, despite the fact that the manoeuvre had been started approximately four hundred yards offshore.

One unusual aspect with regard to tacking the ship was the speed attained when travelling astern, five or six knots being achieved on a number of occasions.

During the period that *Odin's Raven* was on the M.V. *Slettner*, when she was being shipped from Oslofjord after her trials to Trondheim where the actual voyage was due to start, Eddie Kaighin had time to mull over the problems encountered during the trials, and he effected some much-needed alterations. The shrouds, for example, were originally fastened inside the hull to the two frames positioned immediately aft of the mast, just above the deck planking. In this position they had become a positive nuisance when stowing the oars as well as obstructing any movement of the crew fore and aft. He therefore drilled a hole through the second strake and the relevant frames, and passed the shrouds outside the hull secured inside by a figure-of-eight knot; in the new position (Fig. 5) there was the added bonus of the wider-angle thus produced affording a better support to the mast. These shrouds were tightened with a purchase which utilised *Jomfrus* instead of blocks or deadeyes. These were constructed from straight grained oak, unlike the Viking originals which were designed in such a way that the grain was used for extra strength. To compensate for this factor small rope-preventers were fitted to each one as a precautionary measure against breakage.

The final addition to the vessel, prior to her departure from Trondheim, was the addition of a 'Strawkeel', a piece of oak of the same width as the keel, 9″ deep and 9′ long. This was bolted on to the existing keel, the leading edge just aft of the position of the mast step. It was hoped that by virtue of the extra depth gained the leeway would be reduced and the manoeuvring capabilities of the longship increased.

By the time that the last contingent of the crew arrived in Norway, the vessel was fully prepared for the final trials in Oslofjord, the more experienced mariners having grasped the fundamentals necessary to sail her with relative confidence.

AUTHOR'S NOTE – All technical data supplied by the skipper, Eddie Kaighin.

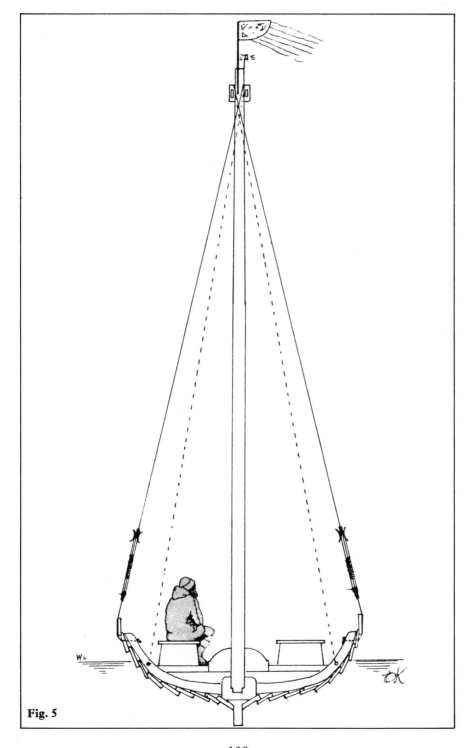

Fig. 5

BIBLIOGRAPHY

ALAN BINNS, *Viking Voyage*, 1980.
A. W. BRØGGER & HAAKON SHETELIG, *The Viking Ships*, 1971.
GEORGE MACKAY BROWN, *An Orkney Tapestry*, 1969.
R. H. KINVIG, *The Isle of Man*, 1975.
MAGNUS MAGNUSSON, *Vikings*, 1980.
DAVID WILSON, *The Vikings and their Origins*, 1970.
G. V. C. YOUNG, *From the Vikings to the Reformation*, 1979.